THE HIGH MOUNTAINS COMPANION

BY IRVINE BUTTERFIELD

DIADEM BOOKS · LONDON

Published in Great Britain by
Diadem Books Ltd., London

Copyright © 1987 by Irvine Butterfield

All trade enquiries to
Cordee, 3a De Montfort Street, Leicester

British Library Cataloguing in Publication Data:
Butterfield, Irvine
    The high mountains companion: the text of Irvine
    Butterfield's "The high mountains of Britain and
    Ireland" in condensed form for practical use.
    1. Mountaineering – Great Britian – Guide-books
    2. Great Britain – Description and travel – 1971 –
       Guide-books
    I. Title   II. Butterfield, Irvine. High mountains
    of Britain and Ireland
    796.5'22   DA632
    ISBN 0-906371-37-6

Printed and bound in Great Britain by
A. Wheaton & Co. Ltd, Exeter

Cover illustration: The Saddle from Sgurr nan Forcan.
Photo: George Burgess

CONTENTS

BEN LOMOND AND THE ARROCHAR ALPS

The seven peaks form a backcloth for the largest inland loch in Scotland and the long sea inlets of the Clyde estuary. They provide panoramic views of the complex coastline and the other mountain groups of the Southern Highlands.

BEN LOMOND

Scotland's most famous mountain provides fine views of the 'Arrochar Alps' and the islands of Loch Lomond.

BEINN NARNAIN   BEINN IME   BEN VANE

Three Arrochar Alps that give a straightforward round above Loch Long, with scrambling opportunities.

BEN VORLICH

The fourth Arrochar Alp can be reached by an enjoyable stroll from near Loch Lomond.

BEINN AN LOCHAIN

This small mountain (a traditional Munro) gives an entertaining scramble to another interesting viewpoint.

BEINN BHUIDHE

Set in drab moorland, this isolated hill has little to commend it other than its solitude.

Recommended Valley Base Arrochar.

Maps O.S. 1:50 000 Sheet 56; Bartholomews 1:100 000 Sheets 44, 45 (Walk 1 only), and 48; O.S. 1:63 360 Sheet *Loch Lomond and The Trossachs.*

Starting Point/Length and time for main itinerary
Walk 1 Rowardennan Hotel (360983). 7 miles/ 3190ft of ascent, 4–6 hours.
Walk 2 The A83 by Loch Long (294050). 11 miles/5700ft of ascent, 7–11 hours.
Walk 3 Ardlui Station (318154). 6 miles/ 3020ft of ascent, 4–6 hours.
Walk 4 Butterbridge (234095). 3 miles/2400ft of ascent, 2–3 hours.
Walk 5 A83 at the head of Loch Fyne (195126). 12 miles/3100ft of ascent, 6–9 hours.

Ben Lomond 3192ft/974m

The popular approach to Ben Lomond's 'steep, steep slopes' can be made either from the Youth Hostel or the Hotel at Rowardennan, from which paths climb to meet some 500ft above the shores of Loch Lomond. The course of the well-worn trail is easily followed up the southern slopes through close-cropped grass and heather. Veering north, it passes the spring known as Halfway Well on the broad shoulder of Sron Aonaich, and continues along to steeper slopes on the back of this spur. The path zig-zags up the most abrupt rise to reach the summit ridge, an undulating crest above the deep eastern corrie, whose streams flow towards the farm of Comer in Gleann Dubh. The path now skirts above

a line of crags to reach the Ordnance Survey post which marks the summit.

Alternative routes
From Loch Dhu on the B829 Aberfoyle to Inversnaid road a good track runs into Gleann Dubh, where, looking west, Ben Lomond dominates the view. Above Comer Farm, rough ground beside streams can be followed into the corrie immediately below the summit, or alternatively, towards the spur on its southern rim. Steep grassy rakes break through the broken crags of the corrie wall, emerging on the summit ridge just below the triangulation pillar. The climb to the ridge east of the summit is steeper than that from Rowardennan, but the solitude and grandeur of this isolated corner rewards the extra effort involved. By following the broad ridge northwards beyond the summit the walker completes the round of this hollow. Below the saddle at the foot of Crùinn a' Bheinn easy grass beside the Caorunn Achaidh Burn provides a pleasant descent to the track in Gleann Dubh, for the return walk to Loch Dhu.

The walker who has made the ascent from Rowardennan need not retrace his steps. Instead, return across the broad ridge to the west of the summit. This leads to the rugged top of Ptarmigan. Ptarmigan's western flank does not lend itself to an easy descent, but the easier gradients of the heathery slopes to the south of the cairn eventually lead to the woods above the

roadhead at Ardess.

The open shelter at Rowchoish, lying just off the forest track of the West Highland Way between Rowardennan and Cailness, blends in well with its surroundings and may be difficult to locate. The ascent of Ben Lomond from this spot, however, involves a steep, arduous flounder through rough scrubby woodland and is not recommended. One and a half miles to the north a route along the south bank of the Cailness Burn proves to be more appealing; grass slopes climb easily to the north ridge of the mountain, by way of the saddle between it and the adjacent hill of Crùinn a' Bheinn. As with all ascents from the west, there are extensive views of the Southern Highlands

---

Beinn Narnain 3036ft/926m
Beinn Ime 3318ft/1011m
Ben Vane 3004ft/915m

The peaks of Beinn Narnain, Beinn Ime, Ben Vane, Ben Vorlich, A' Chrois and The Cobbler, are known collectively as the Arrochar Alps. Good trunk roads skirt the bases of Beinn Ime and Beinn Narnain, and there is a good track from Inveruglas which provides a useful access route from the east to the foot of Ben Vane and the eastern corrie of Beinn Ime.

Beinn Narnain

From Arrochar a footpath is seen to emerge from a forestry plantation above the opposite shore of Loch Long. Climbing beside the boundary fence, it continues up the slope to reach a horizontal terrace crossing the face of Cruach nam Miseag. This is the obvious choice of route to the higher Beinn Narnain beyond.

Rounding the head of the loch, convenient parking spaces are found on both sides of the road at the turn off to Succoth (sign on the right). A Forestry Commission sign 'Argyll Forest Park: Ardgartan Forest' at a gate in the forest fence helps to identify the start of the path which, taking a line to the right of the sign, immediately turns to tackle the steep slope through the trees. Emerging from the pines at a stile, the path continues to a forest track (stiles), which provides the access to the plantations above Succoth. Paths from the Succoth road (at a gate near the bridge across the Allt Sugach) offer alternative starts to the walk.

The path ends at a track (between the Allt a' Bhalachain and the Allt Sugach) on the 1000ft contour where, looking ahead, two rounded tops are seen on the south-east spur of Beinn Narnain. Head towards the dip between them, taking care to avoid the buttresses of Creag an Fhithich on the left. At the col, a bold face of crags and pinnacles on The Cobbler fills the near skyline, on the opposite side of the Allt a' Bhalachain. The ridge continues past blocks and over humps, first in the centre, then left, then to the right to pass under a huge rock. Beyond this a gully to the right of the Spearhead Buttress gives a short scramble to the summit ridge, where the way passes through a gap on the left, and thence to the summit cairns on the plateau ahead. (Note: there is also a cairn on the top of the Spearhead Buttress, just to the left of the gap.)

A second useful path leaves the road immediately to the south of a bridge lying between the two signs to the Torpedo Station. A brick water-tower stands to the left of the ill-defined path which climbs to the left of the Allt a' Bhalachain, to emerge from the forest on to open slopes. A path on the north bank of the stream can then be followed to two huge rocks, the Narnain Boulders, where a tributary provides a useful line of ascent towards the craggy knots on the slopes of Beinn Narnain. From here the col north of Cruach nam Miseag can be reached by a steep climb. Alternatively a less strenuous approach (though still involving scrambling) moves left to avoid the uneven blocks below the first tower, then works through boulders to gain the broken edge below the summit. Several breaks in the crag to the north of the Spearhead Buttress lead to the stony summit crown.

Beinn Ime

To the north of Narnain's triangulation pillar two cairns, standing in line, point the way along the north-west ridge to the broad, grass saddle of the Bealach a' Mhaim. From here the easy grass of Beinn Ime's southern slope rises to a twin-topped crown, the higher north-west top of which is marked by a large cairn.

A shorter ascent of the mountain can be made from Butterbridge, at the head of Glen Kinglas where, above a ruin to the east of the stream, a stream joining the Kinglas Water can be followed to the junction of its two principal tributaries, at the edge of the forest. The stream to the left leads to the Glas Bhealach from where a short, steep ascent to the south leads to the cairn. A route following the stream to the right is longer but less steep.

Ben Vane

From Beinn Ime the best route to Ben Vane is that down the northern ridge to the Glas Bhealach. From this saddle, streams falling to the east are crossed on a contouring route around the northern edge of the deep corrie in front of Ben Vane. After a saddle (at about 1600ft) is crossed, a stiff pull over rough grass terraces brings the small, flat top of Ben Vane into sight, and a cairn at its southern edge.

If climbing the mountain on its own as a short day's outing, the access road to the Sloy dam, leaving the main road near Inveruglas Power Station, might be used (cars can be parked near the gate at the entrance to the road). Halfway to the dam a track turns off to the left across the Inveruglas Water where it begins a gradual ascent into Coiregrogain towards Bealach a' Mhaim. Quit the track after it crosses the stream to make an ascent by the grassy terraces of the mountain's south-east ridge.

The south-east ridge of Ben Vane is rough, with knobbly grass hummocks and here and there a rocky outcrop must be turned. Care should be taken to avoid the crags of the south face. The easiest descent is to the north, where, after a steep drop down the edge of broken escarpments, there is a tiny lochan on a saddle. From here the slopes relent to lead directly down to Loch Sloy. Those returning to Succoth are best advised to use this descent and return by the footpath leading from Coiregrogain through Glen Loin rather than attempt a return by a mountain route.

CHAPTER 1   WALK 3

Ben Vorlich 3092ft/943m
  (north top) 3055ft/931m

Ben Vorlich is a broad-based, twin-topped mountain which sprawls above the northern reaches of Loch Lomond. Picturesque deciduous woods line its lower eastern slopes, very different from the western flank above Loch Sloy, which is broken by minor crags.

The ascent by way of the track to Loch Sloy (the best parking lies just north of the entrance, opposite the power station) and the long south ridge is pleasant but uninteresting, with many false summits before the final top. There is no mistaking the summit, as it is marked by an Ordnance Survey post and several small cairns. Beyond these, a shallow dip then a short rise leads to the north top.

A much more attractive route starts about half a mile south of Ardlui Hotel at the head of Loch Lomond. The walker should locate the second railway underpass to the south of Ardlui Station subway (car parking opposite the subway entrance). Above the railway, heathery slopes lead to the mouth of Coire Creagach. Here a faint path may be followed above the course of a stream amongst scattered birch woods. The trees thin out below a gully (a small dam is hidden from view) where, looking across the stream bed, an almost level terrace will be seen. This provides a useful step on the climb to the crest of the lowest top of a ridge known as Little Hills, which joins the main ridge of the mountain just south of the summit.

Alternatively, to avoid following the stream through its steep-sided gully above the woods, climb the high banks to the right. On the easier ground above, a better view of the ridges ahead unfolds, and streams in the upper corrie lead to grassy ramps that link up with the ridge of the Little Hills. A shorter route to the summit can be found by following a tributary in a hollow behind a short, heathery rib seen to the right. This corrie ends in rough, steep ground, where grassy terraces climb between the outcrops to a point on the main ridge of the mountain a little to the north of its northernmost cairn.

CHAPTER 1   WALK 4

Beinn an Lochain 3021ft (Munro)
  2957ft/901m

The addition of the delightful little peak of Beinn an Lochain to this guide might be considered anomalous, as its status as a 3000ft peak appears to be suspect. The mountain has always been overshadowed by its neighbours, for not only did the early mountaineering pioneers fail to claim it as one of their 'Arrochar Alps', but also the Ordnance Survey maps gave the impression that it was a peak of minor significance, for the height recorded, 2992ft, was that of a point 150 yards south-west of the summit cairn. After careful aneroid measurements Munro came to the conclusion that the mountain's highest point was in excess of 3000ft, the height 3021ft being that adopted. The 1:50,000 series Ordnance

Survey map currently in print, showing a height of 901m (2957ft), has again cast doubt upon the mountain's status but it must here be considered worthy of a mention, if only by virtue of its historical associations with Munro's original lists.

The eastern face of the mountain is its most distinctive feature. Seamed with wet grassy gullies and punctuated by vegetated crags, it rises some 1200ft above Loch Restil, at the head of the Rest and be Thankful Pass. These slopes can be avoided by taking the minor road (B828) into the head of Gleann Mor, above which a long, grassy slope undulates northwards to the summit.

A much more interesting approach takes the north-east ridge starting from the car park at the old bridge over the Kinglas Water. The ridge is obvious, rising from the edge of the stream, its grassy crest climbing in easy steps above the eastern face. The ridge narrows and crags on the

right come into view. These are passed on the left, where the stony ridge gives way to a grassy ramp and a small level platform. Above this is a final knoll and then the summit.

CHAPTER 1   WALK 5

Beinn Bhuidhe 3106ft/948m

Its isolated position and rather uninteresting hump means that Beinn Bhuidhe is often overlooked. There are no other notable heights in the immediate vicinity, and for many visitors it is merely just another summit to be attained.

At the head of Loch Fyne take the minor road to Achadunan. This continues as a track (traffic discouraged) to Glenfyne Lodge and the tiny cottage of Inverchorachan beyond. The last mile, stony and overshadowed by steep wooded slopes, forewarns the walker that a stiff ascent lies immediately ahead.

A stream behind the cottage can be followed to a small, high-level corrie lying at the foot of the final scarp of the two-mile-long summit ridge. Several routes up the numerous gullies in the mountain face above give access to the crest and the summit cone is halfway along, marked by an OS pillar.

The other well-trodden route to the summit starts in Glen Shira, lying to the west of the hill. A private road goes towards the upper reaches of the glen, where it becomes a Land-Rover track to the Shira dam beyond Elrigbeag. This track skirts the western base of Beinn Bhuidhe to cross the Brannie Burn above the site of Rob Roy's House. Beyond the Brannie Burn grass slopes lead to a top, Tom a'Phiobaire, at the south-western end of the summit ridge. The hill narrows on the crown of Stuc a'Chuirn, where the ridge dips before the final knoll of the summit.

CHAPTER 2

THE CRIANLARICH HILLS

Ease of access greatly enhances the attraction of these eleven mountains which can be conveniently ascended from the roads passing through Glen Falloch, Strath Fillan and Glen Lochy. They are more noted for strenuous outings than exceptional views.

BEN MORE   STOB BINNEIN
Two massive mountains, demanding 4000ft of stiff ascent but providing extensive views.

BEINN CHABHAIR   AN CAISTEAL   BEINN A' CHROIN   BEINN TULAICHEAN   CRUACH ARDRAIN
An exceedingly demanding expedition over a succession of craggy tops and steep dividing glens.

BEINN LAOIGH   BEINN A' CHLEIBH   BEN OSS   BEINN DUBHCHRAIG
Ben Laoigh, with its fine winter corries lends this quartet of rather ordinary peaks some extra interest.

CHAPTER 2   WALK 1

Ben More 3843ft/1174m
Stob Binnein 3821ft/1165m
  Stob Coire an Lochain 3497ft/1068m
  Meall na Dige 3140ft/966m

These are the highest mountains south of the Tay and when traversed in a single expedition they offer a strenuous and rewarding day. Stob Binnein is easily identified from afar by its distinctive conical shape. Together with its bulkier twin, Ben More, it rises fully 3000ft above Glen Dochart.

Ben More
Viewed from near Benmore farm the proximity of this mountain and the severity

of its slopes make its ascent appear a daunting prospect. On the lower slopes, above the timberline, a memorial cross marks the site of a death and reminds of possible danger. A hanging corrie, immediately below the summit, can be treacherous and its steep upper section has witnessed several fatal accidents. It is best avoided by a line to the east to approach the summit by the ridge of Sron nam Forsairean. South of the summit, grass and stones provide an easy descent staircase to the Bealach-eadar-dha Beinn.

Stob Binnein (Stobinian)
Beyond the bealach, broken escarpments on the left trim an obvious ridge and shape the pyramid of Stob Binnein, adding attraction to the ascent.

Recommended Valley Base Crianlarich.

Maps O.S. 1:50 000 Sheets 50, 51 and 56; Bartholomews 1:100 000 Sheet 48; O.S. 1:63 360 Sheet *Loch Lomond and the Trossachs*.

Starting Point/Length and time for main itinerary
Walk 1 Benmore (414257). 9 miles/5165ft of ascent, 6–9 hours.
Walk 2 Beinglas (319188). 13 miles/7190ft of ascent, 8–12 hours.
Walk 3 Dailrigh (344290). 15 miles/5300ft of ascent, 8–12 hours.

Those who find the prospect of the hard slog up Ben More too daunting can tackle Stob Binnein first. By following the course of Benmore Burn, and moving onto the upper slopes by a rising diagonal line, the spur of Creagan Liatha can be gained. Its knolly top abuts Stob Binnein where steeper grass leads to an untidy cairn on the summit of Stob Coire an Lochain. Above this, a mossy ridge sweeps up to the crown of Stob Binnein. An alternative ascent of Stob Coire an Lochain can be made from the south by a long ridge which climbs steeply from the Inverlochlarig road.

The approach to Meall na Dige is also much quicker from the south by grassy slopes above Monachyle Glen and the stream of Allt Coire Cheathaich, or alternatively, the broad spread of Am Mam. Small outcrops are easily avoided on the climb to the wide ridge which, to the west of the cairn, is linked to Stob Coire an Lochain.

Ascents from the north leave Meall na Dige awkwardly placed, with re-ascent of Stob Coire an Lochain necessary before a descent is made by either of the ascent routes previously described. Walkers approaching from the south complete their ascents on the summit of Ben More, from which they must either retrace their steps across Stob Binnein to gain Stob Coire an Lochain's southern ridge, or alternatively, make a steep diagonal descent from Bealach-eadar-dha Beinn to the headwaters of the Inverlochlarig Burn for a return to Inverlochlarig.

CHAPTER 2	WALK 2

Beinn Chabhair 3053ft/933m
An Caisteal 3265ft/995m
Beinn a' Chroin 3104ft/946m
(west top) 3078ft/938m
Beinn Tulaichean 3099ft/946m
Cruach Ardrain 3428ft/1046m
Stob Garbh 3148ft/959m

Crianlarich's southern skyline of five knolly peaks, dissected by deep corries has a distinctive character, typified by the rocky crenellations of An Caisteal, the castle. They provide a long and energetic expedition, with many twists and turns, switchbacks and rocky obstacles. In winter the going is very demanding but on a clear summer's day the walking is delightful. The peaks can easily be split into two or three separate expeditions each of which provides an interesting excursion, but climbing the mountains together as a group emphasizes their character to a greater degree and leaves a profounder impression.

Beinn Chabhair

The shortest route to this, the most westerly peak in the group, leaves the Glen Falloch road (A82) just north of the Inverarnan Hotel at a bridge crossing the river to Beinglas farm. To the right of these steadings a path climbs a craggy hillside, so steep that the initial 1000ft of ascent is made in a quarter-of-a-mile. The gradient eases briefly at a moorland track where the rough knolls at the end of Ben Glas are first encountered. Beyond the crag-girt Lochan a' Chaisteil, a further switchback of knots

leads to the final hump of a twin-cairned summit.

Alternatively, after the initial steep ascent, follow the moorland track, and then the banks of the Ben Glas Burn into the boggy hollow of Lochan Beinn Chabhair. This ascent gives a scrambly and demanding route through a steep field of boulders.

An Caisteal

From Beinn Chabhair, the way on to An Caisteal begins with a 1000ft descent to the col to the north-east. This is extremely steep and tricky and requires care, taking a line a little to the north to circumvent cliffs. In winter it should be treated with respect. A climb of equal length and steepness leads to the southern shoulder of An Caisteal, from where a short final rise leads north to the summit

Those who prefer to climb Beinn Chabhair as a separate excursion and thereby avoid this arduous switchback, can approach An Caisteal directly from Glen Falloch, from where the prominent tor on its ridge readily identifies the mountain. The most convenient approach is that by the track which bridges the Falloch near Derrydaroch farm, a route also useful for approaches to Beinn Chabhair's steep north-western flank by way of the Allt a' Chuilinn.

Above Derrydaroch, either of two ridges enclosing the corrie of the Allt Andoran can be climbed to the summit of An Caisteal. To reach the eastern spur, cross the corrie mouth and seek out grassy rakes rising to a scree patch below the ridge south of Sron Gharbh. Known as Twistin Hill, its obvious crest leads to the rocky boss of 'the Castle' which appears to bar further progress. Closer inspection however reveals a path across its top. In gusty conditions this can be avoided by passing the rock on its right. By comparison, the bald, cairned summit seems characterless.

If descending by way of Stob Glas, look for a short, stony ramp due west of the pile. Hummocks crown this ridge, which affords the alternative ascent from Glen Falloch previously mentioned. To continue the major traverse follow a short rib to the south-east which drops 600ft to a col linked to the western slopes of Beinn a' Chroin.

Beinn a' Chroin

Beinn a' Chroin has two tops separated by a 200ft dip. The higher, eastern top is a well-defined hump with a small cairn. Its western partner is a short ridge with two cairned points which might be confusing in mist.

From the eastern top the north ridge provides the best way down to the 1700ft col below Stob Glas, a craggy nose turned on a steep western flank. On an east-west traverse this northwards manoeuvre leads the walker into the head of Coire Earb and,

in mist, needs skilful navigation to locate Beinn a' Chroin's northern ridge. On shorter expeditions descent is easily made by the western bank of the stream to a track in lower Coire Earb, which, passing under the railway, runs down to the road.

Beinn Tulaichean

From the summit of Stob Glas it is easy to skirt the southern slopes of Cruach Ardrain to take in Beinn Tulaichean, before heading back north to the highest peak in the group.

Cruach Ardrain

The knolly southern ridge climbs to a summit cairn sitting on the edge directly above the cleft of Y Gully, a popular winter climb. Continuing the traverse, the way off Cruach Ardrain to the north-east is down steep screes to the wide grassy crest of Stob Garbh. This dips to the hump of Stob Coire Bhuidhe, and it is best to continue along the ridge towards the road before seeking one of the avenues through the woods of Coire Ardrain. These descend to a wider firebreak in the lower corrie and this, in turn, leads to a gap in the forest boundary behind Inverardran on the A85.

On an east-west traverse speedy location of the routes through the forest saves valuable time. That from Inverardran starts on an embankment behind the cottage. A wall runs to a stile in the forest fence giving access to a firebreak up into the woods. Turn right to a wider break and follow the path to a similar break at a higher level. The gap to the left leads to the steep flank of Stob Coire Bhuidhe, and ahead a steep ascent can be made to a dip in the ridge, to the north of Stob Garbh.

A more direct ascent to Cruach Ardrain starts opposite two cottages on the A82 about half a mile south of Crianlarich. A Forestry Commission sign at a gate and stile, indicates a path to a railway bridge, beyond which a climb beside a broken fence, up through a firebreak, leads to a prominent rock on the skyline. Above this easier slopes rise to the rocky scalp of Grey Height and the ridge to Cruach Ardrain. Closer to Derrydaroch, the lower slopes of the Grey Height ridge give an easy ascent above the forest boundary on a climb from the Coire Earb track.

Ascents from Inverlochlarig

Access from this quarter is easier than it used to be, as a track has now been pushed westwards from Inverlochlarig towards the foot of Beinn a' Chroin. Beinn Chabhair is the most distant, and after a short walk along the glen can be climbed from Coire a' Chuilinn by a steep scrambly route up the southern face of the hill. An Caisteal is reached by the Beinn Chabhair – An Caisteal col, and Beinn a' Chroin by a stiff ascent of grassy tiers on an eastern ridge above the Ishag Burn. Beinn Tulaichean's steep southern ridge gives a sharp pull to the summit cairn, whence there is the knolly ridge leading onto Cruach Ardrain. These routes also provide a means of descent from the respective peaks.

The full traverse of the five peaks is never easy. The continual change from ascent to descent can be very tiring. Failure to complete the round does offer some compensation in that the day may be terminated almost at will to leave the remaining hills conveniently grouped for another day.

CHAPTER 2   WALK 3

Beinn Laoigh (Ben Lui) 3708ft/1130m
    (north-west top) 3697ft/1127m
Beinn a' Chleibh 3008ft/917m
Ben Oss 3374ft/1028m
Beinn Dubhchraig 3204ft/977m

This group of mountains, lying some five miles south-west of Tyndrum is dominated by Beinn Laoigh (Ben Lui). On its Cononish side, steep ribs rise to buttress twin peaks on the headwall of Coire Gaothaich. This great scoop holds snow much longer than most others in the Southern Highlands and has long been popular for its winter ascents.

Beinn Laoigh (Ben Lui)

The eastern face of Ben Lui can be seen from the bridge crossing the Fillan on the Crianlarich to Tyndrum road. Nearby, the old schoolhouse at Dailrigh (now used as a barn) lies at the start of the Cononish track. This leads to a sheep-pen on the Allt na Rund. Either of this stream's tributaries can be followed into the mouth of Coire Gaothaich, where there is a choice of routes. On either hand, short spurs abutting the summit ridge climb to narrow rocky crests, each leading to a small conical top. The summit, seen to the left, is marked by a large, untidy cairn. The hanging corrie is dominated by the steep couloir of Central Gully, which is a traditional and popular ascent route in winter for the competent mountaineer.

On the shorter approaches from Glen Lochy, the walker has to negotiate forestry plantations. Start from a car-park opposite a railway bridge spanning the outfall of the Eas Daimh. This is near its confluence with the River Lochy, which is fordable, but there are footbridges to the east and west. That to the east, near the site of the old Glenlochy Crossing signal box (255295), by a stand of mixed trees, was the traditional starting point for the ascent. A newer structure to the west is difficult to see from the road, as it is almost hidden by a small mound. A useful point of reference is a short section of the old road to the north of the present highway. Nearby, a

little to the east, a poor path crosses heathery ground in the direction of a hut, seen on the opposite side of the railway.

From both bridges follow the railway to a stile immediately east of the Eas Daimh bridge. A path, following the left (north) bank of the stream, climbs past a footbridge below the Eas Morag waterfall. Keep to the north bank of the stream, to a stile in the fence at the foot of Ciochan Beinn Laoigh, or cross the stream where it is joined by its largest tributary. The tributary is then followed for a time, and then the path steepens in a firebreak to reach open ground in the Fionn Choirein. At times of spate, cross the Eas Daimh by the Eas Morag footbridge and follow its western bank to a plank bridge on the tributary. Above the forest fence (stile), a useful exit through the corrie headwall is by a patch of rough scree, seen to the left of the broken face of Beinn a' Chleibh. Grassy tiers rise to a col, where, turning to the south-west, along the line of the corrie's rim, a short climb leads to the cairns of Beinn a' Chleibh. The steeper climb to the north-east leads to the summit of Ben Lui.

A more interesting approach to Ben Lui is that along the Eas Daimh (stile in an angled section of the fence close to the stream). Above the trees, craggy bluffs on the Ciochan Beinn Laoigh can be turned on the right. This steep, grassy nose rises to a ridge crest which narrows gradually to the cairned point of the northern summit, above Coire Gaothaich. A short walk along the lip of this great scoop leads to the higher southern top.

Beinn a' Chleibh

The easiest route to Beinn a' Chleibh is by way of the Fionn Choirein as previously described. The steep north-east slopes overlooking this corrie are not really suitable for ascent or descent. The mountain's long western ridge, immediately above Succoth Lodge, is a mass of trees, and nowadays the only route through them starts at the westerly river crossing by the railway hut. From this point, follow the fence to the right until the first angle in it is reached. Continue along a boggy firebreak, which runs straight up the hillside to a stile on the forest boundary. The roughened face of Creag na Cloiche Gile (on the left) is then avoided by continuing above the fence to the top of a broad shoulder, almost due west of Beinn a' Chleibh's summit. Two small cairns mark the top of the easy grass ridge, and on the approach to the mountains's level crown, several cairns are seen, the largest one, on a flat rock near the south-eastern edge of the plateau, would appear to be the

highest point. Other piles nearby are useful guides in mist, indicating the proximity of the broken eastern face. The most southerly pile marks the turn onto the stubby ridge dipping to the col at the head of Fionn Choirein.

Ben Oss

Ben Oss and its near neighbour, Beinn Dubhchraig, when not included in a greater traverse of the four peaks in the group, are usually climbed from Dailrigh. An east-west traverse seems to be preferred as the prior ascent of Beinn Dubhchraig gives an easier start to the day. The near-vertical slopes above the Allt Coire Laoigh preclude any sensible attack on Ben Oss from that quarter, though the climb between it and Ben Lui provides reasonable access to the broad ridge linking the two.

The level summit ridge of Ben Oss runs roughly north to south, and has a cairn decorating its southern extremity. The route to Beinn Dubhchraig goes north along the ridge, which dips, turns eastwards, and climbs across a small cairned top to a col. Beyond this short saddle, the broad stony crest of Beinn Dubhchraig confronts the walker. Seven hundred feet of tiresome plodding leads to the cairn, at the eastern end of an expansive back.

Beinn Dubhchraig

The most pleasant, and the shortest, route to Beinn Dubhchraig starts at Dailrigh. The Cononish track should be followed to the railway, which can be used to bridge the river. Beyond the railway bridge, a track leads to a footbridge over the Allt Coire Dubhchraig, which is crossed to its western bank. The stream is then followed through scattered Scots pines to Coire Dubhchraig. At the head of this heathery hollow either of two broad ridges lead to the summit. A path, which runs a short distance to a fence on the crest above Creag Bhocan, affords a route to the upper slopes. Added attractions are the fine views to be had of Ben Lui's great corries. In mist, the slight arc of this ridge may mislead those seeking the short neck between Ben Oss and Beinn Dubhchraig. In such circumstances, either a south-westerly bearing, or the location of the tiny lochan on the higher slopes are the surest guides.

The traverse of all four mountains is best attempted from Glen Cononish, as this more easily accommodates the short diversion to Beinn a' Chleibh, Ben Lui then being contoured to reach the col at the head of Coire Laoigh for the return across Ben Oss and Beinn Dubhchraig.

LOCH EARN AND CRIEFF

Three mountains standing above Strath Earn, which forms a dividing line between the mountains of the north, and the central lowlands of Scotland. Various ancient rights-of-way and hill-paths provide leisurely starts for the ascents, but the views are unexceptional.

BEN VORLICH STUC A' CHROIN
Steep work on Ben Vorlich, followed by Stuc a' Chroin's rocky staircase enliven this expedition.

BEN CHONZIE
An undistinguished hill, ideally suited to those seeking a carefree stroll to while away an afternoon.

Recommended Valley Base Comrie.

Maps O.S. 1:50 000 Sheets 51, 52 and 57; Bartholomews 1:100 000 Sheet 48; O.S. 1:63 360 Sheet *Loch Lomond and the Trossachs* (Walk 1 only).

Starting Point/Length and time for main itinerary
Walk 1 Ardvorlich (633232). 10 miles/3800 ft of ascent, 5–8 hours.
Walk 2 Invergeldie (743272). 8 miles/2200 ft of ascent, 4–6 hours.

CHAPTER 3	WALK 1

Ben Vorlich 3231ft/985m
Stuc a' Chroin 3189ft/975m

It is difficult to get uninterrupted views of these hills except from a distance. Good paths lead to the peaks from all sides and the walker is soon rewarded with views of many of the highest mountains in the Southern Highlands.

Ben Vorlich
Ben Vorlich has four ridges radiating from its summit, the two northern spurs providing popular routes from the shore of Loch Earn. Cars can be parked on the verges near the entrances to Ardvorlich House, and the estate requests hillwalkers to use the eastern gate. Here, a drive, immediately to the east of a humped bridge, follows a stream, which is crossed on the approach to the house. Across this bridge, turn onto a track to the left where, after a few yards, an estate notice at a gate advises walkers to keep to the waymarked path. Looking ahead, its scar can be seen on the mountain's northern spur. Above the trees, a turn is made away from a second path, which crosses a low pass to the east of the peak. The steep waymarked path is not difficult, and there is ample time to appreciate the views unfolding to the west.

At the western end of Loch Earn, a second track, signposted 'Footpath to Loch Lubnaig via Glen Ample', climbs from the road immediately to the west of a bridge at the Falls of Edinample cottages. An easy walk beside the Burn of Ample leads to a ford, avoided by following the waymarked route to a footbridge below Glenample farm. Here, looking to the slopes of Creagan nan Gabhar, a track is seen climbing the side of the hill to the deep fold of the Allt a' Choire Fhuadaraich. This is reached and followed to a broad corrie, where easy grass slopes lead to Ben Vorlich's north-west spur. Alternatively, ford the stream to gain the heather terraces of Creag Dhubh, and climb by grassy rakes to the memorial cairn at its summit. Here, you join the fence on the ridge to the summit of Stuc a' Chroin.

To the south, the narrow road from Comrie to Glenartney Lodge has a convenient car park opposite a small church, near the roadhead. Beyond the Water of Ruchill bridge, a cottage signposts a ford, which is crossed to follow a track across the open moors of the Monadh Odhar. At the entrance to Gleann an Dubh Choirein, a rougher track turns off up the east bank of the Allt an Dubh Choirein. Continue to a confluence of streams at Dubh Choirein (ruin) and here cross the tributary to the foot of the ridge which rises ahead. This steepens to small outcrops below a narrower crest leading to the summit, a bare table carrying a cairn at its southern end (3224ft/983m), and an Ordnance Survey pillar at the top of the Ardvorlich ridge.

Stuc a' Chroin
From the O.S. pillar, the route to Stuc a' Chroin follows a steep stony ridge to the south-west. In mist, a line veering slightly to the north should first be taken to avoid the vegetated crags of a broken escarp-

ment, though this should not be overdone as open ground running out to the mountain's north-west spur leads into the higher reaches of the Allt a' Choire Fhuadaraich. Beyond the sharp dip to the Bealach an Dubh Choirein, (fence) buttresses and more vegetated crags appear to block the way to the summit of Stuc a' Chroin, but a well-worn path creeps through rocks to the right. In mist, following this route in the reverse direction requires care, and if the head of the path, near the memorial cairn on Creag Dhubh, cannot be located a slight deviation to the north-west will find a surer descent by way of the grassy rakes mentioned earlier (see approach from Falls of Edinample cottages)

Just to the south-west of Dubh Choirein a footbridge spans the Allt an Dubh Choirein to gain heather slopes, which sweep up from a peat-hagged corrie to an escarpment forming the edge of a broad spur. This south-eastern ridge gives an easy pull to the summit prow.

Another route from the south uses the right-of-way from Loch Lubnaig to Loch Earn. The turn-off to Ardchullarie More lies through a gateway in a wall, at a point where the A84 narrows at a bridge on a bend. A signpost just inside the gateway, 'Footpath to Loch Earn via Glen Ample', points to a path left of a barn. This climbs through woods to join the wider Glen Ample track, which crosses a low pass beneath Beinn Each. This steep south-west ridge of Stuc a' Chroin gives a tortuous, grassy ascent to an old fence striding along a knolly crest. This eventually leads to an untidy cairn at the western edge of the mountain's cap, and the higher cairn beyond.

CHAPTER 3	WALK 2

Ben Chonzie 3048ft/931m

This rather featureless hill (also known as Ben-y-Hone) would attract far less attention were it not in excess of 3000ft, for there are many similar rolling tops in the vicinity.

The approach from the north starts at Newton Bridge, in the Sma' Glen. From here a track runs alongside the Almond to Loch Tay (this is a right-of-way but vehicular traffic is discouraged). The foot of the mountain is gained near the derelict cottage of Lechrea some seven miles from Newton Bridge. A bridge to Larichfraskhan is the lowest crossing to the mountain's north-east shoulder, the feature most resembling a ridge on the Auchnafree side. A mile to the west, another cottage, near a small plantation, helps to identify the start of the climb. Ignoring the stalkers' track, which climbs to the Moine Bheag, cross the stream beyond the cottage and ascend the grassy spur with the craggy slopes to its right. Above Lechrea a steeper slope leads to the 2000ft contour. From this level to the summit the moors are featureless, and in mist the great pile of stones at the summit can be difficult to locate.

Three fences converge hereabouts. One line of posts marches north-west along the watershed towards Creag nan Eun, and may be encountered on the final part of the ascent from Lechrea if one navigates a little to the west. Those seeking an alternative return to Glen Lednock, might also choose to follow this boundary to the pass at the head of the Invergeldie Burn. The second line of posts goes eastwards to Glen Turret, and the third follows the ridge to the south, towards point 2759ft/841m, which is a

convenient landmark on the climb from Glen Lednock.

The shortest route to the summit is from Glen Lednock. Starting from the old school at Invergeldie (a large white house – wide verge for parking) a good track runs past the cottage at Coishavachan to a bridge on the Invergeldie burn (hidden behind a clump of pines). Here, on the slope behind the lodge, the old right-of-way path from the lodge road end is joined.

The track continues along the west bank of the Invergeldie Burn and, at a small dam, turns across a ford (usually dry) to shooting butts on the heathery flanks of the hill. By crossing a tributary stream above the first stone butts, an easy climb can be made to the hump ahead (point 2759ft/

841m). Alternatively, follow the track to the fence on the broad ridge to the south of the summit.

Another popular route starts at the Glen Turret dam. From the A85, west of Crieff, take a road marked 'Glen Turret Waterworks' and beyond the distillery bear left at the large Water Board signs. This road leads to the dam car park. From this a track runs along the east shore of the loch to the Turret Burn, which is followed to its source above Lochan Uaine. Here, at the foot of the mountain's north-eastern shoulder, the fence marks the way to the summit. At the top the fence (turning south) provides a useful reference for an alternative walk to the summit of Carn Chois, whose slopes fall towards the dam.

CHAPTER 4

BEN CRUACHAN AND MULL

A loose-knit collection of seven coastal mountains, which are notable for their picturesque views.

BEN CRUACHAN   STOB DIAMH
A superb multi-topped mountain cirque, with spectacular rocky aretes and sensational coastal views.

BEINN A'CHOCHUILL   BEINN EUNAICH
A less strenuous but inferior substitute for the Cruachan walk, but with equally attractive views.

BEINN SGULAIRD
An easy traverse for a lazy afternoon with fine coastal views of Benderloch and Appin.

BEINN FHIONNLAIDH
Scrambling provides the main interest on a mountain hemmed in with forestry and uninspiring slopes.

BEN MORE
A mountain to save for a fine day to gain full benefit from its unique island situation.

CHAPTER 4   WALK 1

Ben Cruachan 3695ft/1126m
  Stob Dearg 3611ft/1101m
  Meall Cuanail 3004ft/918m
  Drochaid Glas 3312ft/1009m
Stob Diamh 3272ft/998m
  Sron an Isean 3163ft/966m
  Stob Garbh 3215ft/980m

Ben Cruachan commands respect, for the traverse of its seven tops, with ascent of 4900ft, is one of the classic expeditions of the Southern Highlands. The traditional start lies near the old railway station at Falls of Cruachan. A poor path leads up the west bank of the Allt Cruachan, passing through woods of oak, hazel and

birch to reach the access road to Cruachan dam. This can be followed to the reservoir's western shore for the lower slopes of Meall Cuanail, the first summit of the west-to-east round. This is seen as a prominent rounded undulation on a broad ridge due south of the main summit. Many prefer to do the round from east-to-west, however, to enjoy longer the views to Loch Linnhe and the Firth of Lorn.

The eastern tops

From the dam, follow the reservoir's eastern shore, before beginning the gradual ascent of the grassy embankments to a col and thence to Stob Garbh, a cairned top perched on the headwall of the mountain's eastern corrie, Coire Creachainn. The traverse continues to the north of this peak,

Recommended Valley Base Oban.

Maps O.S. 1:50 000 Sheets 41, 48 and 50; Bartholomews 1:100 000 Sheet 47; O.S. 1:63 360 Sheet *Ben Nevis and Glen Coe*.

Starting Point/Length and time for main itinerary
Walk 1 Falls of Cruachan (078268). 9 miles/ 4900ft of ascent, 5–8 hours.
Walk 2 Drishaig (133283). 8 miles/3900ft of ascent, 5–8 hours.
Walk 3 Elleric (035489). 4 miles/3050ft of ascent, 3–5 hours.
Walk 4 Elleric (035489). 9 miles/3140ft of ascent, 5–8 hours.
Walk 5 Salen (572431). 19 miles/3500ft of ascent, 8–12 hours.

across a short dip of 250ft to the cairn of Stob Diamh, the highest of the three peaks around the eastern corrie. Those seeking only to traverse these tops may prefer the alternative approach from the Stron-milchan road, where a well-defined track, the route of an old lead-mine railway, runs along the base of the hill to Coire Ghlais. The streams in this hollow, and that of Coire Creachainn are crossed by bridges (not marked on O.S. maps) to gain the long spurs of Stob Garbh or Sron an Isean. From Sron an Isean, the climb to Stob Diamh is steep and uneven and in mist a traverse in the reverse direction requires care, as the ridgeline is difficult to detect.

Drochaid Glas

The next summit along the ridge, Drochaid Glas, lies directly above the basin of the reservoir and the headwalls of a northern corrie. This can also bemuse, for beyond Stob Diamh a large boulderfield is crossed to reach its rocky knob, which has no cairn. To add to the confusion, the summit lies slightly to the north of the main ridgeline. In mist, careful navigation is required to regain the crest, particularly when traversing from west to east when it is better to leave the summit and retrace one's steps for about 20yds, keeping to the south side of the hill as the turn to the east is made. This helps to avoid the possibility of making a false start down the narrow arête which falls towards Glen Noe.

The western tops

To the west of Drochaid Glas, the crest of the ridge is narrower and boulder-strewn, with large blocks appearing on the steeper ground below the main summit, where there is an O.S. pillar.

The ridge continues to a saddle and the peak of Stob Dearg, often referred to as the 'Taynuilt peak'. When descending to this gap in mist, a move to the south should be made as if going to Meall Cuanail. Once clear of the larger stones a westerly bearing can be taken to reach the foot of Stob Dearg. This peak can also be reached on a direct ascent from the Pass of Brander. Above the western end of the pass, follow the Allt Cruiniche to open slopes below the col separating Stob Dearg from the hump of Meall nan Each to the west.

A return to the Stob Dearg – Ben Cruachan col, with some re-ascent towards the latter's summit avoids the slabby face of Coire a' Bhachaill. An easy descent due south then finds the short rise to Meall Cuanail, and the softer grassed slopes beyond which, falling towards the Cruach-an dam, speed the return to the road by the Allt Cruachan.

CHAPTER 4   WALK 2

Beinn a' Chochuill 3215ft/980m
Beinn Eunaich 3242ft/989m

Compared to Ben Cruachan, Beinn Eunaich seems dreary and Beinn a' Chochuill equally apologetic for intruding

upon the eastern skyline of its more imposing neighbour. The peaks look best from Glen Kinglass, where wild corries face the rough flanks of Ben Starav, but this area is so isolated that they are rarely approached from that direction. The most convenient start is from the south-west.

Beinn a' Chochuill

From the tiny bridge over the Allt Mhoille on the Stronmilchan road, a good track rises easily to the pass at the head of Glen Noe. Near the 1250ft contour a short branch goes to the right to cross a south-east rib of Beinn a' Chochuill. From here it is a pleasant plod up on to the flat summit ridge, and an easy stroll to a low cairn half a mile to the west.

Beinn Eunaich

At the eastern end of Beinn a' Chochuill a grassy ridge drops 900ft to a col which is crossed to reach the shoulder of Beinn Eunaich. Views down the rugged Glen Kinglass to the bleak moorland tops of the Black Mount help to break the monotony of the drag to a large summit cairn. Broad grassy slopes fall from the summit to the bump of Stob Maol above the farm at Castles, where they fan out to give an easy glide down to the track.

CHAPTER 4   WALK 3

Beinn Sgulaird 3059ft/937m

This knobbly ridged hill sprawls above the head of Loch Creran. At the head of the loch, on the north side of the River Creran, a lane leads through deciduous woods to a small car-park near Elleric. A track continues past this dwelling to a bridge on the River Ure near Glenure House.

Above Glenure the ground rises sharply and a stream acts as a useful guide to the ridge on the steepest and most direct ascent to the summit cairn. The climbs from Druimavuic and the head of Loch Creran are more leisurely, and better views are obtained from the grassy slopes rising to the first hump on the ridge. This runs north-east along a switchback of dips and rises, first over an unnamed top of 2807ft/856m, a dip of 300ft and then a climb of 70ft to the top of Meall Garbh. A further dip (to 2579ft) is followed by the final rise to the summit. At another dip a third of a mile beyond the summit, the ridge divides. The eastern spur drops very steeply and involves scrambling to reach the River Ure in the glen below. An easier route lies along the main ridge, where steep grass above rocky bluffs sweeps down to the hump of Stob Gaibhre, and the meadows of Glenure.

It is possible to reach the mountain by a tedious route from Gualachulain at the head of Loch Etive, along the line of a forest fence on the Allt a' Bhiorain to the north of Beinn Trilleachan.

CHAPTER 4   WALK 4

Beinn Fhionnlaidh 3145ft/959m

The activities of the Forestry Commission have done much to impede access to this hill, to such an extent that an approach from Glen Etive cannot be recommended.

The most direct route to the summit starts at Glenure to the south-west (see access to Beinn Sgulaird). Here, one of the few access points unencumbered by trees gives an open prospect of the lower slopes of gentle grass rising to Leac Bharainn, above which the well-defined western prow rises to the summit. The climb is enlivened by the gradual appearance of the peaks of Etive and Glencoe. North of the summit are crags above Coire a'Chait and the small nose of Caoran's spur. The opposite flank of the hill is broken, and gives some easy, enjoyable scrambling.

A descent to the north of the hill is inadvisable, as the 1200ft of hillside down to Bealach Caol Creran is extremely steep, in places precipitous, and the forests at the head of Glen Creran very dense.

CHAPTER 4   WALK 5

Ben More 3169ft/966m

Ben More, the highest mountain on the island of Mull, is often one of the last peaks to be climbed by the enthusiastic peak-bagger. Lying towards the west of the island it is some distance from the ferry terminal at Craignure. To take a car across on the ferry just to reach the base of the mountain is costly. The alternative is a bus to Salen and a seven-mile walk to Loch na Keal, where the small island of Eorsa signposts the start of the climb. The first objective is An Gearna, a rounded shoulder above the farm at Disheig.

Above An Gearna, the slope eases temporarily, and again steepens as the hill narrows into the main back of the ridge which runs roughly north-west to south-east across the summit. At right angles to this backbone, the ridge of A' Chioch forms a fine arête above the northern corries and the wide sweep of Glen Clachaig. The eastern slopes are precipitous, and care is needed on the descent to A' Chioch as the drop towards its crest is also steep and a false move could easily lead to difficulties. A compass is of little assistance as the summit of Ben More is composed of magnetic rock, but the direct return to the road should be resisted as the ridge to A' Chioch provides some spectacular views. At the saddle before the rise on to Beinn Fhada, take the easy eastern route off the end of the ridge to reach an ancient right-of-way to the head of Loch na Keal. A well-defined path through a glen joins a wide track leading to the waters of Loch Ba.

GLEN ETIVE
AND GLEN COE

The mountains in this chapter are among Scotland's finest. In Glen Coe intricate routes lead through the numerous cliffs to gain the high aretes and ridges which provide dramatic scrambling. The Glen Etive peaks are less craggy, but offer interesting navigational problems.

BEN STARAV BEINN NAN AIGHENAN GLAS BHEINN MHOR STOB COIR' AN ALBANNAICH MEALL NAN EUN
A demanding and complex walk, with fine views in clear weather and intricate route-finding in mist.

BUACHAILLE ETIVE MOR: STOB DEARG
A magnificent, craggy peak with outstanding views in all directions.

BUACHAILLE ETIVE BEAG: STOB DUBH
A mountain notable for its superb views of the Glen Etive peaks and the high crests of Bidean nam Bian.

BIDEAN NAM BIAN
A classic and extremely strenuous walk on one of Scotland's most complex and interesting mountains.

SGOR NA H-ULAIDH
This hill may not assert itself as forcibly as its neighbours, but its ascent can be just as taxing.

THE AONACH EAGACH: SGOR NAM FIANNAIDH MEALL DEARG
Exposed and exhilarating scrambling on a pinnacled ridge provides one of the great mountain expeditions.

BEINN A'BHEITHIR: SGORR DHEARG SGORR DHONUILL
A superb mountain horseshoe, with varied terrain and constantly changing views.

CHAPTER 5   **WALK 1**

Ben Starav 3541ft/1078m
  Meall Cruidh 3049ft/930m
  Stob Coire Dheirg 3372ft/1028m
Beinn nan Aighenan 3141ft/957m
Glas Bheinn Mhor 3258ft/997m
Stob Coir' an Albannaich 3425ft/1044m
Meall nan Eun 3039ft/928m

These hills are usually approached from Glen Etive, where a track crosses the river to Coileitir farm, about two miles before the roadhead pier. They can be climbed in one expedition or conveniently split into two groups.

Ben Starav
The Etive route provides the best ascent of Ben Starav. A rough moorland path leads to a bridge on the Allt Mheuran, and a cairned path on the west bank. This it leaves gradually to climb by heathery slopes on to a well-defined ridge, buttressed by broken crag on its left. Above the 2250ft contour, the ridge undulates for a short distance on the rise to a narrower crest of broken rock, whose screes cascade towards Loch Etive. The ridge then rises in a graceful rocky staircase to a triangulation pillar (3538ft). The actual

summit is at a cairn a short distance to the south-east, and is one of several viewpoints which encompass the entire range of Cruachan to the south. The top of the mountain is a plateau of bedrock, bordered on the north-east by the craggy rim of a corrie. Across this stonefield, the small cairn on the bump of Meall Cruidh overlooks steep ground falling to ridges running to the south east and north east.

The crest of the south-east ridge contrarily turns south-west, and then curves west to the spur of Stob an Duine Ruaidh. To gain the main ridge to the north-east, move approximately 300 yards east-south-east from Meall Cruidh before heading north-east along first the west, and then the north side of the steeply-angled corrie wall seen on the right. In thick mist careful navigation is needed, as there are cliffs in the angle where the plateau's edge curves to the northern edge of the ridge. These cliffs are seen on the left on the 200ft descent of the rib, which levels out on to a narrow arête of small castellated blocks. If doubtful about the 'castles', keep to the south side of the crest. This avoids awkward exposed moves which, in dry weather, give an entertaining scramble.

Ahead, the ridge lifts gently to the rocky

Recommended Valley Base Glencoe.

Maps O.S. 1:50 000 Sheets 41 and 50; Bartholomews 1:100 000 Sheets 47 and 48; O.S. 1:63 360 Sheet *Ben Nevis and Glen Coe*; S.M.T. 1:20 000 Sheet *Glen Coe*

Starting Point/Length and time for main itinerary
Walk 1 Glen Etive (136467). 18 miles/7700ft of ascent, 10–15 hours.
Walk 2 Altnafeadh (221563). 9 miles/3250ft of ascent, 5–8 hours.
Walk 3 A82 (190562). 6 miles/2800ft of ascent, 3–5 hours.
Walk 4 Achnambeithach (139567). 9 miles/4650ft of ascent, 5–8 hours.
Walk 5 Achnacon (118565). 8 miles/3600ft of ascent, 4–6 hours.
Walk 6 Allt-na-reigh (176566). 4 miles/3000ft of ascent, 3–5 hours.
Walk 7 West Laroch (080578). 10 miles/4000ft of ascent, 5–8 hours.

height of Stob Coire Dheirg, whose cairn signals another twist in the ridge – a steep east-south-easterly drop to meet the ridge running out to Beinn nan Aighenan, on the grassy col to the west of Glas Bheinn Mhor. In mist, careful navigation is required to locate the correct ridge and avoid a short false ridge to the north-east which terminates in an abrupt drop. It is best to veer slightly south from the summit of Stob Coire Dheirg as there are also precipices in the angle between this false ridge and the main ridge to the east of the cairn. There is a trace of a descent path in the screes below the larger rocks around the cairn.

Beinn nan Aighenan (Aighean)

The col to the west of Glas Bheinn Mhor can be approached by a tributary of the Allt Mheuran as the most direct approach to the ridge of Beinn nan Aighenan. This peak has a rough dome which lacks any features of note, and the diversion to its top may, as a consequence, be found tedious.

Glas Bheinn Mhor

Glas Bheinn Mhor is, by contrast, a grassy hill, and though the ascent may seem a ponderous plod, there are fine views across Glen Etive to compensate. The convex slopes delay sighting the summit cairn until the very last moment. To the east of the mossy summit, the drop to the head of the Allt Mheuran follows the edge of craggy ground buttressing the north side of the hill. The last few feet to the col are very steep and several outcrops encountered hereabouts may appear to bar further downward progress. These should be passed on their right, but return to the ridgeline which curves to the north, away from more minor buttresses which appear on the right.

Stob Coir' an Albannaich

It is easy to shorten the walk at this point and return to Glen Etive following the Allt Mheuran. The main itinerary continues up an abrupt steepening towards Stob Coir' an Albannaich. The angle soon eases and higher slopes fan out to a wide grassy summit ridge. On the right (south-east) this narrows to a rocky snout. (Note: walkers going in the reverse direction should beware of this tempting false line of descent. It seems natural to follow the ridge to the end of the snout, but at this point broken terrain denies easy access to the Allt Mheuran gap.)

The approach to Stob Coir' an Albannaich from Coileitir utilizes grassy slopes, rising in steps without interruption for 2000ft. There the slopes ease temporarily, and upward progress continues along a broken edge, to reach a grassy table with a large mossed mound topped by a cairn.

The precipitous face below the summit falls to a saddle in front of Meall Tarsuinn, beyond which Meall nan Eun and the contorted ridges of Stob Ghabhar and Clachlet are seen. The descent to the saddle involves a move to the east of the cairn, followed by a zig-zag course on exceptionally steep slopes with precipitous ground below and to the right.

Meall nan Eun

Meall nan Eun is a decidedly dull, flat-topped hill. It is linked to Meall Tarsuinn by a broad shoulder which runs northwards towards Glen Etive. On the return from the cairn this shoulder directs the walker to the source of the Allt Ceitlein, which leads down to Glen Etive near the farmstead at Glenceitlein.

Approaches from the south

Access to this group of peaks from the Glen Kinglass watershed involves a long approach walk from Victoria Bridge at the west end of Loch Tulla. The track to Clashgour is followed as far as a path which leads to the boggy moors of Loch Dochard, and then easily to a pass at the head of Glen Kinglass. From this point a heather crossing to the west of Lochan na h-Iuraiche gives access to the snout of Stob Coir' an Albannaich. Meall nan Eun is more difficult to get at and is best approached by a route along the north side of the river from Clashgour and round the north-east of Loch Dochard. This route is advised as the cluster of tarns linked by wide streams west of the loch makes the whole valley very marshy.

The western peaks of the group are best approached from the upper end of Glen Kinglass, beyond the pass. Here a bridge spans the river giving access to a blunt rocky spur of Beinn nan Aighenan. Alternatively easier ground alongside the upper reaches of the Kinglass leads to its source at the strategically-placed saddle to the west of Glas Bheinn Mhor.

Whether approached from north or south the traverse of these peaks in a single expedition is a rewarding day, but anyone seeking a shorter day should be sure to include Ben Starav, for it is the finest hill in the group.

CHAPTER 5   WALK 2

Buachaille Etive Mor:
Stob Dearg 3345ft/1022m
Stob na Doire 3316ft/1011m
Stob Coire Altruim 3065ft/939m
Stob na Broige 3120ft/955m

'The great shepherd of Etive' towers above Rannoch Moor, proud guardian at the gates of Glen Coe. This is a mountain for superlatives, and the rambler might be forgiven for being daunted by its overwhelming cragginess as he surveys it from Kingshouse or the Glen Coe road.

Stob Dearg

From Altnafeadh, a fresh perspective shows a gap in the mountain's defences. Here a path leads to a footbridge over the River Coupall and then heads across the moor into Coire na Tulaich which in one long sweep reaches the summit ridge of the mountain. The path can be seen winding its way tortuously amongst the rubble at the corrie headwall and emerging on a stony col a short distance south-west of the summit cairn.

The traverse of the ridge

Stob Dearg is the highest top, but the mountain has more to offer. A splendid high-level traverse above Glen Etive links it to three other recognized tops, the first of which, Stob na Doire, lies just over a mile to the south-west. The stony promenade curves above Coire na Tulaich (note: to find this corrie from the summit in mist, head west-south-west for 300yds and then bear west for a similar distance) then veers to the south-west above the grassy sloped Coire Cloiche Finne, seen to the left. Stob na Doire overlooks a dip in the ridge on the 2600ft contour, from which there is a useful descent to the Lairig Gartain. Beyond the gap, the ridge twists to the north, crossing more stony ground on the rise to the cairn of Stob Coire Altruim. Gentler undulations give easier going on the walk to the final top, Stob na Broige, which is worth visiting for the fine views down the length of Glen Etive. It is possible to drop down the south-west shoulder of this top to Glen Etive (or the Lairig Gartain if continuing to Buachaille Etive Beag) but it is more usual to return to the col between Stob Coire Altruim and Stob na Doire for a swift descent to the Lairig Gartain.

The Curved Ridge

A more demanding ascent of the mountain is by Curved Ridge (an Easy rock-climb, little more than a stiff scramble). The ridge rears up beside the Rannoch Wall, the obvious pink cliff set high on the craggy south-east side of the mountain. The best view of the ridge is from the climbing hut at Jacksonville, where stepping stones lead across the Coupall. From this direction the ridge can be held in view as the mountain is approached. A path leads up screes to a short scramble up the side of a large rocky projection, above which heather terraces give access to the foot of the ridge proper. The climb involves several easy pitches interspersed with modest scrambling, the hardest section being level with the upper part of the Rannoch Wall. Here the ridge narrows and steepens on the upward sweep to the foot of the Crowberry Tower. Moving past the tower, the dark chasm of Crowberry Gully is passed on the right, followed by the mountain's upper wall where a short scramble brings the cairn of Stob Dearg quickly into view.

CHAPTER 5   WALK 3

Buachaille Etive Beag
Stob Dubh 3129ft/958m
Stob Coire Raineach 3029ft/925m

The Glen Coe face of 'The little shepherd' may seem to be a miniature of its grander partner, although the crags on the nose of Stob nan Cabar are not of great significance. To dismiss the mountain on this account would be a mistake, for its traverse gives views of Glen Etive and Bidean nam Bian which are unsurpassed.

Approaching from Glen Coe, the broken face of Stob nan Cabar can be turned on either side, where steep grass and scree are quickly scaled to reach the jumbled cairn of Stob Coire Raineach. The mountain is split into two distinct and separate tops by a saddle in the centre of its stony back. To the south-west of this col, a sharp rise leads to a small top where the ridge narrows to an easy arête, which continues to the table of Stob Dubh. The modest cairn lies a short distance north-north-east of the point marked 3129 on the old one inch maps, but, as the ridge is narrow, it is impossible to miss the highest point. Broken rock and scree break up the slopes on the Lairig Gartain side of the mountain, but these lack the drama of the precipitous face above the Lairig Eilde.

The shortest route to the summit starts in Glen Etive, near the farm at Dalness. A diversion can be made from the Lairig Gartain path onto the ridge which leads steeply to the summit screes. Further along the ridge, at the dividing saddle, stony slopes to the south fan out into the head of Lairig Gartain where a cairned path can be found for the return to Glen Etive, or Glen Coe, though the descent to the Lairig Eilde is a shorter route to the Glen Coe road.

CHAPTER 5   WALK 4

Bidean nam Bian 3766ft/1150m
  Stob Coire nam Beith 3621ft/1107m
  Stob Coire nan Lochan 3657ft/1115m
  Stob Coire Sgreamhach 3497ft/1072m
  Beinn Fhada 3116ft/952m
  (north-east top) 3064ft/931m

The summit of Bidean nam Bian, the highest mountain in the old county of Argyll, hides behind the great buttresses of the 'Three Sisters', but a glimpse of it may be had from near the Clachaig Inn, along the corridor of Coire nam Beith, the most direct route to the western tops.

A track runs from the Glen Coe road to Achnambeithach, but the west bank of the stream falling from the corrie can be followed just as easily. A path twists its way up the grassy slopes into the mouth of a ravine between the spurs of Aonach Dubh and An t-Sron, and thence upwards to cross the stream on the 1750ft contour beneath Stob Coire nan Lochan. Here the stream divides.

Stob Coire nan Lochan
The tributary to the left can be followed up a steep boulderfield to the saddle between Stob Coire nan Lochan and the summit of Bidean nam Bian. Above this col the stones of Stob Coire nan Lochan change colour from red to grey at a fault line crossed a little below the cairn. The ascent from the saddle to Bidean nam Bian is narrower and steeper, with huge buttresses seen on the right (a route which, if used on the descent

and especially in mist, should be treated with caution as there are false leads out to the top of two of the crags set in the angle below the summit ridge).

Stob Coire nam Beith
The right-hand branch of the stream in Coire nam Beith rises high on the slope of An t-Sron, and can be followed to the head of the corrie, where an arduous scree slope gives exits to the ridge at the dips between An t-Sron and Stob Coire nam Beith, and the latter and Bidean nam Bian (the easier route being that to the west of Stob Coire nam Beith). There is also a good stiff climb up the nose of An t-Sron from the lower reaches of Coire nam Beith, or more directly from the Glen Coe road, from opposite the National Trust Information Centre. An interesting chasm cuts into the northern slope of this spur, where steep ground and outcrops can provide odd bits of scrambly entertainment. Rock and grass cover the crest of An t-Sron from where there is a good view of the Church Door and Diamond buttresses, beneath the high tower of Bidean nam Bian. Several cairns dotting the ridge mark the route to the foot of Stob Coire nam Beith, where a well-marked path, (a useful guide in mist) climbs scree above the corrie headwall to the tiny summit cairn, overlooking the very head of the corrie.

Bidean nam Bian
To the south of Stob Coire nam Beith the path dips to follow the curved rim of another corrie headwall to a small bumpy top above cliffs which appear on the left. The summit of Bidean nam Bian awaits.

Beinn Fhada
The ascent of Bidean nam Bian from the east is equally rewarding, as the ridge of Beinn Fhada is particularly fine. The path through the Lairig Eilde should be followed, and beyond the point where it crosses the stream, the climb lies up grassy, rock-strewn slopes offering entertaining route-finding to the ridge above. Breasting the last rise near the spot height of 2661ft/811m the whole range of Bidean nam Bian's many spurs bursts into view.

The north side of Beinn Fhada is precipitous, and its ridge crest an obvious spine. Two cairns on a grassy saddle are passed on the climb to two distinct tops, the first of which, a stony hump marked by a small cairn, is the north-east top of Beinn Fhada. The cliffs on the north side of the ridge become more pronounced, and the finely-honed arête of the centre top, though narrow, has easy passage on its southern side, thus lessening the possibility of wandering too near the edge of the crags in mist. At its south-western end this top has a short scramble down to a narrow gap slicing the ridge. A vertical rock on the opposite wall of the gap is easier than it looks, as the huge block can be turned on

the left (south), where a path on a gritty shelf leads to an obvious scramble up a rocky cleft and a small, firm stance. Here a small ledge, leaning slightly outwards and greasy when wet, calls for one careful move to reach the easier jumble of rock above. The obstacle can be avoided on the left, where steep grass and scree climb back to the ridge for the final pull to the summit of Stob Coire Sgreamhach. Here, at two pink cairns, the main ridge of the mountain turns to the west to a stony saddle at the head of Coire Gabhail, whose vast amphitheatre is now fully exposed to view. An edge of crag is then easily followed, and as the climb to the summit of Bidean nam Bian is a gradual one there is ample time to enjoy the views of the Glen Etive peaks to the south.

If it is not the intention to complete the full traverse of the mountain there is a line of descent from the saddle to the south of Stob Coire nan Lochan into the Lost Valley. This also provides a useful escape route in inclement weather, as the corrie (Coire Gabhail) leads to a narrow ravine and a path down to the road.

CHAPTER 5   WALK 5

Sgor na h-Ulaidh 3258ft/994m
  Stob an Fhuarain 3160ft/968m

The proximity of the more popular peaks of Glen Coe means that Sgor na h-Ulaidh, hidden behind Bidean nam Bian, tends to be overlooked. A track from Achnacon in Glen Coe follows the west bank of the Allt na Muidhe, to a bridge a short distance from the cottage at Gleann-leac-na-muidhe. Nearby, a notice exhorts walkers to take the direct route up the western face of Aonach Dubh a' Ghlinne, a rocky prow guarded by several outcrops and small crags. Two obvious stream gullies, seen above plantations near the cottage, act as guides to the ridge, which is attained after an exhausting clamber of 2000ft. Here there are several tarns nestling in folds between hummocks close to the small cairn of the aptly named Stob an Fhuarain, peak of the well. Looking ahead, the precipitous rock face of Sgor na h-Ulaidh, split by the deep chasm of Red Gully, is seen at the end of an obvious ridge. The remains of an old fence and a low wall should be followed along this crest, especially on the final rise to the summit. Here the fence turns left, away from the northern precipices and up a stony gully on to a short rib, where a turn to the right is made on to the summit rocks a short step from the cairn. The fence continues past another cairn and dips along the broad ridge to the spur of Corr na Beinne. From this ridge another fence shoots down to the right, across ground which is very stony and steep in places. Some 300ft above the valley floor, the fence vaults over a greasy slab, which should be avoided on the right. The banks of the Allt na Muidhe then return the walker to the track at Gleann-leac-na-muidhe.

Access from Glen Creran is made impossibly difficult by huge impenetrable plantations of trees. Glen Etive is no less encumbered, though a gap in the timber leaves a route open to the slopes of Beinn Maol Chaluim, which could be crossed to reach the gap of Bealach Fhionnghaill and the east ridge of Sgor na h-Ulaidh.

CHAPTER 5   WALK 6

The Aonach Eagach:
Sgor nam Fiannaidh 3173ft/967m
  Stob Coire Leith 3080ft/940m
Meall Dearg 3118ft/953m
  Am Bodach 3085ft/943m

The traverse of the Aonach Eagach is not an expedition to be lightly undertaken, for there is a marked degree of exposure at several points along the ridge. The rock-climbing is graded 'easy' but to the rambler this may seem a misnomer. There are two recognized routes to the ridge, the easiest being at the eastern end, where grass slopes behind the cottage at Allt-na-reigh rise to the summit of Am Bodach. At the western end, starting at the Clachaig Hotel, a rough path climbs up the west side of the Clachaig Gully, the deep chasm splitting the steep face of the hill immediately behind the building. This route involves 3000ft of punishing scree slopes. There appear to be several gullies falling to Glen Coe from the ridge, but any temptation to seek access to or from the arête other than at the ends of the chain should be firmly resisted, as most of the accidents on this side of Glen Coe have been caused by walkers trying to avoid, or escape from the centre of the ridge. There is only one route from the ridge, a huge stone-shoot just to the east of Meall Dearg, running down a steep open gully to the road near Achtriochan. This should only be used as a last desperate measure, as the scree is the most diabolical imaginable and the passage by no means easy. An east-west traverse is best, as the climb to Am Bodach is preferable to the grinding scree of Sgor nam Fiannaidh, and the improving vistas to the west are the most enchanting.

Am Bodach and Meall Dearg
Several rocky lumps break up the slopes above the road, but these are easily turned on the right (east) and the climb to the flat crown of Am Bodach should be uneventful. To reach the crest to the north-west, follow the edge of crags to the left of the cairn, where, framed by the gully below, the grass-topped pinnacle of The Chancellor may be seen. A path scratched in the turf, which drops on to an airy stance on

the lip of the northern corrie, hints at exposure to come. This is followed by another rock ledge which dips and twists to to the south side of a narrow rock, where a downward step negotiates the head of a wide gully, whose dramatic shaft sweeps to the floor of Glen Coe. Here, the arête dips slightly and veers to the north, on the gradual pull to a cairn on the grassy hump of Meall Dearg, which looks west to an exciting prospect of the pinnacles.

The Crazy Pinnacles
A line of fence-posts marches along the crest, which narrows beyond the first knoll where a well-trodden path is revealed. Two pinnacles are passed on the south side, a full 3000ft above the Glen Coe road. Just beyond a third pinnacle the path dips to a deep notch. At this point the exposure is quite marked, as the escape from the gap requires a move to the north side of a large rock blocking the ridge. Here an easy climb up a short chimney leads to an uneven pinnacle. This is followed by a delicate arête leading to a similar rocky knob, which is the first of two airy points on the most sensational part of the ridge. On its western edge this tower is a series of grassed knobbles/ of rock, and here the scramble becomes much easier as the path reappears on the dip to a wider crest.

Stob Coire Leith / Sgor nam Fiannaidh
Fence-posts are again reassuring companions on the long easy drag to the next cairn on the peak of Stob Coire Leith. To the west, the ridge levels out to give a relaxing walk to the final peak, Sgor nam Fiannaidh.

A route to the glen near Loch Achtriochtan can be found down steep grass on a line due south of this western summit (also a useful ascent route). Half a mile further to the west, easy-graded scree leads down to the grassy crease marking the head of the Clachaig Gully, where a path should be followed above the rock ribs seen on the right (west) of the deepening chasm – this leads directly to the road at Clachaig Hotel.

CHAPTER 5   WALK 7

Beinn a' Bheithir:
Sgorr Dhearg 3361ft/1024m
  Sgor Bhan 3104ft/947m
Sgorr Dhonuill 3284ft/1001m

Beinn a' Bheithir is an impressive horseshoe of three peaks, commanding the narrows where Loch Leven meets the deep sea-arm of Loch Linnhe. Unimaginative planting has marred access to many of the finer ascents to a ridge which offers splendid panoramas.

Sgor Bhan
The open hillside above West Laroch gives the only uninterrupted climb on the north side of the mountain. From here a

hill-track to the pass at the head of Gleann an Fhiodh (an old route to Glen Creran) gives access to the grassy slopes which climb gradually to steeper heather. The ridge above is wide and easy and carries a path which meanders through rocks to the peak of Sgor Bhan. The face of the north-east ridge, seen to the left, is a forbidding plunge of black stratified slate which cuts across its sharply-angled crest in a series of ledges which dip from north to south. On this route the one steep pitch encountered can be turned by ledges on the south (left).

Sgorr Dhearg
A narrow ridge links the cairn of Sgor Bhan to the summit of Sgorr Dhearg, with its white triangulation pillar. An attendant cairn marks the top of the northern ridge which leads down to Ballachulish Forest. If descending by this spur, the island in the bay to the east of North Ballachulish provides a useful guiding line to the narrowest part of the woods.

The main spine of the mountain falls west-south-west to a grassy saddle at 2450ft. A fence across this gap creeps below the imposing stack of Sgorr a' Chaolais, and drops north towards a stream disappearing into the forest. A track on the west bank of a larger stream further down emerges from the wood near Ballachulish House.

Sgorr Dhonuill
On the west side of the pass steep grass rises to a narrow crest, where crags overhanging the northern corrie are seen to buttress the summit of Sgorr Dhonuill. A path follows the edge of these impressive crags, over rough boulders, to reach a cairn planted firmly in the summit turf.

The mountain's western slopes curve around Gleann a' Chaolais. A rim of very steep stony ground and crags make descent difficult for about a mile west of the cairn. The traverse of a small flat-topped undulation at 2650ft finds a dip in the ridge at the head of a grassy gully. This succours a stream falling to the forest fence, where the track to Ballachulish House should be sought.

Creag Ghorm
To complete the whole horseshoe, the knolly ridge should be followed to Creag Ghorm (2470ft/753m). The strata on this part of the ridge are interesting in appearing to flow across the crest, thereby creating many depressions which hold tiny lochans. Consequently its series of humps and tarn-filled hollows may present some navigational problems in thick mist. The descent from Creag Ghorm to the old piers north of Kentallen on Loch Linnhe is very steep, but following one of the precipitate streams draining this side of the hill is preferable to floundering through the forest at the foot of the northern spur.

BRIDGE OF ORCHY AND THE BLACK MOUNT

The Black Mount group, to the west of the main road, offers rough, stony ridges divided by desolate corries.
The Beinn Dorain chain to the east is grassier, although craggy on the northern and western slopes

BEINN DORAIN BEINN AN DOTHAIDH BEINN ACHALADAIR BEINN A' CHREACHAIN
Steep initial slopes lead to a fine high-level traverse with views across Rannoch Moor to Ben Nevis.

BEINN MHANACH
Hemmed in by greater peaks and Loch Lyon, this hidden mountain proves to be a tedious lump.

STOB GHABHAR STOB A' CHOIRE ODHAIR
A fine walk across stony peaks and above gloomy corries.

CREISE MEALL A' BHUIRIDH
This interesting traverse of the northern Black Mount can be linked conveniently to the Stob Ghabhar walk.

Recommended Valley Base Bridge of Orchy.

Maps O.S. 1:50 000 Sheet 50; Bartholomews 1:100 000 Sheet 48; O.S. 1:63 360 Sheet *Ben Nevis and Glen Coe.*

Starting Point/Length and time for main itinerary
Walk 1 Bridge of Orchy Station (301394). 20 miles/5200ft of ascent, 9–14 hours.
Walk 2 A82 near Auch (317353). 12 miles/ 2800ft of ascent, 5–8 hours.
Walk 3 Victoria Bridge (271423). 15 miles/ 4960ft of ascent, 7–11 hours.
Walk 4 Black Rock Cottage (268531). 8 miles/ 3200ft of ascent, 4–6 hours.

CHAPTER 6	WALK 1

Beinn Dorain 3524ft/1074m
Beinn an Dothaidh 3289ft/1002m
Beinn Achaladair 3404ft/1039m
  (south top) 3288ft/1002m
Beinn a' Chreachain 3540ft/1081m
  Meall Buidhe 3205ft/977m

Beinn Dorain lifts a bold, gully-seamed pyramid to dominate the A82 three miles north of Tyndrum. A line of equally imposing peaks extends to the north-east, their western slopes rising in an unbroken wall above the West Highland Railway and Crannach Wood. The traverse of the four mountains in a single day is an arduous expedition, with almost 6000ft of ascent on a strenuous walk of sixteen miles. Alternatively, Beinn Dorain and Beinn an Dothaidh can be conveniently linked to leave Beinn Achaladair and Beinn a' Chreachain for another day.

Beinn Dorain
The steep south ridge of Beinn Dorain is an unimaginative slog up unrelenting slopes. Even the more acceptable route from Bridge of Orchy station can seem an

exasperating grind to the north end of its ridge, above Coire an Dothaidh. Here, just to the south of a col, two lochans indicate the turning point south to easier slopes rising to a large cairn. In mist, this point might be mistaken for the summit, which is marked by a smaller cairn a few yards further south, across the dip of a narrower ridge.

Beinn an Dothaidh
Returning to the col for the ascent of Beinn an Dothaidh, steer an easterly course to the right of the two tarns to reach the broader spread of the saddle and so avoid the cliffs and treacherous ground which lie ahead. To the north of the saddle, a short sharp rise on to the first of three bumps on the plateau heralds the true summit a quarter of a mile to the north-east. The bump marked 3267 on the old 1" maps (996m) lies a quarter of a mile to the west of the summit proper, which is some 22ft higher and lies near the edge of the northern corrie. The whole western and northern slopes of this hill are steep and precipitous, with the greatest concentration of cliffs above the Allt Coire Achaladair. A steep ridge drops from the summit cairn to the rocky gap at the head of the Allt Coire Achaladair, which provides a useful route to and from the hill.

Beinn Achaladair
Across the gap, a well-defined ridge, flanked by more broken slopes, turns north towards Beinn Achaladair's southern top. The broad ridge beyond is defended on the west and north by steep grassy ramparts. Two cairns grace the edge, the more northerly one, the actual summit, being a few feet higher than its companion.

Beinn a' Chreachain
The ridge now turns to hug the rim of a fine corrie, whose vegetated crags, at a breach in their south-west corner, offer an escape route down to the blackened pines of the Crannach Wood. A broad grassy ridge continues to Meall Buidhe's level crown, which sports three cairns, two at its south-west end, and one to the north-east. The twin cairns mark the highest point, and the head of steep open ground giving a safer descent than the aforementioned corrie-wall breach. Beyond the single cairn lies a short col where the ridge turns eastwards above the scoop of Lochan a' Chreachain to the hump of Beinn a' Chreachain. To the north-east of a small summit cairn, a narrow ridge completes the rim of Coire an Lochain, steepening perceptively as it dips to the Water of Tulla (footbridge), and the track which runs from Gorton to the road near Achallader farm.

CHAPTER 6	WALK 2

Beinn Mhanach 3125ft/954m
  Beinn a' Chuirn 3020ft/924m

Beinn Mhanach owes its name to long-forgotten clerics who, in a bygone age, established a monastery at its foot. Lacking any features of especial note, the mountain, in its lonely corner at the head of Glen Lyon, tends to be passed by. The shortest route to the mountain starts near Auch farm, at adjacent bridges on the confluence of two streams, one of which, the Allt Chonghlais, has a track beside it as far as the deserted shieling of Ais-an t-Sithein. Beyond the cottage, with its copious sheep-pens, steep slopes on the prominent mountain-wall ahead lead to a small cairn on the flat top of Beinn a' Chuirn. To the east, a broad ridge curves away to a larger cairn on the summit of Beinn Mhanach.

The moorland path from the dam in Glen Lyon is a lonely plod, complicated by the need to circumnavigate an arm of Loch Lyon reaching into Gleann Meran, a green vale possessing an unusually large number of sheep-stells. The Allt Meran and the Allt Cailliche are easily crossed a little way upstream, to gain the eastern end of the hill. The long rise to the cairn follows the line of a broken edge, above more ruffled slopes falling away to Gleann Cailliche. Opportunities to vary the return walk are limited, as the head of the loch narrows to the cut of the Abhuinn Ghlas, an uninviting, though not difficult or dangerous, crossing to the trackless southern shore.

CHAPTER 6   WALK 3

Stob Ghabhar 3565ft/1087m
   Aonach Eagach 3272ft/991m
   Sron a' Ghearrain 3202ft/991m
   Stob a' Bhruaich Leith 3083ft/939m
   Sron nan Giubhas 3197ft/974m
Stob a' Choire Odhair 3058ft/943m

The western margin of Rannoch Moor, with its tiny islets set in dark peaty water, backed by the snow-covered mountains, is a memorable picture on a clear winter's morning, and must have induced many to explore the ridges of Stob Ghabhar.

An early start is needed for a leisurely round of the six tops, for it should be remembered that even a traverse of the two mountains offers a challenging walk involving almost 4000ft of ascent. Behind the Glasgow University Mountaineering Club's hut at Clashgour (not to be confused with the cottage to the west) a track beside the Allt Toaig, rises to contour the flanks of Beinn Toaig and Stob a' Choire Odhair. At about 1000ft, turn to the west and climb beside a series of fine cascades on to the south-east spur of Stob Ghabhar. A line of rusty iron posts acts as guide towards, and then along, the ridge-crest of the mountain to pass some 20 yards to the west of the summit cairn, perched on a corrie's edge. Alternatively, follow the Allt Toaig almost to its source, before turning west up scree to the rock bands and grass below the torn crest of Aonach Eagach. To the west of a cairn a narrow notch is encountered, but there is no difficulty and the rocks soon give way to rubble near the fence at the edge of the deep eastern corrie.

Stob Ghabhar
From the summit cairn, the fence follows a stony ridge westwards, along one of the long arms of the hill to the grassy top of Sron a' Ghearrain. This easy walk is followed by a short drop of 150ft to the bare level crown of Stob a' Bhruaich Leith, flanked by the most desolate corries in the Black Mount. The main ridge northwards to Aonach Mor also has some commanding views, and the ridge snout on the attendant spur of Sron nan Giubhas offers a pleasant return route off the hill. But cross the corrie below the tarn and use the saddle between Aonach Eagach and Stob a' Choire Odhair to reach the Allt Toaig track, which is a more pleasant return walk to Victoria Bridge than the boggy plod across the heath of Coireach a' Ba.

Stob a' Choire Odhair
From the head of the track above the University hut, Stob a' Choire Odhair is easily climbed by following a stream towards a short saddle immediately south of the stony summit hump. West of the cairn a rough ridge dips to a broader saddle at the front of Aonach Eagach's broken crags, breached by steep screes providing access slopes to the ridge above. Despite minor crags fringing the slopes to the north of the cairn, Stob a' Choire Odhair lacks the drama of Stob Ghabhar, but offers the compensation of extensive views across Rannoch Moor and the high-walled Achallader hills beyond Loch Tulla.

CHAPTER 6   WALK 4

Creise 3608ft/1100m
   Clach Leathad 3602ft/1098m
   Mam Coire Easain 3506ft/1068m
   Stob a' Ghlais Choire 3268ft/996m
Meall a' Bhuiridh 3636ft/1108m

From the Kingshouse Hotel on the Rannoch Moor the blunt northern shoulder of Creise presents a fine profile, standing in bold silhouette against a southern sky. Meall a' Bhuiridh, the dumpier hill to its left, is familiar to the skier, but the mountaineer may well prefer to climb Creise to avoid the ski-impedimenta. Meall a' Bhuiridh can be taken in later by a detour from the main ridge.

Creise
The finest climb to Creise and Clach Leathad is by way of Sron na Creise, the end of a lengthy ridge which links the four tops west of Meall a' Bhuiridh. From Blackrock Cottage, level heather spreads to the boggy mouth of Cam Ghleann, which should be crossed to gain the lower slopes of Sron na Creise. Its rocky snout should be contoured until Glen Etive comes into view, where steep grass and scree lead to a rake climbing just beneath, and to the west of, several minor cliffs. A stone-filled gully seen ahead rises to more rock ribs on the blunt nose of the upper hill, for the scramble to the cairn of Stob a' Ghlais Choire. Broken crags along the rim of the corrie of the Allt Cam Ghlinne mould the edge of a curved crest rising to the top of Creise to the south. Marked 3596ft on the old maps this cairn has since been raised to the equivalent of 3608ft on the metric maps, to replace Clach Leathad as the highest point on the ridge. From Creise the ridge continues above a bolder escarpment of high crags to the flattened crown of Mam Coire Easain.

Here a narrow stony rib provides a means of descent through a break in the crags to a col at the foot of Meall a' Bhuiridh. In mist, this is difficult to locate as there are no landmarks to act as a guide from the plateau. Under snow, the task is more difficult still, especially when cornices line the edge.

Clach Leathad
The ridge continues to the south, broadening into the stony plateau of Clach Leathad, which splits into two ridges above Coireach a' Ba. The broad slopes of one fall west from the cairn for about half a mile, before becoming progressively steeper on the drop to the Bealach Fuar-chathaidh, a grassy col at the head of Coireach a' Ba. Ahead rises Aonach Mor, whose broad ridge provides a useful link in continuing to Stob Ghabhar, seen two miles to the south.

The ridge bearing east from Clach Leathad's summit is flanked by craggy bluffs above tiny Loch an Easain. There is a gradual incline down to the old road which can be used for the return to Kingshouse, free of the hummocks and bogs of Coireach a' Ba.

Meall a' Bhuiridh
To traverse Meall a' Bhuiridh, the walker must return to Mam Coire Easain to find the rib linking the two mountains. This drops to 3070ft before climbing over rocky ground on a widening crest, which broadens further to the summit of Meall a' Bhuiridh. The alternative ascent from Blackrock Cottage lies along the line of the ski-lift pylons and tows, a route lacking interest, but often preferred if continuing to the neighbouring ridge, as the climb up the rib to Mam Coire Easain is more obvious than its descent.

GLEN LOCHAY
AND LOCH TAY

Thirteen mountains can be explored from a base at Killin. The eastern peaks, particularly Ben Lawers, are very popular but this is compensated by fine views. The less-frequented western peaks are surrounded by other hills which limit the prospects.

BEINN HEASGARNICH   CREAG MHOR   BEINN CHALLUM
A total ascent of over 4000ft makes the ten-mile round of Glen Lochay a strenuous day's outing.

MEALL GLAS   SGIATH CHUIL
Two unexceptional mountains enlivened by fine views of Ben More and Stob Binnein.

MEALL GHAORDIE
Quite the dullest hill in the Southern Highlands.

MEALL NAN TARMACHAN
An 1800ft climb from Lochan Lairige allows easy access to a convuluted and entertaining ridge.

BEN LAWERS   MEALL GREIGH   MEALL GARBH   BEINN GHLAS   MEALL CORRANAICH
MEALL A' CHOIRE LEITH
A grand traverse along an easy, serpentine ridge, which can easily be split into two expeditions.

Recommended Valley Base Killin.

Maps O.S. 1:50 000 Sheets 50 and 51; Bartholomews 1:100 000 Sheet 48; O.S. 1:63 360 Sheet *Loch Lomond and The Trossachs*

Starting Point/Length and time for main itinerary
Walk 1 Badour (431351). 14 miles/6000ft of ascent, 7–11 hours.
Walk 2 Lubchurran (453357). 8 miles/3800ft of ascent, 5–8 hours.
Walk 3 Tullich (516369). 4 miles/2700ft of ascent, 3–5 hours.
Walk 4 Allt a'Mhoirneas bridge (603382). 8 miles/2440ft of ascent, 4–6 hours.
Walk 5 Camusvrachan (620479). 15 miles/7250ft of ascent, 9–14 hours.

CHAPTER 7   WALK 1

Beinn Heasgarnich 3530ft/1076m
   Stob an Fhir-bhogha 3380ft/1030m
Creag Mhor 3387ft/1032m
   Stob nan Clach 3142ft/958m
Beinn Challum 3354ft/1025m
   (south top) 3270ft/997m

These peaks lie in the ancient deer forest of Mamlorn at the head of Glen Lochay, through which the Scottish kings once hunted stags. Sheep are nowadays just as likely to be encountered.

Beinn Heasgarnich
The forest's highest peak, Beinn Heasgarnich, is a great whaleback which runs north from the meadows of Glen Lochay to the desolate waters of Loch Lyon. Snow lingers late in its high corries, and a small tarn lying high in Coire Ban Mor is often fed by melting snow well into June or July.

It is almost 3000ft from the cottage of Badour to the summit, with many streams to indicate a grassy way to the ridge. This is reached close to a small cairn on the bland top of Stob an Fhir-bhogha, where a broad ridge veering to the north points to two more slight undulations on the way to the summit hump of Beinn Heasgarnich, a half-mile distant.

The eastern slopes of the mountain are steep grass, with numerous springs feeding the Allt Tarsuinn, which in its turn falls to open moorland, where another watercourse draining Lochan Achlarich can be followed to the road at the head of the Lairig nan Lunn. The reverse of this descent provides the speediest route to the summit, as the road crosses the pass on the 1700ft contour, though vehicles are denied access from the north by a locked gate at the foot of the hill.

Above Loch Lyon dam, the best route lies along the shoulder of Meall a' Chall, passing the tiny Lochan nan Cat on a climb to the steeper slopes of the north-east ridge. Approaches to Coire Heasgarnich and the north-west spur lack variety and interest except under snow.

On a crossing to Creag Mhor, the long descent of the south-west ridge of Stob an Fhir-bhogha offers the line of least resistance, but beware the dreary bogs at the head of the Bealach na Baintighearna. A tiny lochan lies on the direct line for the steep ascent route to the top of Creag

Mhor. A more westerly line, towards the source of the Allt Fionn a' Glinne, provides an easier ascent.

Creag Mhor
Creag Mhor is steeper than Beinn Heasgarnich and the round of Coire-cheathaich makes a pleasant excursion taking in both tops of the mountain. The steep grassy spur of Sron nan Eun, above Batavaime, offers only token resistance. Beyond the small top of the Sron, the broad crest eases temporarily before rushing up another 500ft to Creag Mhor's slim summit cairn at the junction of three ridges. Here, the spine of Sron nan Eun meets the spur of Meall Tionail and a broad western slope of the hill, which turns an arm around the precipitous headwall of Coire-cheathaich to the poorly-cairned Stob nan Clach. The end of this ridge is exceptionally steep, and care is needed on descents south-east of the cairn. In thick mist, it is advisable to look for the easier gradients lying to the south, above the corrie of the Allt Lairig Mhic Bhaidein.

To the south-west, an open col on the 2400ft contour links Creag Mhor to Cam Chreag, whose level summit is easily traversed to reach a narrow col at the foot of Beinn Challum. Cam Chreag can also be contoured on its eastern slopes to reach this col.

Beinn Challum
This deep wedge formed by the Allt Challum accentuates the height of Beinn

Challum's spire when seen from Glen Lochay. On ascents from the head of this glen, the walk to the foot of the eastern spur is made much easier by a level track, seen on the slopes behind the cottages of Badour and Batavaime. At the end of the track, a stream which has been diverted into a cut-off dam provides a guide to the small outcrops on the nose of the hill. These are turned on the right to gain a broad grassy ridge, commanding fine southward views. The summit peak lies ahead, at the western end of the ridge.

For a more challenging climb to the cairn, follow the Allt Challum towards its source, and ascend the steep grass and scattered rocks supporting the north-west spur. In dry conditions, a rocky gully which leads to the ridge a little west of the cairn may have even more appeal.

To the south of the cairn a steep bank falls to a ridge, split longitudinally by a short, scree-filled trough. The narrow arête formed leads to the southern top.

Being such a fine viewpoint, many visitors approach the mountain by a popular route from the south. This starts at the dog-legged bridge across the Fillan, near Dailrigh (useful parking space west of the bridge). Nearby, the farm-track to Auchtertyre gives ready access to fields below the railway. Here, look beyond the tracks and head for the nearest hump of Creag Loisgte to climb in a long diagonal across its western flank. Another track crosses the river and railway, and by Kirkton farm (sign just west of a layby on the south of the road) to the lower slopes of Creag Loisgte.

Nearer to Crianlarich a track to Inverhaggernie (signed for Allt Chaorain Guest House) has been pushed further up the hill for forestry purposes. At the farm keep to the left, cross a small hump-backed bridge, and follow the track which passes under a railway viaduct to reach the high ground. Here, a wall acts as a useful guide to the crest of Creag Loisgte. The route continues along a broad ridge, with Beinn Challum dominating the immediate horizon, and giving a stiff climb up the final rise to the top. It is normal to return by the same route, but those seeking to return to Dailrigh can descend by the north-west ridge to a sheltered track on the Allt Gleann a' Chlachain, which leads back to Auchtertyre.

CHAPTER 7   •   WALK 2

Meall Glas 3139ft/960m
   Beinn Cheathaich 3076ft/937m
Sgiath Chuil 3016ft/935m
   Meall a' Churain 3007ft/918m

These hills on the south side of Glen Lochay, are notable only for their height.

Access from the south is by a dull track to Auchessan farm, to the east of Loch Iubhair, followed by a tedious ascent to either summit.

Sgiath Chuil

The climb from Glen Lochay is hardly less exciting, and is made by simply keeping to the east of the stream behind Lubchurran cottage and following a broad heathery ridge leading to the cairned top of Meall a' Churain, beyond which a level ridge leads to the hump of Sgiath Chuil. Small knots of rock guarding the summit on the south and west offer the possibility of an interesting descent but even this is an illusion as they are quite easily avoided.

Meall Glas

The slopes to the west of the Sgiath Chuil to Meall a' Churain ridge give a steep, stony descent on the half-mile fall to the pass 1000ft below. The opposite slopes of this divide are more gradual, but the contours tighten near outcrops below the summit of Beinn Cheathaich, whose cairn has a triangulation pillar for company.

A quarter of a mile south-west of the pillar, a small top with a cairn (2980ft/908m) is passed at the eastern end of a featureless, broad-backed ridge, which bends in a shallow crescent around the wide basin of Coire Cheathaich. A casual stroll soon finds the gentle rise to the larger cairn of Meall Glas. The north-west ridge provides an obvious descent to the Lochay above Batavaime, where a bridge gives access to the track down the glen. Alternatively, a direct line across the upper slopes of Coire Cheathaich leads back to Lubchurran. The descent to the south takes an open ridge of rougher ground followed by rocky outcrops, which have to be threaded to reach the Allt Glas, and then the Allt Riobain, and thence further descent to the meadows of Auchessan.

CHAPTER 7   WALK 3

Meall Ghaordie 3410ft/1039m

The blunt cone of this mountain rises above the general level of a long broad ridge separating the glens of the Lyon and the Lochay. The two spurs of Creag Laoghain and Creag an Tulabhain, on its northern flank, terminate in vegetated crags, but on the south side the slopes just west of the farm at Tullich provide a monotonous ascent of some 2700ft.

The ascent from the north is a little more interesting. Cross the river to the old farmstead at Stronuich. Behind the house, the corrie of the Allt Laoghain provides easy grassed ramps to the source of a stream about half a mile below the summit. More easy grass leads up to the summit, with its O.S. pillar.

CHAPTER 7   WALK 4

Meall nan Tarmachan 3421ft/1043m
   Meall Garbh 3369ft/1026m
   Beinn nan Eachan 3265ft/995m
   (east top) 3110ft/948m
   Creag na Caillich 2990ft/916m

The Tarmachan Ridge, as it is popularly known, is within easy reach of the road across the Lochan na Lairige pass. As this crosses the 1800ft contour, any additional climb to the cairn of Meall nan Tarmachan is modest, making this a good hill for a lazy day.

The shortest route to the main summit starts at the Lochan na Lairige dam. A stream, falling from a high corrie on the steep slopes to the west, indicates a direct route up on to a short grassy table south-west of a rough escarpment above the loch. This escarpment can be traversed by starting from the large cairn at the head of the pass. From the grassy platform rock-studded slopes carry the ridge south-west to the diminutive summit knoll with a small cairn.

Another route starts at a small bridge over the Allt a' Mhoirneas, just above the National Trust car park, where a track follows the contours beneath a broad ridge, whose easy grass climbs to a conical knoll on the 3000ft contour. A dip to the north of this leads to the last 400 feet of terraces leading to the cairn. The main ridge heads south-west across several knolls. In mist, three little tarns on the first small col, among the undulations, together with the rusty iron fence posts, act as guide to the ridge crest, which narrows at this point, above the escarpment of Coire Riadhailt. A narrow grassy arête pushes further west to another knoll – Meall Garbh.

Meall Garbh juts out slightly to the north of the arête and, when moving onto the narrow crest heading west, it is necessary to veer south for a short distance in order to avoid the crag under the northern edge. A rib, which drops south from the crest about 50 yards east of the knoll provides an easy escape from this point.

A few yards west of Meall Garbh, the arête drops to the gap of the Bealach Riadhailt, a deep trench cutting right across the ridge. Beyond this, a broader ridge, sprouting knolls and hummocks (confusing in mist), leads to a cairn on the eastern hump of Beinn nan Eachan. A sharp dip, followed by a gradual rise leads to the cairn on the grassy western top.

A broad ridge to the north leads to Meall Ton Eich. This spur is a pleasant walk, and from it an easy descent can be made to the north-east to regain the Lochan na Lairige road.

The main ridge continues in a westerly direction from Beinn nan Eachan with an escarped face on its southern edge. This soon develops into the more robust crags that support the hump of Creag na Caillich, which is gained by veering to the south. Its height, resurveyed at 916m, or 3005ft, compares with that recorded on the one-inch maps as 2990ft, and the metric 'Munroists' can thereby add another 'top' to their lists. The peak's lacerated eastern face denies the walker a direct descent to the Allt a' Mhoirneas track, and he must, therefore, follow the drift of the slope south of the cairn before turning to cross the broad basin of the corrie beneath the southern scarps of Beinn nan Eachan.

CHAPTER 7   WALK 5

Ben Lawers 3984ft/1214m
   Creag an Fhithich 3430ft/1047m
Meall Greigh 3280ft/1001m
Meall Garbh 3661ft/1118m
   An Stuc 3643ft/1118m
Beinn Ghlas 3657ft/1103m
Meall Corranaich 3530ft/1069m
Meall a' Choire Leith 3033ft/926m

Ben Lawers, the ninth highest mountain in Scotland, is the central point of a ridge which never falls below the 2500ft contour, and as well as being noted for its profusion of wild alpine flowers is one of the most popular mountains in the Southern Highlands.

The land over 1500ft, overlooking Loch Tay is the property of the National Trust, who have an information centre and car park beside the Lochan na Lairige road. A well-worn tourist path goes from this point, crossing the summit of Beinn Ghlas, to reach Ben Lawers.

The greater traverse of the range is a strenuous day's expedition and, if returning to the starting point, the most useful base is Milton Roro in Glen Lyon.

Meall a' Choire Leith
Above Milton Roro, follow the west bank of the Allt a' Chobhair below the rough neb of Sron Eich. Steep grassy slopes lead to a ridge above Coire Ban and thence to Meall a' Choire Leith. From the summit cairn a wide slope dips south-south-east to a col at 2550ft above the broad sweep of Coire Gorm to the west which provides a useful

ascent route from the Lochan na Lairige pass. Above Coire Liath, on the east flank, the col narrows into a ridge of 500ft of gently graded grass leading to a small cairn and a fence on the highest point of Meall Corranaich.

Meall Corranaich
Others ways up Meall Corranaich include a route from the head of the Lochan na Lairige pass which is a weary plod, and, more popular, a ridge running south-west from the summit to a point above the National Trust car park. This is enlivened by a number of small tops. A cairn sits above the 3000ft contour, where this ridge runs almost level for a short distance, and, in mist might be thought to mark the summit, but the absence of the march fence should be noted, and upward progress maintained.

Beinn Ghlas
The main ridge crest drops sharply from the summit of Meall Corranaich to a col at the head of Coire Odhar, (the march fence provides a useful guide) rising again in a fine sweep to the south-east. Above the northern scarps of Beinn Ghlas, the crest veers to the east, where an insignificant cairn, on the edge, peers down into the rift of the Allt a' Chobhair.

Ben Lawers
The ridge to Ben Lawers goes north-east, to a col badly scarred by the rut of the tourist path. The path keeps to the crest before climbing severely eroded slopes to the summit which is equipped with an indicator, a cairn, and a triangulation pillar.

From the summit various descent routes are possible. A ridge runs south-east to merge into the wide, grassy eastern flanks of the hill. The shorter, rock-strewn south ridge also widens quickly, and although there is a marked depression on the south for a time, this too fans out into broad green slopes above the cottages to the west of Lawers. Those opting to ascend the mountain from the south, should note that only one parking space exists on the A827, (near the turn off to Craggantoll farm) a road confined by fences and walls.

The main spinal ridge is the northern arm of the mountain, the eastern banks of which are rough and steep, and support a small cairned summit, Creag an Fhithich, on a buttress overlooking Lochan nan Cat.

When approached on a descent from the summit of Lawers, this top is hardly prominent and is easily by-passed on the west, especially in mist, though it does appear as an obvious hump when seen from An Stuc, the next hill along the ridge.

An Stuc
The cairn on the short grassy table of An Stuc is surrounded on all sides by very steep slopes, which are particularly precipitous and craggy above Lochan nan Cat. After crossing the summit the descent to the gap at the foot of Meall Garbh is abnormally steep for grass, and should be approached with caution when wet, for it is the sharpest gradient encountered on the ridge. In icy conditions, a slight deviation to the less severe slopes above the Fin Glen is advisable. Under snow, its ascent on an east-west circuit of Lochan nan Cat can be entertaining, and even in summer there are some delightful grassy scrambles here.

Meall Garbh
There is a gradual rise to the cairn at the western end of Meall Garbh. From a level crown a broad ridge falls north-north-west towards Glen Lyon, to give a useful return route to Milton Roro. A little to the south-east, across a shallow depression, a second cairn, standing on a rocky knob, is a better vantage point for glimpses of Ben Lawers and An Stuc, enhanced by the deep trough of Lochan nan Cat.

Meall Greigh
From Meall Garbh, the ridge takes a wide easterly swing to an expansive crest leading towards Meall Greigh, a route requiring careful navigation in thick mist on account of the slight curvature of the ridge and almost-level nature of the ground. The top of Meall Greigh is a green table, with two cairns standing about 150 yards apart, the actual summit being marked by the south-east cairn. The southern flanks of the hill drop easily to the Lawers Burn, where a path may be found leading to Machuim farm and the road at Lawers, a route which is equally useful as the start of the shorter round of the eastern tops.

Those wishing to return to Milton Roro are faced with the unenviable chore of retracing the route back to the northern spur of Meall Greigh, or descending the northern slopes of Meall Greigh to gain the valley of the Inverinain Burn and thence to Inverinain.

RANNOCH
AND GLEN LYON

Rich heather carpets the lower slopes of these seven hills, which all have broad easy ridges and wide horizons. Schiehallion, though included in this group, is so different in character that it might be better placed in a group on its own.

CARN MAIRG CREAG MHOR MEALL GARBH CARN GORM
A traverse of four mountains providing a straightforward stroll along a broad, featureless ridge.

SCHIEHALLION
Schiehallion is a graceful and arresting peak, easily climbed and offering fine views.

STUCHD AN LOCHAIN
A hill of character, giving a pleasant ridge walk above an attractive mountain tarn and crags.

MEALL BUIDHE
This undistinguished mound, climbed easily from Loch Daimh, is notable for its extensive views.

Recommended Valley Base Aberfeldy.

Maps O.S. 1:50 000 Sheets 42, 51 and 52; Bartholomews 1:100 000 Sheet 48.

Starting Point/Length and time for main itinerary
Walk 1 Invervar (666483). 11 miles/4550ft of ascent, 6–9 hours.
Walk 2 Braes of Foss (750559). 5 miles/2470ft of ascent, 3–5 hours.
Walk 3 Loch an Daimh (510463). 5 miles/1950ft of ascent, 3–5 hours.
Walk 4 Loch an Daimh (510463). 5 miles/1600ft of ascent, 2–3 hours.

CHAPTER 8	WALK 1

Carn Gorm 3370ft/1029m
Meall Garbh c.3200ft/963m
 Meall Luaidhe 3035ft/925m
 An Sgor 3002ft/924m
Carn Mairg 3419ft/1042m
 Meall Liath 3261ft/1012m
 Meall a' Bharr 3315ft/1004m
Creag Mhor c.3200ft/981m

A broad six-mile ridge along the northern side of Glen Lyon, never far from the 3000ft contour links this group of eight tops, which are best ascended from Invervar, in Glen Lyon. Here, through densely planted timber, a path uses one of the few convenient gaps. Starting at a gate opposite the telephone kiosk in the hamlet, it climbs along the east bank of the Invervar Burn. Above the timberline, broad spurs rise from the stream, and its tributary, the Allt Coir' Chearcaill, to the individual peaks. It is, however, more usual to aim for the most westerly peak, Carn Gorm, or Creag Mhor to the east.

Carn Gorm
For the more gradual ascent of Carn Gorm, keep to the east bank of the Invervar Burn,

until the stream divides near the 1000ft contour, where the western tributary should be followed, to be crossed a little way above a derelict wooden hut which appears on a knoll ahead. The slopes thus gained give an ascent seeming to lack purpose, until the steep grassy rib leading to the summit of Carn Gorm is reached. The well-formed top sports a small cairn. The broad spread of the main ridge appears almost flat, with promises of a speedy high-level traverse to Carn Mairg. Along the north-east spur, a fence dips to the small abrupt cone of An Sgor. The iron posts keep to a stony crest to pass a low cairn. The fence now crosses increasingly stony ground to the flat top of Meall Garbh, which, in addition to its quartzite-capped summit cairn, has two other cairns to the east. These lie about 70 yards south of the march fence, and are possibly used by local stalkers as waymarkers to the featureless spur of Meall Luaidhe (656510), a top marked by an insignificant heap of stones.

In mist, the march fence is more than useful on the downward turn to the north-east, to a bare level crest which continues to Meall a' Bharr, the true summit of which is at the cairn on its eastern end.

Carn Mairg
Another dip over equally uninteresting terrain leads to the steady drag on to the stone-capped Carn Mairg, whose steep southern flank falls to the bowl of Coir' Chearcaill. The ridge to the east of the cairn dips to Meall Liath. From here the southern slope leads down to a wide grassy ridge, which makes a lazy curve around the

head of Gleann Muilinn and on to Creag Mhor.

Creag Mhor
In mist, the cairn at the western end of this hill might well be confused with the true summit, lying a quarter of a mile to the east. Here another cairn sits on a small outcrop, which scarcely rises above the general level of a mossy plateau.

The best descent is from the western cairn, where, at about the 1750ft contour on the west bank of the Allt Coir' Chearchaill, a bothy track serving a two-roomed bothy and stable can be followed down to a point overlooking the woods of Invervar. From this point it is best to descend by the rib to Invervar Burn, where the path is regained for the return to the road.

The northern approaches
Neither the forest track through Coire Carie, or the track from Inverhadden into Glen Sassunn seem particularly attractive when the walker is faced with a tiresome plod through acres of heather which deny him access to outliers of the range.

CHAPTER 8	WALK 2

Schiehallion 3547ft/1083m

Schiehallion, which is also known as Schichallion or Sidh Chaillean, is one of the most popular vantage points in the Southern Highlands. This peak is famous for its appearance — seen from the road to the west of Kinloch Rannoch it appears as a perfect cone. However, from the famed Queen's View at the eastern end of Loch Tummel the hill appears as a broad-backed ridge, which is really what it is.

The most favoured route to the summit starts near Braes of Foss (car-park) from where a path leads up the heathery eastern slopes of the mountain. To the east of the farmhouse on the south side of the road, there is a gate, beyond which the path quickly takes shape, as, following the east bank of a tributary of the Allt Kynachan, it climbs to the shoulder immediately ahead. This moorland ground gives way to stonier terrain, and along the crest of the ridge cairns mark the route to summit rocks, which support a triangulation pillar and a cairn commanding a fine view down the length of Loch Rannoch.

Another popular route starts near Glengoulandie farm, (restricted roadside parking) where a path runs from the southern boundary of the deer-park into the narrow entrance to Gleann Mor. This should be followed for about a mile, where, reaching the wider trough of the glen, the heathery slopes at the eastern end of the mountain (Aonach Ban on the map) can be tackled. Here the hill-path is very indistinct, but the going easy enough, and by continuing in a line almost due west it soon reappears in the heather at a higher level.

The steepest route starts near Tempar farm near Kinloch Rannoch (limited parking). Above the steading, follow a land-rover track climbing the hill beside the Tempar Burn to find an obvious path which appears on the left. Here the climb begins in earnest, as the western ridge follows a determined and direct line all the way to the summit.

The most direct ascent takes the northern slopes starting west of Braes of Foss at the spot height 1114ft/340m. This is a rougher but quicker way than the other routes.

CHAPTER 8   WALK 3

Stuchd an Lochain 3144ft/960m
 Sron Chona Choirein 3031ft/918m

There are higher hills in the vicinity, but Stuchd an Lochain's true character lies in its hidden crags and corries, which are not revealed to the traveller on the Glen Lyon road, who sees only the towering spur of An Grianan, and the nose of Meall Dubh above Cashlie.

A path climbs beside the Allt Cashlie to reach the mossy plateau between the tops of Sron Chona Choirein and Stuchd an Lochain, and a little further along Glen Lyon a track from Pubil follows the Allt Camaslaidh to boggy ground near its source, on the open hillside below the eastern corner of Stuchd an Lochain's summit cone. A more popular ascent of the mountain starts at the head of a narrow road, running to the foot of the dam at the eastern end of Loch an Daimh (sometime Loch Giorra). A rough access track runs to the head of the dam wall, and rough grass above gives a swift rise towards the ridge. The crest, reached to the east of the small stony dome of Creag an Fheadain, carries a broken fence, which can be followed to a cairn. These rusty posts continue along the top of a broad ridge on the headwall of Coire an Duich. A spur to the south of this hollow meets the main ridge, at a cairn on the plateau of Sron Chona Choirein. The ridge leads west, crosses another slight bump, and follows the fence on a slight curve to the north to the abrupt hump of Stuchd an Lochain. The highest point is on the edge of a craggy face above Lochan nan Cat.

An interesting variation is possible to liven up the return route. Take the broad ridge back towards Sron Chona Choirein until it is possible to descend the grassy eastern end of the corrie headwall to Lochan nan Cat. Below the tarn, a burn tumbles from the corrie and this can be followed to the moors along the margins of Loch an Daimh for a pleasant walk to the dam.

CHAPTER 8   WALK 4

Meall Buidhe 3054ft/931m
 (south-east top) 3004ft/915m

The hills to the south-west of Loch Rannoch, along the margins of Rannoch Moor, are a sprawl of bare, rounded grass tops, and even Meall Buidhe (also known as Garbh Mheall) the highest of their number is of little interest.

The easiest approach is from the dam at Loch an Daimh (Loch Giorra) to the south. At the eastern end of the loch, easy grass slopes provide the way alongside an open gully, whose depression is the best guide to the broad slopes below the mountain's south-east top. There are few landmarks on the lower hill, and on ground so featureless it as all too easy to find oneself on the southern rim of Glas Choire. However, the edge can be followed in a westerly direction, on the line of an escarpment. This turns northwards immediately below the south-east top, which presents to the walker a short grassy ramp of 150ft at the top of which is a cairn, looking to another slightly larger pile on a higher point, a few yards to the north-west.

Beyond this cairn, there is a slight dip to a wide, flat ridge, where a path, keeping to the eastern escarpment, passes several cairns to one pile larger than the rest, identified by several quartzite blocks in its untidy heap. The whole summit of Meall Buidhe is almost denuded, with only a covering of close-cropped grass and small stones, but for such an unremarkable hill the views are very extensive.

To climb the hill from the north, a good forestry track runs from Bridge of Gaur at the west end of Loch Rannoch (near the school) to meet a similar track by the Allt Sloc na Creadha beneath the north-west shoulder of the hill. From the head of the track a small tributary of this stream can be followed to the broad saddle between Garbh Mheall and the summit of Meall Buidhe. The name Garbh Mheall is sometimes given to the whole mountain by local inhabitants, whereas the Ordnance Survey use that name merely for the minor top at the north end of the ridge.

BEN ALDER AND LOCH OSSIAN

Remote and fabled peaks with long approaches to eerie bothies, followed by grand high-level walks over the tops in one of Scotland's last unspoilt wilderness areas with associations with Prince Charlie, and other sombre legends.

BEN ALDER   BEINN BHEOIL
A high plateau in a region of romantic isolation, giving fine expeditions.

CARN DEARG   GEAL CHARN   AONACH BEAG   BEINN EIBHINN
An elegant ridge-walk with length, variety and interest.

BEINN NA LAP   CARN DEARG   SGOR GAIBHRE
Featureless hills overlooking Rannoch Moor set in great tracts of deer forest.

STOB COIRE SGRIODAIN   CHNO DEARG
A comfortable round above the woods of Laggan and Moy.

Recommended Valley Base Laggan.

Maps O.S. 1:50 000 Sheet 42; Bartholomews 1:100 000 Sheet 51.

Starting Point/Length and time for main itinerary
Walk 1 Ben Alder Cottage (499680). 8 miles/ 3400ft of ascent, 4–6 hours. (Rannoch Mill (506576) to Ben Alder Cottage walk-in 8 miles/ 700ft of ascent.)
Walk 2 Culra (523762). 15 miles/4450ft of ascent, 7–11 hours. (Dalwhinnie to Culra walk in 9 miles/ 200ft of ascent.)
Walk 3 Corrour (355664). 14 miles/4550ft of ascent, 7–11 hours.
Walk 4 Fersit (350782). 8 miles/3000ft of ascent, 4–6 hours.

CHAPTER 9   WALK 1

Ben Alder 3765ft/1148m
Beinn Bheoil 3333ft/1019m
Sron Coire na h-Iolaire 3128ft/955m

This is one of the great isolated mountain massifs of Scotland and whichever direction is chosen to reach it the remoteness of the mountain's situation is always apparent.

Access from the south
Two approach routes from the south in most common use are those from Corrour Station, and from near Bridge of Ericht at the west end of Loch Rannoch.

Corrour Station can only be reached by using the railway. The approach from here follows the forestry track to Corrour Lodge at the head of Loch Ossian, and the indistinct path along the south bank of the Uisge Labhair until it peters out on the peat-hagged moorland under the slopes of Beinn a' Chumhainn. This hill should be turned on its northern flank to gain a high valley and a stalkers' path, which runs along the foot of Ben Alder to Ben Alder Cottage (McCook's Cottage) beside Loch Ericht.

The Loch Rannoch approach starts from a mill (506578) on the north side of the road at the west end of the loch (between the two entry drives to Rannoch Lodge). A good track crosses the moors to reach a bridge on the Cam Chriochan, beside Loch Ericht. A useful marker at the approach to the plantation south of Lochan Loin nan Donnlaich is a cairn indicating the start of a moorland path, which cuts alongside the forestry boundary to provide a short cut. From Cam Chriochan a grass-grown track then crosses the heath to a group of old Caledonian pines, about a mile south of the Alder Burn, there to peter out in the peat-hagged moor which lies before Alder Bay. The bridge near McCook's Cottage is swept away from time to time, so be prepared for a lengthy detour upstream.

Ben Alder
The east bank of the stream behind McCook's Cottage carries a path towards the Bealach Breabag, which should be left near its summit, where a steep climb up broken escarpments to the west leads to a ridge high above Garbh Choire. On the half-mile walk above the cliffs of this deep hollow, the other great crags buttressing the eastern edge of the plateau are seen, and a turn to the north beyond a small hump should lead to a shallow depression cutting across the route to the summit. This, and a small tarn at about 3700ft (considered by many to be the highest lochan in the Highlands) are the only features on an expansive plateau. To locate the summit, which lies roughly north-north-east, follow the line of a slope which slides off to the right towards the edge of the cliffs. At the highest point a triangulation pillar stands inside a low wall of jumbled stone, with a tiny cairn nearby.

Beinn Bheoil
To the east of the Bealach Breabag, a short, easy slope leads to Sron Coire na h-Iolaire. Cairns mark both ends of this short spur, which is set at right angles to the mile-long ridge of Beinn Bheoil, and from the higher eastern cairn there are fine views of Loch Ericht stretching south to the edge of the moors. To the north of the western cairn the ridge drops to a stony saddle, which broadens to grassy banks supporting Beinn Bheoil's mound of slabby stones. The longer northern ridge of the hill fans out to the dark peaty moors where the Culra/ Bealach Breabag path may be found.

Access from the north-east
This track, and the path through the Bealach Dubh, are both good routes to Ben Alder from the north from Pattack and Culra, (see Walk 2). The Bealach Breabag path pushes up the northern slopes to the east shore of Loch a' Bhealaich Bheithe. Set back on the opposite shore the great north-east face of Ben Alder throws down two prominent ridges known as the Long and Short Leachas. The northerly spur, the Long Leachas, gives a fine scramble, slightly exposed in places on a vegetated ridge high above the Bealach Dubh. The easier scrambles of the Short Leachas, on the opposite wall of Coire na Leith-chais, are worthwhile for the views of Loch a' Bhealaich Bheithe. The ascent of either ridge, followed by a traverse of Ben Alder and Beinn Bheoil, is the most varied and interesting expedition that these mountains have to offer.

The Bealach Dubh route follows the path along the broken north-western flank of Ben Alder. About three-quarters of a mile east of the top of the pass (2300ft) the route leaves the path and takes a southerly course up the burn draining an obvious, steep corrie. The summit plateau is reached some distance north of the cairn. Ascents from the top of Bealach Dubh or from Bealach Cumhann to the south, lead to the most featureless part of the plateau and are not so interesting.

Given the variety of these northern approaches and the increasing popularity of McCook's Cottage, it is well worth considering Culra as a base.

CHAPTER 9   WALK 2

Carn Dearg 3391ft/1034m
  Diollaid a' Chairn 3029ft/922m
Geal Charn 3656ft/1132m
  Sgor Iutharn 3350ft/1014m
Aonach Beag 3647ft/1114m
Beinn Eibhinn 3611ft/1100m
  Mullach Coire nan Nead 3025ft/921m
  Uinneag a' Ghlas-choire 3041ft/922m

Anyone visiting these four mountains, set in the heart of the wilderness of the Ben Alder Forest, must give due consideration to the distances from the nearest road or railway. It is six miles as the crow flies from Luiblea on the Loch Laggan road to the summit of Beinn Eibhinn, and slightly more from Corrour on the West Highland railway. To the north lies Dalwhinnie, ten miles from Culra, at the base of Carn Dearg. An itinerary starting from here is probably the best alternative though even this involves a long walk back through the Bealach Dubh if returning to Culra. Other options include a complete traverse of the range from Corrour to Dalwhinnie and a round of the peaks from Loch Laggan to the north (see access notes for Chapter 11, Walk 1). The peaks could also be picked off piecemeal on shorter days but, on balance, the described way seems best, despite its length.

All of this assumes that one can drive to Loch Pattack. Part of this northern route is a private estate road, and if permission can be obtained to take a vehicle as far as the boathouse at Pattack (547787), the walker is then two-and-a-half miles from the open shelter at Culra, the most advantageous base. The most direct path leads to the Lodge along the south side of the Allt a' Chaoil-reidhe (using a footbridge). An alternative track follows the shore of Loch Pattack (bridge over the feeder stream) and the lower slopes of Carn Dearg.

Carn Dearg
Carn Dearg rises to the south-west of Loch Pattack, its heathery ruffs culminating in a broad ridge with a stony peak. Its southern flanks are just as easily ascended from Culra, though with a steeper pull to the summit cairn. A second cairn, a little to the south, looks down an edge of the ridge, which here dips to a flat saddle, and the hump of Diollaid a' Chairn. Beyond this top, the ridge narrows, and ahead, buttressed by walls of broken crag falling to corries on either hand, steep terraces rise to the plateau of Geal Charn. Loch an Sgoir, seen in the hollow to the left, backed by the steep screes of Sgor Iutharn's narrow arête, is a perfect example of a lonely mountain lochan.

Sgor Iutharn
This is a subsidiary top divorced from the main spine of the ridge. It is notable for its

impressive Lancet Edge. From Culra, this appears as a stone arrowhead guarding the narrows of the Bealach Dubh. The path through the pass gives easy access to the lower slopes of the edge with wide grassy ledges, which twist and turn around and over small outcrops. The arête becomes narrower as more rocky height is gained, and at one point a rock platform, above an almost-vertical wall of scree, gives an impressive glimpse of Loch an Sgoir, before the jumbled blocks of the wider crest announce the approach to the low hump of Sgor Iutharn's cairn. Lying at the western end of the hill (482739) the skeletal remains of a light aircraft mark the turn to face a scarp supporting the flat moss of Geal Charn. As it is off the main route, this ascent might be added as a short day's outing after the rigours of the traverse of the main chain.

Geal Charn
Returning to the main ridge, the next peak is Geal Charn - a broad expanse of green buttressed on the north by crags which sweep around the hill eventually defining the north-east spur which provides the route of ascent from Diollaid a' Chairn. Once on the plateau, several minor undulations appear on the perimeter of a large shallow saucer, whose mosses feed streams falling to Loch an Sgoir. Even in clear weather the summit cairn is difficult to see, and to detect the heap of stones it is best to aim for the escarpment above Coire na Coichille at the western side of the mossy flats. Peaks to the south gradually come into view, and looking in this direction the cairn is discovered shortly before the long slope, which leads west-south-west to a grassy saddle at the foot of Aonach Beag.

Aonach Beag
This is the easiest summit in the range, and approached from Geal Charn, it offers a short, sharp rise to a small cairn, which commands a fine view south-east to the vast plateau of Ben Alder, and another to the west to the peaks of the Grey Corries and the Ben Nevis group. At the cairn, a right-angle turn is taken to the south-west for a descent down rough terraces that slant down to a narrow col above Lochan a' Charra Mhoir.

Beinn Eibhinn
Ahead lies a quick, scrambly pull to the curve of a broad ridge, which rises to the cairn of Beinn Eibhinn, seen at the corrie lip. The stony ridge continues beyond the cairn to fan out as a broad shoulder above the Allt Gualainn a' Charra Mhoir. Further to the west, another wide slope dips to a small cairned top (3000ft/910m) at the junction of two spurs, Mullach Coire nan Nead and Uinneag a' Ghlas-choire. In mist, two tiny pools on the broad ridge to the east of this cairn should not be

confused with the larger lochans at the foot of the scarp below it. There, two larger water holes, lying in rough identical hollows, feed streams on opposite sides of the mountain, and should be passed to reach the larger cairn of Mullach Coire nan Nead, lying on stony ground to the west.

From the cairn (3000ft/910m) a second ridge heads south to a stony gap, which cuts straight across the ridge to form a 'window', as the name of adjacent top (Uinneag a' Ghlas-choire) implies. The cairn is on the broad spur beyond and does not appear to be on the highest point, though on such uniform ground this may well be an optical illusion.

Having collected these two minor tops the best descent route, to avoid the boggy ground in the valley of the Uisge Labhair, is a diagonal line down slopes to the east of the window to meet the valley below Coire a' Charra Bhig. Here one can cross to the stalkers' path on the opposite hillside and thence to the Bealach Dubh.

Other approaches
A good track runs from Luiblea, at the west end of Loch Laggan, to the ruin at Lubvan, below Beinn a' Chlachair. The Allt Cam should then be followed to reach the broad shoulders of Beinn Eibhinn, at the start of the five-mile traverse to Carn Dearg. Steep ground to the north of Carn Dearg's cairn leads to the treacherous Allt Cam (An Lairig), which is not always easy to cross, to reach a high-level path crossing the Bealach Leamhain (between Beinn a' Chlachair and Mullach Coire an Iubhair) to the Lubvan track on the return to Luiblea.

Those attempting to explore the range from Corrour find the broad heathery slopes of Beinn Eibhinn well-guarded by the peat-hagged moorland of the Uisge Labhair. Once on the ridge however, a fine walk takes in all the summits, leaving a choice of returning through the Bealach Dubh, heading north for Loch Laggan via the Bealach Leamhain, or continuing to Loch Pattack and Dalwhinnie.

CHAPTER 9   WALK 3

Beinn na Lap 3066ft/937m
Carn Dearg 3080ft/941m
Sgor Gaibhre 3124ft/955m
  Sgor Choinnich 3040ft/929m

The three mountains above Loch Ossian are broad, rounded ridges, and were it not for the fact that their summits breast the 3000ft contour, they might attract nothing more than a passing glance. Even so, their isolation may awaken the curiosity of inquisitive ramblers searching for a quiet corner, for the hills of the Corrour Forest are some distance from the road, and the railway, skirting the northern fringe of Rannoch Moor, provides the only link with the outside world.

Beinn na Lap

The approaches from the north from Fersit or Loch Laggan by Strath Ossian, or the deep valley of Allt Feith na h-Ealaidh (Allt Feith Thuill), are dauntingly long and deter all but the most determined walkers.

The easiest ascent is by the broad ridge, which rises from the Corrour Station/ Strathossian House track, above the west end of Loch Ossian. The bald, rounded slope above the woods of Ossian is unbelievably easy, but if choosing to traverse the hill from Strathossian House beware the boggy ground to the south of Loch na Lap. A few crags under the eastern edge of the ridge, to the north of the cairn, can be threaded without difficulty, in descent, to reach the woods beside Loch Ossian (look for gaps to the west).

Carn Dearg

Carn Dearg can be climbed with equal ease from the south-west end of Loch Ossian. Near the Youth Hostel, follow a moorland path rising gradually through the heather slopes above the track to the head of the loch. Where the path turns south, head directly up the slopes towards the summit, which is reached at a cairn overlooking the drab northern scoop of Coire Creagach, and the ruins of Corrour Old Lodge on the edge of the moor to the south.

Sgor Gaibhre

To the north-east, Carn Dearg throws out a broad ridge to the saddle of Mam Ban, beyond which is seen an easy green slope rising to the point of Sgor Gaibhre. The dramatic slant of the green buttresses on the eastern slope of this hill also mould the saddle connecting it to the twin peak of Sgor Choinnich, whose cairn similarly looks down to the pool of Lochan a' Bhealaich and the dull sprawl of the moors. The broad ridge to the north-west of this cairn provides a useful line of descent to avoid the boggy moors on either hand.

Ascent from the Rannoch Road

A mile-and-a-half east of Rannoch Station, near Loch Eigheach, a track signposted 'Road to the Isles' should be followed to the foot of Sron Leachd a' Chaorruinn, at the start of the long drag along the southern spur of Carn Dearg. Alternatively keep to the east bank of the Allt Eigheach and climb to Beinn Pharlagain. Its crest is a series of knolly tops, the highest of which lies at the northern end of the hill, above two tarns looking along a broad ridge to the saddle due south of Sgor Gaibhre. These two routes, when linked, give a carefree round of Coire Eigheach, with a nice prospect of Schiehallion to the east.

Those starting at Corrour Station have the opportunity to complete the circuit of Loch Ossian and climb all the peaks in one go, and though this may involve a race against the clock to catch the last train in the evening, it adds a little spice to the conquest of three otherwise unremarkable hills.

CHAPTER 9   WALK 4

Stob Coire Sgriodain 3211ft/976m
  (south top) 3132ft/960m
Chno Dearg 3433ft/1047m
  Meall Garbh 3206ft/977m

These mountains form a pleasant horse-shoe above the forests of Laggan and the Spean, and are a popular short day's expedition from the roadhead at Fersit, south of Tulloch Station.

Stob Coire Sgriodain

A track crosses the railway, passes through a gate, and runs east along the fringes of woods which cloak the hillside above Loch Treig. Sheep pens beyond the trees lie at the foot of the rough ground rising to the steeper rock and heather nose of Sron na Garbh-bheinne, at the end of the ridge climbing to the point of Stob Coire Sgriodain. Slopes plunging to Loch Treig appear on the right, where outcrops are threaded on the blunt snout below the narrower ridge leading to the summit cairn. With Loch Treig now fully 2000ft below, there are uninterrupted views across its head to the brown moors of Rannoch and Buachaille Etive Mor beyond. The nearer view is dominated by the twin humps of Stob Coire Easain and Stob a' Choire Mheadhoin, and to the north Creag Meagaidh sprawls above a thick carpet of conifers. A sharp dip beyond the cairn leads to a grassy trough, which guards the rise to a second cairn on the small escarped bump of the hill's southern top. Here the crest turns east to another bump at 3025ft/925m

Chno Dearg

The hill now curves to the level crown of Meall Garbh, to the south-east. Steep crags to the east of its cairn form the headwall of a corrie, dominated by the swollen hump of Chno Dearg to the north. Its convex slopes make its ascent uninteresting, but the attainment of the untidy heap of stones that marks the summit brings into view the lonely Loch Ghuilbinn, below the Beinn Eibhinn massif.

An easy descent to the north leads to the Strath Ossian/ Fersit track.

BEN NEVIS, THE MAMORES AND THE GREY CORRIES

Twenty mountains, including eleven major peaks, all focussed around Ben Nevis, provide magnificent expeditions including two extended ridge-traverses of great sporting challenge. The Aonachs and the Grey Corries could be combined into a longer expedition.

MULLACH NAN COIREAN   STOB BAN   SGURR A' MHAIM   AM BODACH   STOB COIRE A' CHAIRN
AN GEARANACH   BINNEIN BEAG   NA GRUAGAICHEAN   BINNEIN MOR   SGURR EILDE MOR
The Mamore traverse is one of the most demanding and sporting of Britain's major hill-walks.

BEN NEVIS   CARN MOR DEARG
Britain's highest mountain can be a grinding bore if tackled on a poor day by the ordinary route, though a well-thought-out plan of campaign provides a magnificent outing.

AONACH BEAG   AONACH MOR
Two 4000ft peaks, somewhat upstaged by Ben Nevis, but still offering fine walking and splendid views.

STOB BAN   STOB CHOIRE CLAURIGH   STOB COIRE AN LAOIGH   SGURR CHOINNICH MOR
The peaks of the 'Grey Corries' provide a classic ridge-walk in a very remote location.

STOB A' CHOIRE MHEADHOIN   STOB COIRE EASAIN
Unexceptional peaks enlivened, in clear conditions, by wide and enjoyable panoramas.

CHAPTER 10   WALK 1

Mullach nan Coirean 3077ft/939m
(south-east top) 3004ft/917m
Stob Ban 3274ft/999m
Sgurr a' Mhaim 3601ft/1099m
Stob a' Coire Mhail 3250ft/991m
Sgor an Iubhair 3284ft/1001m
Am Bodach 3382ft/1032m
Stob Coire a' Chairn 3219ft/983m
An Gearanach 3230ft/985m
An Garbhanach 3206ft/975m
Na Gruagaichean 3442ft/1055m
(north-west top) 3404ft/1036m
Binnein Mor 3700ft/1128m
(south top) 3476ft/1059m
Sgurr Eilde Beag 3135ft/956m
Sgurr Eilde Mor 3279ft/1008m
Binnein Beag 3083ft/940m

These ten mountains, linked by a ridge which rarely strays below the 2500ft contour, are known collectively as 'The Mamores'. The traverse of the range in a single day is a considerable undertaking, a task not made any easier by the additional re-ascents from the two outlying summits of Sgurr a' Mhaim and An Gearanach on a return to the main ridge. Sgurr Eilde Mor, which is also known as Sgurr na h-Eilde, also set at some distance from Binnein Mor by a divide which is the largest encountered between peaks. However, the

traverse can be split into shorter walks on circuits of the northern corries. Steall Hut, reached by a path (and wire footbridge) from the head of Glen Nevis, and Meanach shelter, provide useful bases for such expeditions. Those using the Meanach shelter will need to cross the Amhainn Rath, which in spate conditions can be difficult. The military road across the Lairig Mor to the south, gives easy access to the broad shoulders of the western tops, and a landrover track from Kinlochleven to Luibeilt provides another useful route to the 1100ft contour below the eastern tops. The latter track can also be reached more directly, by following either of two moorland paths which climb from the Grey Mare's Tail waterfall access track, starting near the Episcopal church in Kinlochleven.

Mullach nan Coirean
Mullach nan Coirean, a bald hill of red granite, lying furthest to the west, is the most easily reached summit in the group. From the Glen Nevis road, although it is possible to negotiate the barrier of forestry above the Youth Hostel to gain the north ridge, a shorter and better approach takes the east bank of the Allt a' Choire Dheirg, which should be crossed above the woods to gain the north-east spur of the hill. This ridge, which is quite narrow in places, climbs to meet the north ridge a few yards to the north of the summit cairn. This is also the culmination of a third broader

Recommended Valley Base Fort William.

Maps O.S. 1:50 000 Sheet 41; Bartholomews 1:100 000 Sheets 48, 50 and 51; O.S. 1:63 360 Sheet Ben Nevis and Glen Coe.

Starting Point/Length and time for main itinerary
Walk 1 Achriabhach (143683). 21 miles/9400ft of ascent, 12–18 hours.
Walk 2 Ben Nevis Distillery (125757). 13 miles/5800ft of ascent, 7–11 hours.
Walk 3 Glen Nevis (167691). 14 miles/4880ft of ascent, 7–11 hours.
Walk 4 Coirechoille (252807). 21 miles/6630ft of ascent, 10–15 hours.
Walk 5 Fersit (350782). 8 miles/3350ft of ascent, 4–6 hours.

ridge, reached from Blar a' Chaoruinn (car-park) on the military road. This approach crosses the blunt top of Meall a' Chaoruinn before swinging eastwards to Mullach nan Coirean.

The main ridge to the south-east is a broad plateau of red granite, and the rise to the high point of the south-east top (3004ft/917m) is so imperceptible that it is possible, in thick mist, to pass the cairn without realising. The barren ridge arcs slightly to the north at this point, to another top, buttressed on the north by splintered crags looking directly across the glen to Ben Nevis. A slabby gully is passed, and here a path scrambles up broken rock on to the head of a granite crag, which is then followed for another half-mile to a long, almost level, saddle, at the head of a wide heather corrie above the croft of Tigh-na-sleubhaich, seen below.

Stob Ban

Here the presence of grass indicates mica-schist rock at the start of the climb to a small prominent top about a third of a mile to the north of the grey summit scree of Stob Ban. (There is a steep, exhilarating ascent from Achriabhach, in Glen Nevis, to this cone, which is the highest point on a blunt prow of terraced crags and outcrops.) A few hundred feet of rough scree separates this tiny horn from the quartzite cairn of Stob Ban, perched near the edge of massive crags. Below lies a wild glen, hemmed in on the opposite wall by the long, serrated ridge of Sgurr a' Mhaim. If a limited round of the peaks of Choire Dheirg is undertaken it is best to tackle Stob Ban first as it is the harder ascent. The south-west ridge of Stob Ban stumbles over shattered stone to a steep nose above Tigh-na-sleubhaich, providing a very steep descent back to the military road.

Sgor an Iubhair

The main ridge drops steeply to the east to a wide pass at the head of Coire a' Mhusgain. On the east wall of this corrie, a stalkers' path makes a gradual ascent from the foot of the north-west ridge of Sgurr a' Mhaim.

Grassy terraces climb from the pass to Sgor an Iubhair, a cairn at the junction of a subsidiary ridge running out to the higher peak of Sgurr a' Mhaim. This narrow arête (known as the Devil's Ridge) reaches a high point at 3250ft on Stob a' Coire Mhail, and, at one point, is broken by crags at the narrow spine. Here care is needed to negotiate rocks propped against the western slope of the ridge. Ahead wider slopes lead to the cairn of Sgurr a' Mhaim.

Sgurr a' Mhaim

The summit of Sgurr a' Mhaim is a dome of sharp, whitish-grey quartzite blocks. Many doing the Mamore chain elect to leave this peak for a separate ascent from Glen Nevis by the obvious north-west ridge from Achriabhach. Here a gate opens to a path which eases the climb up grassy terraces to the steeper slopes above. The north-east ridge above Steall (wire footbridge) is another clamber up a steep grassy staircase. A more interesting route still, takes the Allt Coire a' Mhail above the Falls of Steall to the foot of the east ridge. This rib is separated from the north-east ridge by a small corrie tucked into the hill. This east ridge gives a fine scramble for about 800ft to a pinnacle near the foot of a narrower rib close to the north-east ridge, immediately below the summit. The views from the cairn are rewarding for the whole length of Glen Nevis and its attendant peaks are seen.

Am Bodach

East of Sgor an Iubhair the main ridge dips to a saddle at 2800ft, served by a path which climbs from the military road at the foot of Coire na h-Eirghe. Ahead, another 600ft of easy grass leads to the cairn of Am Bodach. The ridge then turns north-east to another grassy col on the 2800ft contour, which is also served by a rough path from Mamore Lodge to the south. Ahead, more easy grass rises gently to Stob Coire a' Chairn.

Stob Coire a' Chairn

The summit of this hill is a flat-topped dome, where the main ridge makes a right-angled turn to the south-east. The summit has never been named on the Ordnance Survey maps, being simply identified by spot-heights 3219ft/983 metres, and as with all tops in the Mamores, sports the usual cairn.

An Gearanach

To the north, a steep grassy face falls to the rocky spine of An Garbhanach which in places is little more than the upper edge of huge tilted slabs, forming a narrow arête running a further 600 yards to the cairn of An Gearanach (985m), where broader terraces provide the steps for a stalkers' path climbing from the Falls of Steall.

Na Gruagaichean

To the south-east of Stob Coire a' Chairn there is a col at 2500ft where a second path drops to the Allt Coire na Ba, and the track to Mamore Lodge. The ridge now pulls easily to the twin summits of Na Gruagaichean, also known as A' Gruagach, a rather featureless hill-top with a hint of crags on the slopes above Coire na Gabhalach. A shallow dip of 200ft between the cairns is followed by a similar dip of about 300ft to the north-east. The ridge then rises up to the south summit of Binnein Mor.

Binnein Mor

From the north and south this mountain appears as a graceful spire. Views from the west, of which that from Sgurr a' Mhaim is probably the most notable, show a long ridge throwing down grey screes. The summit, at 3700ft, lies at the north end of this narrow crest beyond the south top. The north-north-east ridge, falling from the cairn to a lochan on a wide saddle at its foot, is wet and slabby, with patches of crumbling moss. The drier north-north-west spur is therefore the one usually selected for descents and ascents on this side of the mountain.

Binnein Beag

To the north of the tarn stands Binnein Beag, which gives a pleasant scramble to a cairn overlooking the watershed of Glen Nevis. The round of Coire na Gabhalach, starting either with the stiff ascent of An Gearanach in the west, or with Binnein Beag to the east, provides an enjoyable traverse across the intervening tops of Binnein Mor, Na Gruagaichean and Stob Coire a' Chairn.

Sgurr Eilde Mor

The paths and track from Kinlochleven make access to the eastern tops much easier. A cairned stalkers' path also helps, as it climbs under the flanks of Na Gruagaichean on a steep, exposed slope to the zig-zags on the snout of Sgurr Eilde Beag, the south-eastern spur of Binnein Mor. Here, a branch of the path continues at a lower level, under the towering walls of Binnein Mor, to three tarns on a boggy saddle, to the west of Sgurr Eilde Mor. Above the largest pool, grassy slopes give way to steeper gradients of loose rock which, from below, appear as a short ridge. Small, angled slabs encountered above the western face of the hill form a narrow edge, at the top of which a large cairn marks the summit of another longer ridge pointing to the head of Glen Nevis. Approximately ten yards to the south-south-east, a smaller cairn acts as guide to steep, rocky terraces, which give a stumbly descent to the stream fed by the three lochans, for a return to the track.

On a full traverse of the Mamores a west-to-east circuit is best. From Binnein Mor it is best to re-track south and descend the spur of Sgurr Eilde Beag to the stalkers' path, climb the short north-west ridge of Sgurr Eilde Mor, and retrace one's steps to the path. Binnein Beag can then be reached by an indistinct path crossing the head of Coire a' Bhinnein, and that mountain is ideally placed for the return walk down Glen Nevis.

CHAPTER 10   WALK 2

Ben Nevis 4406ft/1344m
  Carn Dearg (SW) 3348ft/1020m
  Carn Dearg (NW) 3961ft/1221m
Carn Mor Dearg 4012ft/1223m
  Carn Dearg Meadhonach 3870ft/1180m
  Carn Beag Dearg 3265ft/1006m

Ben Nevis is usually translated from the Gaelic as malicious or venomous mountain, though some consider 'Nevis' to be a corruption of 'nibheis', meaning cloud or heavens. What cannot be disputed is that whichever choice is adopted, it will be equally apt, for the mountain is frequently enveloped in cloud and mist, often accompanied by some of the vilest weather imaginable.

Ben Nevis

Its great bulk looms large above Fort William, and the adjacent peaks, though breasting the 4000ft contour, are overshadowed by 'The Ben', which deceptively hides its gigantic cliffs behind the outlying shoulder of Meall an t-Suidhe. The old pony track from Achintee, at the foot of Glen Nevis, joined by a path from the Glen Nevis Youth Hostel, encourages visitors, as it gives the impression that there is an easy passage to the summit, which, being the highest in Britain, has an added attraction. It is not uncommon to meet ill-clad and abysmally-shod tourists struggling up the mountainside seduced by fine weather in the valley. Such is the popularity of the 'Tourist route' that severe erosion has resulted in the disappearance of parts of the pathway, and although efforts have been made to stabilise the worst of the landslips the ugly scars remain. The numerous cairns also add to the general untidiness about the ruined observatory, the indicator, and the Ordnance Survey post near the cliff-edge, which vie with each other for the privilege of marking the summit.

Anyone wishing to see the cliffs from below should take the path along the Allt a' Mhuilinn. A track through the Ben Nevis Distillery yard crosses the railway to the south bank of the Allt Coire an Lochain, which is followed to a bridge on the route of the disused aluminium company railway. On the opposite side of the stream, a boggy path cuts the contours in an obvious diagonal towards the corrie of the Allt a' Mhuilinn (ignore the access track crossed at about 500ft). The path from the Golf Club car park crosses the course in a bee-line for the nearest slopes to an obvious stile. A tortuous boggy track winds up through thickets of silver birch and hazel to the entrance of a wide corrie by a dam and forestry road end. The path from the Ben Nevis Distillery comes in from the right near the top of the steep section. The path continues up the wide valley on the east bank of the Allt a' Mhuilinn and eventually reaches the CIC Hut, which, at 2250ft, lies at the foot of the cliffs. Here the path doubles back on itself, skirts the base of the crags of Carn Dearg (north-west) to the boggy saddle of Lochan Meall an t-Suidhe, to meet the Achintee track. This continues across the face of the mountain, to climb above the deep trench of the Red Burn to a series of wide zig-zags leading to the scree and boulders of the summit plateau. Approaching the last rise, the path runs perilously close to the edge of several gullies which cut back into the face of the cliffs. Care is needed in mist, as any snow may be corniced and project several feet over the void.

For emergencies there is a small metal bivouac shelter perched on the ruined observatory wall. Similar shelters lie in an angle above the tiny lochan in the head of Coire Leis, and on the crown of Carn Dearg, several yards due north of the metal indicator post at the top of Number 4 gully.

Carn Dearg (south-west)

The ascent of the mountain by way of Carn Dearg (south-west) or the Allt Coire Eoghainn is seldom attempted, as the climb from the road in Glen Nevis is a steep, murderous flog of fully 4000ft up slopes strewn with gullies and clifflets. The summit is thus best approached from the Achintee track. At the head of the zig-zags, take the path which meanders to the right, and at a cairn near the southerly point of the curve, below a steep bank, take a SSW bearing. In clear conditions Stob Ban, seen across the hidden trough of Glen Nevis, can be used as a guiding point. A second cairn lies on a line from the path to a third pile at the top of a steep scree-slope, which falls 700ft to a short grassy ridge topped by a pencil-slim cairn.

Carn Dearg (north-west)

The cairn of Carn Dearg (north-west) sits out to the north of the path, beyond a vast spread of scree at the head of the Red Burn. From the summit of Ben Nevis, the cliff-edge can be used as a guide to a walk which enjoys airy glimpses down the gullies to the Allt a' Mhuilinn (careful compass work is needed in mist, the No 4 gully indicator post is a useful landmark). The cairn lies almost on the point of a spur noted for its dramatic view of the bold profile of Tower Ridge. To the north and west of the cairn there are fringes of broken crag, and care is needed when steering back towards the path above Lochan Meall an t-Suidhe. It is better, if seeking the Achintee path, to take a southerly bearing towards the refuge shelter, and a line of cairns which mark out a route towards the head of the Red Burn.

Carn Mor Dearg

The finest approach to Ben Nevis is that along the arête of Carn Mor Dearg, reached from the north-west by way of the Allt a' Mhuilinn. Here, heathery slopes give an easy rise to the nose of the hill, where a cairn marks the summit of Carn Beag Dearg. This is little more than a lump on the bare stony crest running south-east to Carn Dearg Meadhonach. On the eastern face of this hill pinnacled buttresses fall away to the Allt Daim. The ridge rises gradually to the summit of Carn Mor Dearg. From the summit a steeply-angled ridge drops 1300ft to the east to a col marking the watershed between the Allt Daim and the Allt Coire Giubhsachan. The mountain can be approached by an enjoyable route from Steall ruin following this latter stream and the east ridge.

The way to Ben Nevis follows the celebrated Carn Mor Dearg arête which skirts round the head of Coire Leis. From Carn Mor Dearg, and along the ridge, there are fascinating views of some of the grandest cliffs in all Scotland. In summer the arête, though narrow in places, is little more than a scramble. The traverse of the ridge under snow is a different proposition entirely, and is regarded as one of Scotland's classic winter routes. Carn Mor Dearg is seldom climbed for its own sake, and this opportunity to link two 4000ft peaks in a single expedition should not be missed. At the southern end of the arête a notice bears the legend 'Abseil posts 50ft intervals for roping down only'. Below, a line of iron posts plots a route down a stony rib into the head of Coire Leis. It is also possible to climb to the ridge from the corrie, taking a rough path which skirts the base of the cliffs. At the foot of the north-east ridge of Ben Nevis, a massive jumble of rocks on the corrie floor can be avoided by keeping to the edge of the basin, where broken rock-terrace steps provide a useful ladder to the upper headwall, which leads to two cairns a few yards to the south of the abseil posts.

The final steep rise to the summit of Ben Nevis begins at the notice on a stony path threading among huge boulders, heading firstly to the south-west and then veering gradually round to the west, keeping well clear of the cliffs to the right. Near the top a line of iron posts at approximately 25 yard intervals provides another guide to the plateau, which only comes into view when a group of cairns suddenly appear near the observatory. In descent, when doing the round of peaks in the opposite direction, the iron posts indicate a line keeping well clear of the cliffs. From the lowest post it is important to work across the slopes to the east to gain the col above Coire Leis – it is all to easy to lose too much height on the southern slopes and miss the col.

CHAPTER 10	WALK 3

Aonach Beag 4060ft/1236m
Stob Coire Bhealaich 3644ft/1100m
Sgurr a' Bhuic 3165ft/965m
Aonach Mor 3999ft/1219m
Stob an Cul Choire 3580ft/1097m
Stob Coire an Fhir Dhuibh 3250ft/983m
Tom na Sroine 3015ft/918m

Guarded on the north by the dense woods of the Leanachan Forest, and to the west by the great bulk of Ben Nevis, the most obvious and direct approach to these peaks is from Glen Nevis starting at the gorge of the Water of Nevis (car-park at roadhead).

Aonach Beag

Above Steall ruin, a stream rising on slopes to the north-east can be followed for a time to gain height on the steady pull to Sgurr a' Bhuic. A saddle at about 2950ft to the north sets this top apart from Aonach Beag, and its slopes lead to the rocky ridge and cairn of Stob Coire Bhealaich. (n.b. It is worth noting that the eastern slopes of this 'top' are particularly steep and require care above the crags at the head of Coire an Eoin should an approach from that quarter be contemplated.) To the north-west, the dome of Aonach Beag heaves its flat field of stones above impressive buttresses of black crag, and of the twin cairns near the edge, the western pile is the higher.

Aonach Mor

The saddle to the north-west is narrow and stony at its lowest point some 400ft below the summit cairns, and ahead, to the north, a blunt acre of rocky ground rises towards Aonach Mor, a summit which, according to the one-inch maps, fails by a foot to reach the princely height of 4000ft. As if to compensate, a large cairn makes good the deficiency. This hill is separated from Carn Mor Dearg by the deep cut of the Allt Daim, reached by descending the very steep bank below the Aonach Mor/Aonach Beag saddle. When returning to Steall this slope and the Allt Coire Guibhsachan, rising on the south side of the gap provides a worthwhile route. The south-west ridge of Aonach Beag could also be used for descent and gives a shorter, though less interesting route to the main summits.

Aonach Mor has three subsidiary tops, all points along its north-east ridge. The route to the first top, Stob an Cul Choire, lies to the east of the summit cairn, where a line of cliffs appears to bar downward progress. A search slightly to the north reveals a steep ramp, leading to a short saddle at the start of the ridge, which is buttressed on its southern flank. When taking in these peaks they are best traversed from north to south. This allows the final ramp to Aonach Mor to be approached from below where the route is more obvious. In mist the descent of this section will be even more complex, a factor equally relevant on the drop to the saddle north of Aonach Beag.

A descent of 300ft to the east of Stob an Cul Choire finds a point where the rough crest turns to the north, up a short rise of 50ft, to the bump of Stob an Fhir Dhuibh, which looks across two wild corries to the cragged summits of both the Aonachs. The ridge proceeds northwards from this point, along the line of a sharp eastern escarpment, to Tom na Sroine, and slopes fanning out to the woods of Leanachan. This route, if used as an approach for a north/south traverse of the mountains, is best made from Tom na Brataich on the old Fort William – Spean Bridge road, to the south of the railway. (Access from the A82 at Torlundy (143771 — on a bend), and Leanachan access (208811 — railway underpass). Follow the track through the woods, across the junction (track from the minor road to Creag Aoil — an alternative access — on the right), and beyond the disused Aluminium Company light railway, near the head of the track, look for a firebreak to the open slopes above. Ahead lies the steady climb to Coire an t-Sneachda and the main ridge of Aonach Mor, with the ridge of Aonach an Nid seen to the left.

Contour below the snout of this ridge, and cross the Allt Choille-rais to the east, to gain the northern slopes of the obvious cragged end of Tom na Sroine's ridge.

CHAPTER 10	WALK 4

Stob Ban 3217ft/977m
Stob Choire Claurigh 3858ft/1177m
  (north top) 3719ft/1134m
  Stob a' Choire Leith 3625ft/1105m
  Stob Coire Gaibhre 3134ft/955m
  Stob Coire na Ceannain 3679ft/1121m
Stob Coire an Laoigh 3657ft/1115m
  Stob Coire Easain 3545ft/1080m
  Caisteal 3621ft/1104m
  Beinn na Socaich 3303ft/1007m
  Stob Coire Cath na Sine 3542ft/1080m
Sgurr Choinnich Mor 3603ft/1095m
  Sgurr Choinnich Beag 3175ft/966m

The long file of the 'Grey Corries' is best seen on the drive south to Fort William, from a point near the Commandos' War Memorial above Spean Bridge. The name 'Grey Corries' is a local one, and appropriate for a range covered with quartzite screes. Access is by a minor road from Spean Bridge Hotel, which follows the River Spean to Coirechoille farm, from which a track climbs by an old drovers' route to the Lairig Leacach. A small, one-roomed shelter at the head of the track lies at the start of the climbs to Stob Choire Claurigh and Stob Ban.

Stob Ban

The Allt a' Chuil Choirean separating these two mountains gives access to the ridges which rise steeply to the extremities of both peaks, the ascent of Stob Ban being the easier of the two, as only the final 400ft are particularly rough. The northern face, below the grey stacked stone of the summit cairn, is exceedingly precipitous, and the descent to a small tarn on the saddle at the foot of this broken edge is best attempted by taking a slight diversion to the west.

Stob Choire Claurigh

Above the saddle, there is an abrupt pull of 1000ft of unstable scree, which becomes progressively worse on the approach to the large summit cairn of Stob Choire Claurigh. The ascent of this mountain's east ridge is equally uncompromising as the rise to the 3000ft contour is a struggle up the steepest walls of the pass. The final 700ft to Stob Coire na Ceannain follows the line of an obvious ridge, which is narrower still on the arête above Coire na Ceannain, lying to the west of the cairn. From this, huge blocks and scree lift to a similar stack, the north top of Stob Choire Claurigh. The straggling arm of a north ridge, seen as a craggy edge above Coire na Ceannain, dips to the point of Stob Coire Gaibhre, which in turn falls to the head of the woods on the Lairig Leacach track. As an ascent this is the most direct route to the ridge, but it

leaves the outlying tops inconveniently placed.

Stob Coire an Laoigh

The main ridge lying to the west is a high barrier of splintered rock. Grey curtains of rock spill into corries on either hand, but anyone anticipating exposed scrambles will be disappointed, for Stob a' Choire Leith and Stob Coire Cath na Sine are little more than undulations on a broad crest, with cairns standing like mileposts to mark westward progress to the rough cap of Stob Coire an Laoigh. Caisteal's summit is the narrowest, buttressed on both sides by high crags which support a cairn, lying in the angle of a dog-leg twist of the ridge, overlooking the wild Coire Rath. To the north, this hill throws out a spur, escarped on its eastern edge, but this is little favoured as an ascent or descent route to the higher summit of Stob Coire an Laoigh to the west-south-west. A mere 50ft in height separates the cairns, and the ridge between the two is almost level, and remains so until Stob Coire Easain. The bold northern ridge of this top, Beinn na Socaich, falls to the bowl of Coire Choimhlidh, and the track-bed of the disused aluminium company railway for the return walk to the Lairig Leacach track. In the reverse direction this affords a speedy access to the easiest ascent to the ridge.

Sgurr Choinnich Mor

There is a loss of height of approximately 600ft between Stob Coire Easain and Sgurr Choinnich Mor to the south-west, and a similar dip to the smaller peak of Sgurr Choinnich Beag beyond. These peaks are awkwardly placed, leaving a choice of a tiresome retracing of route to Stob Coire Easain or an equally unsatisfactory descent down to Allt Coire an Eoin, if a return to Spean Bridge is sought. An alternative would be to traverse the group based on an approach up Glen Nevis or to climb the peaks on a separate expedition from Glen Nevis starting at Steall ruins. Take a diagonal route across the flanks of Sgurr a' Bhuic to the saddle west of Sgurr Choinnich Beag, a precursor to the more majestic horn of Sgurr Choinnich Mor.

To the south-east, Meanach shelter (265685), most conveniently approached from Glen Nevis, provides another base from which an east-west traverse of the whole ridge can be made. A moorland path from the cottage to the Lairig Leacach runs along the Allt nam Fang, and this gives a lift to the upper slopes of Stob Ban.

CHAPTER 10	WALK 5

Stob a' Choire Mheadhoin 3610ft/1106m
Stob Coire Easain 3658ft/1116m

Although classed as separate mountains, these peaks are divided neither by great distance nor substantial loss of height. Founded on the same broad base, a steep, wide ridge running south-west to north-east above Loch Treig, they are best approached from the north along the spur of Meall Cian Dearg.

Stob a' Choire Mheadhoin

A good road runs from the A86 in Glen Spean to the cottages at Fersit, at the north end of Loch Treig, where a track can be followed from the roadhead to the dam wall, and the track-bed of the disused aluminium company railway, beneath the slopes of Meall Cian Dearg. The pull from the loch-side to the 2500ft contour is heather, broken by small outcrops, which, like the few gullies on the steeper upper slopes, can be avoided by contouring along the slope to the south. On the open ridge, two small rises followed by short level stretches give a long drawn-out plod, which becomes progressively stonier on the rise to the hump of Stob a' Choire Mheadhoin, whose cairn is found near the southern edge of its flattened top.

Stob Coire Easain

To the south-west there is a short, stony dip to a saddle, followed by an abrupt 500ft rise to a well constructed cairn on the bare crown of Stob Coire Easain. The western slopes of this hill fall away sharply to the deep gash of the Lairig Leacach, which provides the other alternative access track. The long crag-fringed spur of Irlick Chaoile, to the south, drops to the lonely and desolate corner at the head of Loch Treig, which despite its isolation, still has shepherds residing at Creaguaineach Lodge, served by a rough track and moorland path connecting it to the tiny railhead at Corrour. All of these offer descent possibilities but most walkers prefer to drop to the open moors of Coire Laire, or retrace their steps along the ridge to Fersit.

CHAPTER 11

LAGGAN, CREAG MEAGAIDH AND THE MONADHLIATH

Fourteen rounded mountains overlooking Loch Laggan, all with wide ridges and flat summits. The main summit – Creag Meagaidh – offers one of the most dramatic corries in Scotland which forms the centrepiece to an otherwise unexceptional collection of peaks.

BEINN A'CHLACHAIR   CREAG PITRIDH   MULLACH COIRE AN IUBHAIR
Three mountains which make an enjoyable outing, with interesting views of the Ben Alder Forest.

BEINN TEALLACH   BEINN A' CHAORUINN
A combination of peaks giving an easy round conveniently close to the main road.

CREAG MEAGAIDH   STOB POITE COIRE ARDAIR   CARN LIATH
Straightforward walking along the rim of a deep mountain cirque, much more demanding if the tops are included.

A'CHAILLEACH   CARN SGULAIN   CARN BALLACH   CARN BAN   CARN DEARG   GEAL CHARN
The Monadhliath peaks are unrelentingly tedious. Geal Charn's isolation often prompts a separate ascent.

CHAPTER 11	WALK 1

Beinn a' Chlachair 3569ft/1088m
Mullach Coire an Iubhair 3443ft/1049m
   Sron Garbh 3357ft/1026m
Creag Pitridh 3031ft/924m

These three mountains are a fine day's walk involving a little under 4000ft of ascent, on a circuit from Luiblea at the south-west end of Loch Laggan. Across the heather to the east of the Amhainn Ghuilbinn, a track runs around Binnein Shuas with a branch to Lubvan and the main route on to Lochan na h-Earba. From the southern corner of the lochan a wide moorland path climbs to Bhealaich Leamhain which is centrally placed between the three peaks.

Beinn a' Chlachair

Starting from Lubvan, Beinn a' Chlachair's summit is reached by a direct climb to the rim of Coire Mor a' Chlachair, an impressive cirque which adds character to the face of an otherwise featureless, bulky hill. The summit cairn lies near the edge of this corrie. The broad, bare back of the hill leads north-east towards Bhealaich Leamhain. At the end of this ridge, turn the crags on the left (north) and descend a steep slope falling to the pass.

Mullach Coire an Iubhair (Geal Charn)

On the opposite side of the pass, crags bar a direct ascent and are excuse enough to follow the path along its western flank, which leads to easier slopes spreading to the summit. Here, a short spine of rock, surmounted by an Ordnance Survey pillar and an imposing cairn, lies above a huge field of rubble. To the east the rubble fans out to a flat saddle and then Sron Garbh, seen as a broad ridge curving around the northern corrie.

Recommended Valley Base Laggan

Maps O.S. 1:50 000 Sheets 34, 35, 41 and 42; Bartholomews 1:100 000 Sheet 51.

Starting Point/Length and time for main itinerary
Walk 1 Luiblea (432830). 15 miles/4050ft of ascent, 7–11 hours.
Walk 2 Roughburn (377813). 11 miles/3760ft of ascent, 5–8 hours.
Walk 3 Aberarder (483873). 17 miles/4510ft of ascent, 8–12 hours.
Walk 4 Glen Banchor (693998). 18 miles/3600ft of ascent, 8–12 hours.

Creag Pitridh

Creag Pitridh hardly merits its mountain status, for its small boss of steep terraced grass and miniature crag barely rises 500ft above the saddle separating it from Mullach Coire an Iubhair, from which it can be easily and quickly climbed.

All these mountains can also be climbed from Pattack, where the Blackburn hut (544817) provides shelter, and comforts enhanced by adequate supplies of fuel in the nearby woods.

From Blackburn, a path to the Bhealaich Leamhain runs under the heathery knoll of Meallan Odhar to a crossing of the stream draining Loch a' Bhealaich Leamhain. Beyond this ford, the heathery slopes of Beinn a' Chlachair rise easily to the ridge. This route also serves as a useful return for those choosing to traverse the group in the reverse direction. This alternative approach follows a path along the Allt Dubh to the foot of Sron Garbh, seen as a rough nose, which is easily turned on heather terraces to reach a summit cairn perched on a large rock.

CHAPTER 11   WALK 2

Beinn Teallach 2994ft/915m*
Beinn a' Chaoruinn 3453ft/1052m
  (south top) 3437ft/1050m
  (north top) 3422ft/1045m

The broken scarps of Beinn Teallach are a mirror image of the bolder crags on the eastern face of Beinn a' Chaoruinn, which also runs northwards from the forests of Loch Moy.

The initial approach track passes through plantations adjacent to the road, the gate immediately across the road from Roughburn cottages providing the easiest access to the foot of both hills. In the forest the track divides and the branch to the left should be followed to the gate to a sheep-pen at the boundary fence. The best way of tackling the peaks is to do them as a round of the glen of the Allt a' Chaoruinn, taking Beinn Teallach first.

Beinn Teallach
Open ground fronting the Allt a' Chaoruinn should be crossed to reach the fence of another plantation on the opposite bank of the stream. Here a path rises gradually to an old iron fence, beyond which smooth heather slopes climb to a broad crest, which, as the ascent continues, is gradually delineated on the right by steeper slopes punctuated by craggy knots. The stony summit sports a large cairn slightly west of the main line of the mountain's spine, which continues northwards to give a short descent through outcrops to a cairn in the pass of Tom Mor. A path beside the Allt a' Chaoruinn will return the walker to the sheep-pen gate, or alternatively he may climb steep banks of grass on the opposite side of the pass to the great back of Beinn a' Chaoruinn. This is reached by way of a broad ridge to the north-north-west of the grassed knobble of the mountain's northern top.

Beinn a' Chaoruinn
From this point a bleak ridge runs due south above a line of broken crags, seen

falling away to the left into Coire na h-Uamha. Beyond a shallow depression, where the cliffs cut back into the plateau, the wide crest rises to the slender pencil of a cairn on the centre top, which, resurveyed at 1053 metres, is now classed as the mountain's summit, a privilege previously enjoyed by the south top. Climbers tackling Beinn a' Chaoruinn first may prefer the more exacting climb to this summit up the narrow ridge from the floor of Coire na h-Uamha, which, at its foot is signposted by a pinnacle. Unfortunately the lower corrie is now extensively forested and access is therefore restricted.

Continuing along the ridge, a further depression is followed by an easy rise to the stony south top, marked by two cairns, which look out across the Laggan valley to the hills above Loch Treig. Heather terraces tumble down the southern end of the mountain's ridge and these should be crossed diagonally to reach the forest fence below the knot of Meall Clachaig, and the fence then followed to the sheep-pen for the return to Roughburn.

CHAPTER 11   WALK 3

Creag Meagaidh 3700ft/1130m
  Creag Mhor 3496ft/1065m
  Puist Coire Ardair 3591ft/1070m
  Meall Coire Choille-rais 3299ft/1027m
  An Cearcallach 3250ft/993m
Stob Poite Coire Ardair 3460ft/1053m
  (east top) 3441ft/1051m
  Sron Garbh Choire 3250ft/991m
Carn Liath 3298ft/1006m
  Meall an-t-Snaim 3180ft/969m
  A' Bhuidheanach 3177ft/966m
  Stob Choire Dhuibh 3006ft/916m

Guarded by plantations, the corrie of the Allt na h-Uamha and the green groove of the Moy Burn, though affording direct routes to Creag Meagaidh's cairns, deny the walker the more pleasurable approach of the path climbing to Coire Ardair. Above Aberarder farm, its long lazy arc turns through the straggling woods of Coill a' Choire to a tarn at the foot of an impressive array of cliffs, one of the largest precipices in Scotland, whose gullies in winter give exhilarating ice-climbs.

The path works up into a high corrie below the northern end of the cliffs and then rises steeply to a distinctive col known as 'The Window' at 3100ft. This opening, filled with jumbled blocks and scree, allows access to the broad plateau of Creag Meagaidh and the long ridge of Stob Poite Coire Ardair. It is one of the main landmarks of this group, the key to any rapid descent, and difficult to locate from the plateau in misty conditions.

Creag Meagaidh
The flattened top of Creag Meagaidh is marked by a small cairn, dwarfed by a

larger pile nearer the edge of an escarpment to the north-east. To the south a large expanse of mossy grass dips to the head of the Moy Burn, and the buttressed spurs of Meall Coire Choille-rais and An Cearcallach.

A line of crumbling cliffs on the north-eastern flank of Meall Coire Choille-rais drop to a deep tarned hollow dominated to the north by Puist Coire Ardair and Creag Mhor. Lying on a broad spur to the east of the summit plateau, these tops are buttressed on the northern flanks by the cliffs of Coire Ardair. The broad nose of Creag Mhor (also known as Sron a' Choire) is best reached from the bridge over the Allt Coire Ardair, a little to the west of Aberarder farm, or, alternatively, direct from the Laggan road. A finer ascent leaves the Coire Ardair path in a climb up steep grass, beside a broken edge, looking directly onto the higher walls of Puist Coire Ardair. Lochan a' Choire gradually comes into view, and there are more airy glimpses of it from the cliff-edge on the rise to the cairn of Creag Mhor, and the higher Puist Coire Ardair.

Stob Poite Coire Ardair
On the north table of 'The Window' wire and rusty posts in the scree straggle to the untidy cairns of Stob Poite Coire Ardair. A broad ridge continues eastward to Sron Garbh Choire (also known as Sron Coire a' Chriochairean) and Meall an-t-Snaim — an easy traverse, interrupted briefly by a curious deep furrow across the ridge. Carn Liath's cairn marks the highest point at the eastern end of this ridge.

Carn Liath
A broad slope above the Coire Ardair path rises to the flattened crown of this hill, which, to the north-east of its cairn, carries a broad ridge to the rounded top of A' Bhuidheanach whose cairn sits above the slabs of Coire nan Gall, one of the few breaks in the broad flanking slopes. The rolling crest here allows carefree walking to Stob Choire Dhuibh and an enjoyable finish to a round of the tops. A diagonal descent across the open face of the hill, leads easily to Aberarder farm.

Easy slopes to the north of the range can be reached from Lubh-chonnal at the head of Glen Roy, or Drummin and Garvamore on the Corrieyairack Pass road, but the expansive moors along the Spey are marshy, and few reconnoitre the hills from this quarter.

---

*A height of 2994ft given on the one inch maps appears to be confirmed by a height of 913m (2995ft) on the 1:50,000 second series Ordnance Survey maps. The 1:25,000 maps published later give a height of 915m (3001ft) confirmed by the Ordnance Survey, making this the last 'Munro'.

CHAPTER 11   WALK 4

A' Chailleach 3045ft/930m
Carn Sgulain 3015ft/920m
Carn Ballach 3020ft/920m
Carn Ban 3087ft/942m
    Snechdach Slinnean 3011ft/918m
Carn Dearg 3093ft/945m
    (south-east top) 3027ft/922m
Geal Charn 3036ft/926m

Ascents of these mountains are from the south, as no roads penetrate the featureless moors on the headwaters of the Findhorn. A road from the centre of Newtonmore runs as far as a wooden bridge over the Allt a' Chaoruinn, where it is replaced by a rutted track, which continues to a house at Glenballoch. The western end of this glen is served by a track crossing from the Laggan road to a lone cottage at the head of Strath an Eilich.

A' Chailleach

A' Chailleach is best ascended from the Allt a' Chaoruinn, where heather clothes a slope which rises past the wooden hut of the Red Bothy (687022) to a long back of the hill. The large cairn, a familiar landmark seen from the A9, appears ahead, and is soon within reach. The hill boasts an escarpment on its eastern slope, but for the most part conforms to the drab pattern of the neighbouring plateau.

Carn Sgulain

The peat-hagged Allt Cuil na Caillich, to the north, and a meagre 350ft below A' Chailleach's cairn is the only significant dip encountered, and looking ahead the drier mosses and stones rise a similar height to the cairn of Carn Sgulain, which like Carn Ballach and Carn Ban is a mere undulation on a dreary plain.

Carn Ballach

Carn Ballach's cairns scarcely merit a glance in the passing, as even in clear weather the higher elevation of the north-east top appears debatable, for a trifling eleven feet are said to be all that separate the two piles of stones. The iron posts of a boundary fence continue along the broad ridge, which here runs to the south-west.

Carn Ban (Carn Mairg)

Carn Ban's cairn huddles round one of the rusty posts, which here turn to indicate the way to the lochan on the flat-topped Snechdach Slinnean. A wide ridge also strikes off to the south-south-east, dipping a mere 160ft to the narrower crest of Carn Dearg, flanked by a broken edge above Gleann Ballach.

Carn Dearg

On a short table near this edge stands a tiny cairn, and a similar pile, a quarter of a mile to the south-east, identifies a second top. To the west, the hill falls away to Loch Dubh, where a small wooden hut signposts the head of a path to Glen Banchor. The eastern escarpment of Carn Dearg's ridge fades into broad slopes of heather tumbling towards the stony Allt Ballach, which should be crossed well above the derelict Dalballoch cottage to avoid the wet flats beside the River Calder by keeping to the side of the hill until the track at Glenballoch is reached.

Geal Charn

Geal Charn is linked to Carn Ban by an extraordinarily lengthy ridge. It can be included in the main itinerary but it is probably better to climb it on a quick excursion from the road near the Spey dam at Laggan. A good track goes high into Glen Markie, where a bridge across the Markie Burn may be found beneath the slopes of Beinn Sgiath. Heather terraces rise to the cairn of this flat-topped spur, which is linked to Geal Charn by a narrow neck above the deep cragged hollow of Lochan a' Choire. The large summit cairn, on its flat field of stones, looks north to a depressing wasteland, typical of the Monadhliath. Most retrace their steps, but anyone seeking a different route off the hill could follow the curve of the precipitous ground above the eastern corrie, to the slopes falling to the Allt nam Beith, and the Glen Markie track.

DRUMOCHTER
AND GLEN TILT

A disparate collection of twelve mountains. In the main they are broad, rounded, heathery hills notable for their isolation and lack of popularity. Beinn a' Ghlo is a massif of considerable stature and interest, however.

GEAL-CHARN A' MHARCONAICH BEINN UDLAMAIN SGAIRNEACH MHOR
Mountains easily traversed from Drumochter, and offering interesting views across Loch Ericht to Ben Alder.

MEALL CHUAICH
A boring hill with an equally drab outlook. Its main merit is that it can be climbed quickly.

A' BHUIDHEANACH BHEAG CARN NA CAIM
Rounded featureless hummocks that form the eastern side of the Pass of Drumochter.

BEINN DEARG
An isolated peak in the middle of an area of uninteresting rounded heather tops with below-average views.

CARN A' CHLAMAIN
This hill, situated in an interesting position above Glen Tilt, provides a pleasant walk.

BEINN A' GHLO: CARN LIATH BRAIGH COIRE CHRUINN-BHALGAIN CARN NAN GABHAR
A fine three-summited massif, with steep-walled corries and wide ridges which demand strenuous effort.

Recommended Valley Base Blair Atholl

Maps O.S. 1:50 000 Sheets 42 and 43; Bartholomews 1:100 000 Sheet 51; O.S. 1:63 360 Sheet *Cairngorms*.

Starting Point/Length and time for main itinerary
Walk 1 Balsporran (628792). 15 miles/3800ft of ascent, 7–11 hours.
Walk 2 Cuaich (654867). 8 miles/ 2000ft of ascent, 4–6 hours.
Walk 3 Wade Bridge (640827). 9 miles/2000ft of ascent, 4–6 hours.
Walk 4 Old Blair (867667). 15 miles/2900ft of ascent, 6–9 hours.
Walk 5 Glen Tilt (908720). 7 miles/2300ft of ascent, 3–5 hours.
Walk 6 Marble Lodge (898717). 13 miles/4200ft of ascent, 6–9 hours.

CHAPTER 12   WALK 1

Geal-charn 3005ft/917m
A' Mharconaich 3185ft/975m
Beinn Udlamain 3306ft/1010m
Sgairneach Mhor 3251ft/991m
   Mam Ban 3011ft/918m *

Of the drab heathery mounds bordering the Drumochter Pass, A' Mharconaich, with its snout, and Geal-charn, with its distinctive cairns, are the most readily identified.

Geal-charn
From Balsporran cottage railway crossing, a path to the head of Coire Fhar provides the initial start to a direct line of ascent to

---

* Not listed in Munro's Tables, but almost certainly qualifies as a 'top', as it is as distinctive as Mealla'Chaoruinn on the opposite side of the pass.

---

the ridge, north-east of the three cairns, which are not just below the summit, but at about 2750ft, and are handy waymarks to the shattered pile of that cairn, lying half a mile due west. The summit is broad and level, and Loch Ericht stays in sight on the shallow dip to the south of the cairn, where the path from Balsporran is seen to emerge on to a saddle, at the head of Coire Fhar.

A' Mharconaich
A' Mharconaich, the next peak to the south, is a broad whaleback of easy turf with an old fence marching part way along its ridge. This reaches a height of 3174ft (967m) and at this point the fence, along the line of the regional boundary, makes a downhill turn towards Drumochter Pass. A cairn here may be thought to mark the highest point of the mountain. The summit, however, lies half-a-mile to the north-north-east, almost at the edge of the bold escarpment looking down on the pass.

Beinn Udlamain
After retracking across the summit ridge of A' Mharconaich the rusty fence is followed across a wide saddle to the south-west to reach another broad back climbing to the levelled crown of the un-named top (3213ft) on the northern nose of Beinn Udlamain. Here, a cairn stands to the north of a turn in the fence, which continues to a barren plateau where only the summit cairn breaks the smooth line of the near horizon. On the stony ridge to the south, the fence passes a small refuge,

which looks across the head of Coire Dhomhain to Sgairneach Mhor's western top.

Sgairneach Mhor
It is best to leave the fence before it reaches the foot of the slope in search of a shorter crossing of the boggy col. On the opposite side, continue on an easterly bearing, especially in mist, as this helps to locate the cairn on the most westerly hump of this bulging hill (3053ft/931m).

The metrication of the maps has given a firm height to the top of the broad-backed Mam Ban ridge to the south. In mist, this top, Mam Ban, is best located by taking a line due south from the two cairns (3160ft/963m) at the south-western end of the plateau but in clear conditions it might be easier to skirt this shoulder and reach Mam Ban before returning to climb the final rise to Sgairneach Mhor. A cairn, seen as a point on the near horizon from the saddle to the north, marks the far-from-obvious high point of a flat field of stone studded moss. If Mam Ban is left until last, some contouring to the north-east will be required to gain Sgairneach Mhor's eastern spur for the logical descent.

On a return to the ridge the two small cairns at 3160ft/963m mark the turn along the broad summit to a third cairn to the north-east. This tall pillar sits beside the triangulation post at the summit, a short distance from the edge of broken cliffs ringing Coire Creagach. This height has, over the years, been variously recorded as 3160ft, 3210ft and 3251ft, which is now confirmed by its metric equivalent of 991m.

From Sgairneach Mhor's triangulation post the walker, descending the eastern spur, speedily reaches the thick heather above Coire Dhomhain. There is a track on the opposite side of the Allt Coire Dhomhain which leads to the railway (underpass) and the road, near the summit sign of the Drumochter Pass, about two and a half miles south of Balsporran.

CHAPTER 12   WALK 2

Meall Chuaich 3120ft/951m

Very little can be said about this hill north-east of Dalwhinnie, except that it rises above the 3000ft contour. It can be approached and climbed easily from Dalwhinnie or with slightly more interest from Glen Tromie.

A gated access track, leaving the A9 near Cuaich cottage (Sign: no authorised vehicles, no dogs) runs to Loch Cuaich dam, at the mountain's foot, from which the ascent is little more than a short, sharp walk up broad heathery slopes. The hill can also be climbed from the east, where there is a track through Glen Tromie. From the deserted cottage at Bhran the tree-lined banks of the Allt na Fearna can be followed to the upper hill, and further up the glen, near Gaick Lodge, a steep zig-zag path, climbing Sgor Dearg, reaches a wide plateau which dips northwards to a gap on the 1800ft contour. Fortunately, a good fence along this broad ridge provides a useful guide to the summit of Meall Chuaich, which possesses a large cairn.

CHAPTER 12   WALK 3

A' Bhuidheanach Bheag 3064ft/936m
  Meall a' Chaoruinn 3004ft/916m
  Glas Mheall Mor 3037ft/928m
Carn na Caim 3087ft/941m

These peaks are mere undulations on the plateau east of the Drumochter Pass. On this side the ascent is straightforward, if prosaic; the slopes are easy heather, seamed here and there with shallow gullies.

There is an alternative route from the Gaick Pass to the east. A rough track runs from Dalnacardoch Lodge (722704) on the A9 to Sronphadruig Lodge. The wild Cama Choire, or curved corrie, lying above the headwaters of Edendon Water, is the one real feature of the massif, and an easy heather ascent of the tops can be made from the lodge in a brisk round of this corrie.

A' Bhuideanach Bheag
From Drumochter it is not easy to identify

the climb to Meall a' Chaoruinn, but a useful guide is to take an easterly bearing from the TV mast, seen to the west of the road, south of Balsporran cottages. An easier rise lies to the north, where a more easterly course can be followed through the heathery fold of Coire Dubhaig to the cairn. Above this point the hill rises another 60ft, to reach a fence which should be followed to an Ordnance Survey post, in an angle where the posts turn north towards Carn na Caim. There is an uninteresting walk out to Glas Mheall Mor, seen across the bare plateau to the east-south-east.

Carn na Caim
North of A' Bhuidheanach Bheag, the fence crosses a peaty col at the head of Coire Chuirn, the only ravine on the west side of the plateau. Beyond this, the ugly scar of a track is seen climbing from the road south of Dalwhinnie to the crown of the hill. The fence continues to Carn na Caim, which has two barely-discernible tops on either side of a shallow depression, on ground so featureless that it is difficult to detect the cairns. Here, the fence divides, and although one branch runs towards Dalwhinnie, the slopes are so widely contoured that any route back to the road serves.

CHAPTER 12   WALK 4

Beinn Dearg 3304ft/1008m
  Beinn Gharbh 3050ft/932m

Beinn Dearg is situated in the Grampian range eight miles north of the A9 at Blair Atholl. All routes to the mountain, of necessity, lie on its southern flanks and involve long walks to reach it. The easiest route follows the ancient track of the Minigaig Pass, a right of way which starts at Old Blair, running northwards as a wide track to a hut on the Allt Sheicheachan. Beyond this stream a moorland path drops to Bruar Water near Bruar Lodge. The lodge is also served by another track (rough but motorable – seek permission from Atholl Estates) from Calvine on the A9. The best route to take in the main peak and the top is a path following the Allt Beinn Losgarnaich a little to the north of the lodge. This climbs steeply to the broad heathery spread of Beinn Gharbh which, in turn, rises easily to the stony summit of Beinn Dearg to the south. A path, seen earlier, climbing from the lodge to the south-west ridge of Beinn Dearg, is then used for a speedy descent to the Bruar Water. Either of these paths provide a much crisper ascent than that above the Allt Sheicheachan path, which is characterised by the tiresome heather of the spur of Druim Dubh.

The mountain can also be tackled from

the Glen Tilt track (motorable – seek permission from Atholl Estates) by following Gleann Diridh and climbing the expansive slopes of Beinn a' Chait, two miles to the south-east. The Tilt is crossed by a bridge to the east of Marble Lodge followed by a walk back down the north bank through birch woods to a footbridge over the Allt Diridh and the entrance to Gleann Diridh. This approach is somewhat tedious, but the inclusion of Beinn Mheadhonach on a circuit of the glen makes for a more satisfying expedition.

CHAPTER 12   WALK 5

Carn a' Chlamain 3159ft/963m
  (north top) 3123ft/952m

As an easy day after the traverse of Beinn a' Ghlo (Walk 6), this hill's ascent can round off a visit to Glen Tilt in the Forest of Atholl.

Two miles south-west of Forest Lodge in Glen Tilt, (motorable track – seek permission from Atholl Estates) there is a long easy spur just to the east of the Allt Craoinidh. The initial climb of 700ft is quite steep, but once overcome there is easier walking along the crest of a heather ridge, which appears ahead as a graceful arc curving upwards to the summit. Above a low crumbling wall, running across the slope, the ridge flattens slightly on the edge of Grianan Mor (the big sunny place). A cairn stands here, and in thick mist may be confused with the summit cairn, which appears at the top of a sharp stony rise, above the head of the corrie on the left. Schiehallion is seen away to the west as a turn is made from the diminutive cairn of the north top to the flat peat of Braigh nan Creagan Breac. A broad ridge leads steeply down to the bridge over the Tilt to the east of Marble Lodge.

The pull from the hut on the Tarf, along the tributary of the Feith Uaine Mhor, is a peat-hagged flounder to the heather of Meall Tionail. A boggy saddle to the south of its cairn is followed by an easy, grassed rise to the cairn of Carn a' Chlamain. In good weather this route, as a completion of a south/north traverse, can be quicker than the route up the Tilt and the Tarf, as a useful preliminary to reach the Tarf bothy for an expedition up An Sgarsoch and Carn Ealer (Chapter 15, Walk 3).

CHAPTER 12   WALK 6

Beinn a' Ghlo:
Carn Liath 3197ft/975m
Braigh Coire Chruinn-bhalgain
  3505ft/1070m
Carn nan Gabhar 3677ft/1121m
  Airgiod Bheinn 3490ft/1061m

Carn Liath, a familiar landmark when motoring north along the A9 through the pass of Killiecrankie, hides the main bulk of Beinn a' Ghlo, which is not seen until passing Blair Atholl. A track from Old Blair to Forest Lodge on the Tilt can be used, with Estate permission, for vehicular access to the foot of the mountain.

Carn Liath
Behind Balaneasie Cottage on the south bank of the Tilt (path from bridge east of Marble Lodge), grassy banks rise to the upper reaches of the Fender Burn, where the clump of pines beside Craig-choinnich Lodge acts as guide and landmark to the steep heather-clad slopes beyond. These can also be reached from the derelict cottage at Aldandulish, served by a grassy but motorable track, which is a continuation of a narrow road from the Old Bridge of Tilt.

It is a hard pull to Carn Liath's cairn, on a distinct point overlooking the wide sweep of Beinn a' Ghlo's eastern corries, and the whalebacks of its other tops. Ahead, a ridge dips along a sharpened crest to a gap at the foot of the narrow bank on the 900ft climb to Braigh Coire Chruinn-bhalgain.

Braigh Coire Chruinn-bhalgain
To the right (east), steeply-pitched walls sweep away in a wide arc to the flanks of Airgiod Bheinn, shaping the ridge towards this southern snout of Carn nan Gabhar. On the opposite flank, the dumpy hill-top of Braigh Coire Chruinn-bhalgain falls precipitately towards the Tilt.

Carn nan Gabhar
The sharp rise from the col above the corrie bowl of Glas Leathad leads abruptly to the broad ridge between Carn nan Gabhar and Airgiod Bheinn. Those intending to descend by the north ridge of the mountain should here make the short diversion to Airgiod Bheinn before retracing steps northwards along the plateau to a field of blocks supporting the cairn of Carn nan Gabhar. The Ordnance Survey post sits on a slab of rock and should be passed to reach a low mound of stone a few yards to the north-east, some 3ft higher.

The mountain is wildest to the north, with outcrops and broken crags around the tarn of Loch Loch. This route of ascent can be approached from the A924 by a private road to Daldhu in Gleann Fearnach. A track into Glen Loch almost reaches the foot of a scrambly route up the face of Coire cas-eagallach (the steep fearful corrie), and the easier scree on steep slopes to the south.

Those returning to Glen Fender can cross Airgiod Bheinn whose heathery nose gives a swift descent to the Allt Coire Lagain, which can be followed to a track below Carn Liath for a return to Glen Fender. Walkers returning to the Tilt will find that the shortest route re-traverses Braigh Coire Chruinn-bhalgain, followed by a steep descent down its western slopes. The wooden footbridge near Clachghlas is a useful river crossing. Alternatively – more circuitous but far more satisfying – is a descent down Carn nan Gabhar's northern ridge to the bridge below Allt Fheannach, to complete the finest traverse of the mountain.

AVIEMORE AND THE WESTERN CAIRNGORMS

Nine mountains encompassing the largest area in Britain above the 4000ft contour. Long walks across the wild plateaux overlook some of the grandest corries and most magnificent cliffs in Scotland. The Cairngorm ski-lift eases access to the first two walks.

CAIRN GORM
A walk heading west from the main summit to the remote tops skirts above fine cliffs and corries.

BYNACK MORE   A' CHOINNEACH
When approached from Cairn Gorm, these two mountains provide a leisurely walk with interesting views.

GEAL-CHARN   SGOR GAOITH   CARN BAN MOR   MEALL DUBHAG   MULLACH CLACH A' BHLAIR
The five Munros of Glen Feshie, which give easy level walking above the 3000ft contour.

BRAERIACH: BRAIGH RIABHACH
A varied expedition along the craggy rim of the greatest high-level plateau in Britain.

Recommended Valley Base Coylumbridge

Maps O.S. 1:50 000 Sheets 36 and 43; Bartholomews 1:100 000 Sheets 51 and 52; O.S. 1:25 000 Sheet *High Tops of The Cairngorms*; O.S. 1:63 360 Sheet *Cairngorms.*

Starting Point/Length and time for main itinerary
Walk 1 Coire na Ciste (998074). 9 miles/2700ft of ascent, 4–6 hours.
Walk 2 Glenmore Lodge (992097). 14 miles/3100ft of ascent, 6–9 hours.
Walk 3 Balachroick (853013). 20 miles/3650ft of ascent, 8–12 hours.
Walk 4 Loch an Eilein (896086). 24 miles/3810ft of ascent, 10–15 hours.

CHAPTER 13   WALK 1

Cairn Gorm 4084ft/1245m
  Sron a' Cha-no 3300ft/1028m
  Cnap Coire na Spreidhe 3772ft/1151m
  Fiacaill a' Choire Chais 3700ft/1141m
  Stob Coire an t-Sneachda 3850ft/1176m
  Fiacaill Coire an t-Sneachda 3500ft/1125m
  Cairn Lochan 3983ft/1215m
  Creag an Leth-choin 3448ft/1053m
    (north top) 3365ft/1026m
  Fiacaill na Leth-choin 3500ft/1083m

Cairn Gorm is a high mountain plateau with one main summit and nine tops. It is the easiest 4000ft peak in Britain, and can be ascended very quickly if the chairlift on the Ptarmigan restaurant is used. From the restaurant there remains an easy 500ft slope to the summit. Alternatively, use can be made of the service track on the eastern slopes of Coire Cas, which continues as a broad stony path, marked with posts, to the mountain top. Despite this ease of ascent to the main peak, it is worth remembering that the featureless nature of

the plateau thus gained, combined with the cliffs that bar the way to safety along its north-western flank, can pose serious problems in bad weather. The Cairngorm accident of 1970, when six people died in a blizzard during a forced bivouac on the slopes of Cairn Lochan is a grim reminder of the potential dangers of this high massif, so temptingly accessible.

If a complete traverse of the tops is sought an ascent to the plateau at its northern end will be required. Above the Coire na Ciste car-park, a heathery rib to the east of the Allt na Ciste leads to the ridge above Coire Laogh Mor and the tiny cairn of Sron a' Cha-no above the ragged bluffs, overlooking Strath Nethy. Those using the Pass of Ryvoan approach can take the track to Nethy hut, and follow the bank of the Nethy to the foot of this ridge, or climb more directly to the cairn of Mam Suim at the end of the ridge.

A broad ridge rises easily from Sron a' Cha-no to Cnap Coire na Spreidhe, following the line of escarpments above Strath Nethy. On the approach to Cairn Gorm, the path from Coire Cas towards the spring of the Marquis' Well is a busy throughfare, as evidenced by the immense cairn on the summit, and the radio relay station and weather station nearby.

Wide corries to the south-east of the plateau merge into stonier ground which ends abruptly by a sharp drop of cliffs and bluffs to Loch Avon. The path down the Allt Coire Raibeirt is one of the few safe routes through the cliffs to the loch, and much used by climbers visiting the Shelter Stone crags.

Going westwards the rim of Coire Cas leads to the top of Fiacaill a' Choire Chais which can also be approached by an easy heathery ridge on the western lip of the hollow. The broad back of the mountain now turns to the south, along the headwall of Coire an t-Sneachda, to the cairn of Stob Coire an t-Sneachda, a stony hump above several minute tarns. Further to the west Fiacaill Coire an t-Sneachda pokes a broken ridge towards Loch Morlich. A break on the crags where this spur abutts the ridge provides a pleasant easy scramble to a cairn at the eastern end of Cairn Lochan. Huge blocks, lining the great walls above the tarn in Coire an Lochain, are seen on the walk to another cliff-top cairn on the point of Cairn Lochan.

To the west the mountain runs to the edge of crags above the Lairig Ghru, and easy slopes along the western fringe of Coire an Lochain to Fiacaill na Leth-choin, at the northern edge of the Miadan Creag an Leth-choin. Here there may be a temptation to follow the stream falling to Coire an Lochain, but this should be firmly resisted, especially when snow lies on the corrie wall, as this is very prone to avalanche. To the north-west, Creag an Leth-choin (Lurcher's Crag) is seen perched atop crags at the northern entrance to the Lairig Ghru, and a quarter of a mile to the north another insignificant cairn, sitting at the end of this spur, overlooks gentler slopes which fall towards Loch Morlich and the Lairig Ghru path. In the dip of the Allt Creag an Leth-choin, a useful path leads through the heather for the return walk to the Coire Cas car park.

CHAPTER 13   WALK 2

Bynack More 3574ft/1090m
  Bynack Beg 3162ft/ 964m
A' Choinneach 3345ft/1017m

Approached from the Pass of Ryvoan, the traverse of these two hills might be combined with that of the northern tops of Cairn Gorm (Walk 1) on a round of Strath Nethy.

Bynack More

A good forest track through the Pass of Ryvoan leads to a junction near Ryvoan. Here the track branching right to the Pit Fyannich (Nethy Hut) should be followed to cross the Nethy to the Lairig an Laoigh path, which reaches the 2500ft contour at the foot of Bynack More. A wide ridge to the south can then be followed to a rocky rib leading to the summit, with, if desired, a short easy detour towards the Nethy on a crossing of the crusty heap of Bynack Beg. The ridge to the south of Bynack More's cairn runs to granite tors, known as the Little Barns of Bynack, a convenient landmark at an altitude several feet higher than the larger blocks of the Barns on the slopes facing the Lairig an Laoigh.

A' Choinneach

To the south-west, A' Choinneach's broad spread is quickly traversed to an insignificant cairn overlooking Strath Nethy, where the valley can be used for the return or Cairn Gorm traversed, according to taste.

Coming from Cairn Gorm and taking the peaks in the reverse direction, one first encounters a steep tumble of 1300ft above the Feith Buidhe to The Saddle, at the head of Strath Nethy. The view along Loch Avon from this col is particularly fine, and must surely rank as one of the most engaging in Scotland. The rise from the Saddle to the level crown of A' Choinneach has little interest. Classified as a 'mountain' by Munro, it remained so until the Brown and Donaldson 1981 list demoted it to the status of a 'top'. It is worth noting that to the east of the cairn, an easy slope falls towards the Lairig an Laoigh path near the shelter at the Fords of Avon, a useful four-man refuge. If continuing to Bynack More, head directly for the Little Barns of Bynack, as the tors are the surest guide to the mountain's summit ridge.

CHAPTER 13   WALK 3

Geal-charn 3019ft/920m
Sgor Gaoith 3658ft/1118m
  Sgoran Dubh Mor 3635ft/1111m
  Meall Buidhe 3185ft/976m
Carn Ban Mor 3443ft/1052m
Meall Dubhag 3268ft/998m
Mullach Clach a' Bhlair 3338ft/1019m
  Diollaid Coire Eindart 3184ft/974m

The finest approaches to this chain of 'Munros' are those along Gleann Einich, which from Coylumbridge and Loch an Eilein follow woodland tracks to a complex of paths to the west of the tiny Lochan Deo. Leave the Gleann Einich track before the river crossing, near the foot of Creag Dhubh, on a heathery ascent to Clach Mhic Cailein, the Argyll Stone. From this, the lengthy ridge rises gradually to a sizeable cairn at the end of Sgoran Dubh Mor.

Further up the glen (beyond the deep ford) there is a more dramatic route along the western shore of Loch Einich. The path, known as Ross's path, climbs steeply above the head of the loch to A' Phocaid (the pocket), a high corrie ringed by a wall of broken crags. These are threaded to reach the pool of Fuaran Diotach (the breakfast well) on the plateau's edge, south of Sgor Gaoith. The problem with this approach is that the rest of the peaks are a little too distant for a satisfactory itinerary. The Sgor Gaoith group could therefore be kept for a short day, leaving the other peaks to be tackled from Glen Feshie on another visit.

Glen Feshie, with its shorter approaches, is also better suited as a starting point for traversing all the peaks in a day. From the roadhead at Achlean (853976) an easy footpath above the Allt Fhearnagain climbs to an expansive shoulder to the south of Carn Ban Mor. To the west of the River Feshie, another minor road runs to Carnachuin (locked gate at Tolvah). It is worth remembering the footbridge over the river half-a-mile south of Stronetoper, as it allows woods to the east of the river to be avoided when returning from the head of the glen. Beyond Carnachuin another bridge crosses the river from where a track leads right through woods to Ruigh-aiteachain. A branch straight ahead climbs directly to the Moine Mhor, the big moss, along a shoulder overlooking the deep scoop of Coire Garbhlach.

Geal-charn

Leaving the Achlean road just north of Balachroick, a path climbs through scattered woods above the Allt Ruadh to peter out on heather slopes which clamber to the rough grass of Geal-charn's summit.

To the south-east of the cairn, an undulating ridge crosses a slight dip marked with a small cairn to the grassy lump of Meall Buidhe, and the steep 500ft bank below the large cairn on Sgoran Dubh Mor.

Sgor Gaoith

The ridge of Sgoran Dubh Mor, buttressed by steep broken crags above Loch Einich, is a fine battlement which enjoys unparalled views to Braeriach. At the highest point, an airy table, peering over a drop to Loch Einich, supports a few stones and a narrow up-ended slab on this, the summit of Sgor Gaoith.

Carn Ban Mor

To the south more easy grass leads to Carn Ban Mor, an indeterminate top crowned by a squat cairn, the largest of several confusing piles scattered about the undulations of an extensive plateau. In mist, only diligent map and compass work helps to identify the correct cairn. A little to the south-west of the summit, an incipient watercourse, where the unsightly remains of an old corrugated iron hut lie, marks the site of a bothy at the head of the Allt Fhearnagan path.

Meall Dubhag

Slopes dip to Meall Dubhag a little further to the south, passing a small howff (890964) on a ridge so broad that in mist a south-westerly bearing may well be needed to locate the largest, and most westerly of the two cairns on the levelled top of Meall Dubhag, which lies slightly to the west of a fold in the ridge, on a point overlooking Coire Garbhlach. This deep hollow cuts back into the plateau, and a detour round it must be made to reach the long dragging slopes of Mullach Clach a' Bhlair, seen to the south, where the ugly scar of the Moine Mhor track is joined for the walk to the cairn.

Mullach Clach a' Bhlair

Mullach Clach a' Bhlair marks the turning point for most walkers, who can opt for an easy descent to Ruigh-aiteachain by the wide ridge dropping to Druim nam Bo. The persistent may push on to a distant cairn at the end of the track. Diollaid Coire Eindart is not a top to get excited about, and its acres of monotonous peat are best left to the fanatical 'Munroist'.

Anyone staying at Ruigh-aiteachain, wishing to traverse the hills in the opposite direction, will find a useful path a few yards south of the shelter (about halfway between it and a fork in the path). This climbs through shrubs and heather, to emerge on the point of Creag na Gaibhre, a top with a fine view to the head of Glen Feshie, which improves on the climb to the tiny Lochan nam Bo and the broad shoulder of Druim nam Bo.

CHAPTER 13   WALK 4

Braeriach:
Braigh Riabhach 4248ft/1296m
  Stob Coire an Lochain 4036ft/1235m
  South Plateau 4149ft/1265m
  Sron na Lairig 3875ft/1184m
  Stob Lochan nan Cnapan 3009ft/918m

Seen from Aviemore as a deep corridor through the heart of the Cairngorms, the Lairig Ghru offers the best access to the high remote plateaus of Braeriach, and Ben Macdui (Chapter 14, Walk 3).

Northern access to the Lairig Ghru
There are a number of possible starting points to reach the entrance of the Lairig Ghru. From the B970 (Aviemore/Feshie-bridge road) turn off to the Loch an Eilein car park, (signpost near a monument enclosed by iron railings). A forest track along the north shore of the loch leads to a complex of tracks near Lochan Deo, where, by keeping to the most easterly trail, a similar track from Coylumbridge is joined. From Lochan Deo, take the track which terminates at the Allt Druidh, where the Cairngorm Club footbridge provides a safe crossing to the well-trodden path climbing to the Sinclair Hut (958037), at the entrance to the pass. Another route starts at the north-western corner of Loch Morlich and goes by way of the Rothiemurchus Hut. A shorter footpath to the Sinclair Hut leaves the Coire Cas road opposite a car park just above the forest boundary. After crossing a footbridge on the Allt Mor, the stream is followed for about a mile to be re-crossed (ford) on a turn to the south-west, where the path

pushes through the heather of an obvious pass, known as the Chalamain Gap, to a short steep descent to another ford below the Sinclair Hut. This refuge sits on an elevated terrace and cannot be seen from the bank of the stream, and a waymarked path climbing a crude staircase is the only sure guide to it.

Braigh Riabhach (Braeriach)
To the south of the hut there is a gradual pull along the heather shoulder of Sron na Lairig to a higher shoulder above the pass (cairn). This broad ridge turns westwards in a broad arc, rising between the sweep of Coire Beanaidh and ragged escarpments above the Lairig Ghru. Buttresses then appear on the left as the edge of a huge wall of cliff, rimming Coire Bhrochain, is followed to the summit cairn of Braeriach, perched almost on the lip.

A more varied ascent approaches up Gleann Einich. From Lochan Deo a track runs into the glen, and here, on the mountain's western flank, broad slopes climbing between Coire an Lochain and Coire Bogha-cloiche give a laborious 2000ft climb to the cairn of Stob Coire an Lochain. Alternatively continue towards Loch Einich. Shortly before the loch a path cuts up the hill to the Allt Coire Bogha-cloiche and then continues as a long gradual ascent to the Allt Coire Dhondail, to be followed by zig-zags which emerge from the head of Coire Dhondail 600ft below the cairn of the South Plateau (Carn na Criche), found a mile to the east. Between this windswept pile and the main summit lies the largest area of high tundra in Britain. At its centre, below the Einich Cairn (4061ft/1237m), a tiny spring at the source of the Dee

bubbles from a mossy patch, at the foot of a small grassy bank, identified by a miniature cairn of white quartzite. The infant stream runs through gravel beds to be joined by other springs, (the 'Fuaran Dhe' – Wells of God), before winding across the plateau to plunge over 400ft cliffs at the head of Garbh Choire Dhaidh. A large snow bridge sometimes seen here often lasts well into the summer. These Falls of Dee can be seen from below, when approaching a break in the crags on a steep, bouldery route from the Garbh Choire shelter to the plateau.

Braeriach boasts a pointless and distant top – Stob Lochan nan Cnapan (Tom Dubh). Those who wish to take this in during a Braeriach traverse might consider starting up Ross's Path from Gleann Einich or from Achlean in Glen Feshie (see Walk 3). From the edge of the Moine Mhor, Stob Lochan nan Cnapan (Tom Dubh) may be discerned above the streams feeding the Eidart. Its ascent involves a considerable detour from whichever route is chosen on traverses of the neighbouring tops. This is one for the real enthusiast, the most meaningless 3000ft 'top' in all Britain, for here lies the ultimate in desolate wilderness, a landscape so featureless that it almost defies man's ability to use map and compass. Devoid of landmarks, in mist, only the oozy drains of the plateau's few streams offer guides of any consequence. When frozen by winter blizzards even these fail to assist, and dead reckoning by compass is the only sure guide to the safety of the glens below.

BRAEMAR AND THE EASTERN CAIRNGORMS

A vast area of high land, where winter lingers later than anywhere else in Britain. Distance and weather here can tax the stamina of the fittest walker, but good approach paths and flat, stony terrain allow great distances to be covered.

THE DEVIL'S POINT   CAIRN TOUL
One of the finest ascents in the Cairngorms, which can be extended by adding Braeriach.

MONADH MOR   BEINN BHROTAIN   CARN CLOICH-MHUILINN
Remote, featureless mountains requiring stamina, determination and perseverance.

BEN MACDUI   CARN A' MHAIM
A high mountain plateau pitted with wild crag-rimmed corries and hidden tarns.

DERRY CAIRNGORM   BEINN MHEADHOIN
Part of the Macdui massif, offering a similar walk with some interesting rock features.

BEN AVON: LEABAIDH AN DAIMH BHUIDHE   BEINN A' BHUIRD
With the tops included the traverse of these two massifs is an expedition of exceptional challenge.

BEINN BHREAC   BEINN A' CHAORRUINN
A grassy moorland walk, which in clear conditions offers interesting perspectives of the Ben Macdui group.

CHAPTER 14	WALK 1

The Devil's Point 3303ft/1004m
Cairn Toul 4241ft/1291m
  Stob Coire an t-Saighdeir 3950ft/1213m
  Sgor an Lochain Uaine 4150ft/1258m

A half-mile east of the Linn of Dee, a track runs to Luibeg and Derry Lodge in Glen Lui, continuing as a moorland path to the southern entrance to the Lairig Ghru, on the most pleasant walk to the foot of Cairn Toul. Here a footbridge crosses the swift-flowing Dee a little below Corrour bothy, a popular shelter much used by walkers crossing the pass or seeking a night's bivouac near the base of the great mountains around it.

The Devil's Point

The black arrowhead of The Devil's Point (from the Gaelic Bod an Deamhain) towers above the tiny cottage. A stream on the slopes of Cairn Toul helps to locate a path up the hillside, on to the saddle where the ridge of the Devil's Point meets the waist of Carn Toul. This narrow spine, flanked on both sides by falls of rock, runs out to the cairn of the Point.

Cairn Toul

To the north-west of the saddle, convex slopes rise to the narrowing ridge of Stob Coire an t-Saighdeir, above a plunge to the right which becomes craggy towards Cairn Toul (also known as Carn an t-sabhail). On

the summit is a large cairn, inside a windbreak wall. The great cliffs above Lochan Uaine also support the sharp horn of Sgor an Lochain Uaine, more popularly known as The Angels' Peak. The long slant of the narrow ridge can be followed to the col at the end of the South Plateau top of Braeriach (Chapter 13, Walk 4). By continuing the traverse on a round of the tops above the An Garbh Choire, the Lairig Ghru path then provides a scenic return route to the Linn of Dee. The alternative is a drop from the col to Loch nan Stuirteag and Glen Geusachan (Walk 2), or a return by the ridge. Ramblers traversing these peaks sometimes find that the Sinclair Hut and Corrour bothy can be used to advantage, especially if contemplating a longer expedition across more of the Cairngorm tops.

CHAPTER 14	WALK 2

Monadh Mor 3651ft/1113m
Beinn Bhrotain 3795ft/1157m
Carn Cloich-mhuilinn 3087ft/942m

The easiest track to these hills is that which follows the Dee from Linn of Dee to White Bridge, where tracks to either Glen Geldie (across bridge) or Glen Dee can be taken. Three miles of tedious heather lie between the Geldie Burn and the summit cairns of Beinn Bhrotain, and the slopes from the head of the track along the Dee, south of

Recommended Valley Base Braemar

Maps O.S. 1:50 000 Sheets 36 and 43;
Bartholomews 1:100 000 Sheets 51 and 52;
O.S. 1:25 000 Sheet *High Tops of The Cairngorms*; O.S. 1:63 360 Sheet *Cairngorms*.

Starting Point/Length and time for main itinerary
Walk 1 Corrour (981958). 8 miles/2750ft of ascent, 4–6 hours. (Linn of Dee to Corrour – 8 miles.)
Walk 2 Corrour (981958). 12 miles/2700ft of ascent, 5–8 hours.
Walk 3 Linn of Dee (068898). 21 miles/4510ft of ascent, 9–14 hours.
Walk 4 Linn of Dee (068898). 19 miles/3600ft of ascent, 8–12 hours.
Walk 5 Allanaquoich (117911). 32 miles/5700ft of ascent, 13–20 hours.
Walk 6 Linn of Dee (068898). 18 miles/2650ft of ascent, 7–11 hours.

Corrour, are little different. The walk through Glen Lui (Walk 1) is more picturesque, and combined with a return by the Dee adds variety to a round of the hills. Anyone staying at Corrour may consider a longer combined ascent with Cairn Toul (Walk 1), and for the sake of convenience the walk is described as a traverse from this point. In returning to Corrour from the south, a detour may be necessary to cross the Dee at White Bridge, as this river and the Geusachan Burn can be difficult to negotiate.

Monadh Mor

The heathery margins of the west bank of the Dee can be followed to the entrance of Glen Geusachan, where the bank of the Geusachan Burn should be followed to the head of the glen. Here a break in the escarpments of Monadh Mor allows an easy climb to be made, beside a stream falling from Loch nan Stuirteag.

At the northern end of Monadh Mor, grass rises easily to a field of stones, giving a pleasant stroll to the first and highest of two cairns on the twin barrows of the summit plain.

Beinn Bhrotain
It seems natural to follow the eastern edge of the hill to the neck of Coire Cath nam Fionn, where a turn to the south-east sees the start of the rise to Beinn Bhrotain's highest point, marked by an Ordnance Survey pillar and two cairns. To the east a third solitary cairn sits at the head of slopes to crags above the Dee, which can be reached by taking a more southerly route down the Caochan Roibidh.

Carn Cloich-mhuilinn
Alternatively, by descending a little to the west of Coire an t-Sneachda, near the source of the Allt Garbh, a shallow col is crossed to reach an innocuous mound. The rise of barely 200ft to the ragged cairn of Carn Cloich-mhuilinn is one of the easiest imaginable, and the descent to the Dee further recommends this lazy hill.

Though greater distances are involved, it is possible to reach these three peaks from Glen Feshie, by following the Moine Mhor track to the centre of the plateau near Stob Loch nan Cnapan or Tom Dubh (see Chapter 13, Walks 3 and 4), on a crossing which is perhaps the most psychologically intimidating walk in Britain. The traverse of Monadh Mor and Beinn Bhrotain may seem no less monotonous, and the return from Carn Cloich-mhuilinn to the Geldie/Feshie path involves another traverse across inhospitable moors. Just east of the River Eidart the footpath splits into two, the higher route leading to a footbridge which was purposely built at this dangerous crossing after several people had come to grief. A few yards to the west, a tumbledown hut provides poor shelter, and should not be counted on in an emergency. Ahead, the path down Glen Feshie becomes progressively more reliable as it descends to the woods south of Ruigh-aiteachain.

CHAPTER 14   WALK 3

Ben Macdui 4296ft/1309m
  (north top) 4244ft/1295m
  Stob Coire Sputan Dearg 4095ft/1249m
  Sron Riach 3534ft/1110m
  Carn Etchachan 3673ft/1120m
Carn a' Mhaim 3402ft/1064m

Ben Macdui, its five tops and its satellite peaks, Carn a' Mhaim, Beinn Mheadhoin and Derry Cairngorm are so inconveniently scattered that even the most zealous 'Munroist' might find it tiresome to sweep

them all into one day. The latter two plus six tops are therefore grouped into Walk 4 leaving a managable but still awkward expedition based on Ben Macdui.

The construction of the road to Coire Cas detracts from the rigours of the Cairngorms, and on a walk to Macdui may well do the walker a disservice by denying him the benefit of a gradual attunement to his surroundings. Ben Macdui (also known as Beinn Mhic Dhuibh) can be reached from Cairn Gorm (Chapter 13, Walk 1) by a long level walk across the plateau. Several crude paths in the turf lead to the head of the Feith Buidhe and the stony rise to Macdui's north top. But this approach is unsatisfactory for Britain's second highest peak, and for a fuller appreciation of its magnificence it should be approached from the glens of the Derry or the Dee or from the Lairig Ghru.

The Lairig Ghru
The Lairig Ghru (see Walk 1 and Chapter 13, Walk 4) cuts through the mountains between Braeriach and Ben Macdui on its twenty-eight mile passage from Aviemore to Braemar, and is a fine walking expedition in its own right, which should not be lightly undertaken.

At its highest point, near the regional boundary, the pass reaches an elevation of 2733ft and, just below the summit on the south side, the path disappears for a time in a large boulderfield near the Pools of Dee. On the steep, eastern wall of the pass, the March Burn provides a useful guide to the plateau near Lochan Buidhe, and the path to the summit of Macdui. Another route from the Lairig Ghru follows the Allt Clach nan Taillear, one mile north of Corrour Bothy. Those wishing to quit the plateau quickly to lose height in bad weather might well chose these streams for descent. In poor conditions, particularly if iced, they are not easy and the March Burn in particular should be treated with respect.

Ben Macdui
The upper hill is a vast boulderfield, whose highest point is crowned by an Ordnance Survey pillar and an indicator, erected by the Cairngorm Club in 1925. On a clear day the views are extensive and embrace the whole of northern Scotland.

Ascent from Glen Lui
The shortest route from the south is the path from Luibeg Bridge which follows the east bank of the Luibeg Burn to the foot of Sron Riach. This allows a direct assault on the higher ridge under which lie the corrie walls of Lochan Uaine, whose drab grey crags support the stony point of Stob Coire Sputan Dearg, and the summit of Macdui seen beyond.

Loch Etchachan
To the north-east of Macdui's summit, deep rocky folds contain Loch Etchachan,

the largest tarn in the Cairngorms above 3000ft. This can be reached by a long walk up Glen Derry. A line of rock terraces rises, from its western fringe to the bare stone of Carn Etchachan, a cairned top at the edge of the cliffs which tumble to the great boulder of the Shelter Stone, at the head of Loch Avon. Those approaching from the March Burn, and wishing to visit this top, might opt to traverse to it first before heading to the summit of Ben Macdui.

Nearby, there is a scrambly route up the Garbh Uisge Beag to the summit plateau of Macdui. A rough path in the boulderfield to the east of the Shelter Stone climbs to the grassy level at the northern corner of Loch Etchachan. Crossing to the eastern side of the water, it meets the path from Coire Etchachan beside a small pool at the foot of Creagan a' Choire Etchachan, seen to the south.

Carn a' Mhaim
The ridge linking Carn a' Mhaim to Ben Macdui is the only one of its kind in Cairngorms, an exhilarating arête commanding a fine prospect of the Devil's Point and Cairn Toul. It is best reached in a steep ascent from Luibeg Bridge. The arête can then be followed to Allt Clach nan Taillear for a further ascent to the plateau. Alternatively it could be added at the end of a north-south traverse of the peaks. The cairn lies some 300 yards south of the point marked 1037 (3329 on the one-inch maps) and from it steep heather falls away to the pass linking the glens of the Lui and the Dee. Care is needed on descents from this cairn, as the ground is loose and very steep. and many consider it prudent to return along the ridge to the easier slopes, on the eastern flank, at the foot of Macdui.

CHAPTER 14   WALK 4

Derry Cairngorm 3788ft/1155m
  Little Cairngorm 3350ft/1040m
  Sgurr an Lochan Uaine 3150ft/983m
  Creagan a' Choire Etchachan
    3629ft/1108m
Beinn Mheadhoin 3883ft/1182m
  (south-west top) 3750ft/1163m
  Stob Coire Etchachan 3551ft/1082m
  Stacan Dubha 3330ft/1013m

Although these are really satellite peaks of Ben Macdui (Walk 3) they are perhaps best climbed as a separate expedition.

Derry Cairngorm
The Luibeg track runs to the base of Carn Crom (2847ft/890m) above the woods in Glen Derry, and its south-eastern spur provides a long heathery ascent leading to a broad bank of stones. Little Cairngorm's rough heap, is scarcely more than an undulation on this stony ridge, as it heads north to Derry Cairngorm, where several

large boulders, heaped into an obelisk, mark the summit.

The hill spreads northwards to the steep bluffs of Creagan a' Choire Etchachan above the rough basin of Coire Etchachan and, to the north-east, crags buttressing the flat-topped Sgurr an Lochan Uaine curve around the tiny tarn which gave the top its name. Seen from Derry Cairngorm, this is no more than a bump near the cliff-edge, but from Glen Derry it is much more pronounced.

Beinn Mheadhoin

After crossing Creagan a' Choire Etchachan there is an easy descent to Loch Etchachan from where Beinn Mheadhoin can be tackled. This great hill sits at the head of Glen Derry, looming large above the Coire Etchachan path, which provides a convenient ladder to its western end, where a broad back rises from the Loch Etchachan saddle. The south-west top is an unremarkable lump on the ridge, which continues to the actual summit, a huge tor surmounted by a cairn, reached by an easy scramble on the rock's northern side. Of the other two tops, Stacan Dubha, above Loch Avon, is the finest viewpoint. Stob Coire Etchachan, to the south of the summit, peers into Coire Etchachan from the top of a line of crags, and as the fall to Glen Derry is steep on this side of the hill, care is needed in mist when hunting for the cairn, which is almost indistinguishable from the bouldery ground on which it stands. It is best, when descending, to avoid the slopes below and contour west to Loch Etchachan.

CHAPTER 14   WALK 5

Ben Avon:
Leabaidh an Daimh Bhuidhe
    3843ft/1171m
    (south-west top) 3729ft/1135m
    E. Meur Gorm Craig 3075ft/935m
    W. Meur Gorm Craig 3354ft/1021m
    Stob Bac an Fhurain 3533ft/1076m
    Mullach Lochan nan Gabhar
    3662ft/1122m
    Stuc Gharbh Mhor 3625ft/1120m
    Stob Dubh an Eas Bhig 3563ft/1063m
    Carn Eas 3556ft/1089m
    Creag an Dail Mhor 3189ft/972m
Beinn a' Bhuird 3924ft/1196m
    (south top) 3860ft/1177m
    Cnap a' Chleirich 3811ft/1172m
    Stob an t-Sluichd 3621ft/1106m
    A' Chioch 3500ft/1050m

When seen from Glen Clunie, Ben Avon crowds the skyline above heathery hills north of the Dee, and the rocky blisters along its crest distinguish it from its equally imposing neighbour Beinn a' Bhuird. Of all the high tops in the Cairngorms, the barren summit of Ben

Avon (also known as Beinn Ath-fhinn) is the most difficult to reach, and walkers should be prepared for a long day.

Access routes to Ben Avon

To the east, a track from the Lechd road (A939) runs along the River Gairn to the ruined lodge at Loch Builg, a distance of 7 miles. Even from here, there are more miles of mountainous terrain to cross to reach the summit tor.

To the north, the Tomintoul to Inchrory road is only public as far as Delnabo (locked gate). Prior permission may be obtained to take a car to Inchrory, thus saving a six-mile walk but even then the mountain is still distant. This approach might be suitable for an ascent of Ben Avon and the two northern tops of Beinn a' Bhuird, with a return along Glen Avon.

On balance however, approaches from the south are preferable, as these traverses can accommodate crossings of Ben Avon and Beinn a' Bhuird and the tops above Glen Derry. West of Braemar a narrow road from Mar Lodge to Allanaquoich gives way to a private track to Balnagower Cottage, which continues through woods to a moorland path at the approach to the ruins of Slugain Lodge. Alternatively in drought conditions the Dee itself might be forded, saving some distance. Ahead, an indistinct path pushes north into the broad basin of the Quoich Water to reach the Clach a' Chleirich, the priest's stone, at the entrance to a corrie backed by the ridges of Ben Avon and Beinn a' Bhuird.

Ben Avon

Above the Quoich Water, heather slopes lead to Creag an Dail Mhor, and the cairn of Carn Eas to the north, where the mile-long drag across the plateau to the south-west top begins. The main summit beyond seems a very distant two miles, though the 300ft rise to it, across a carpet of orange-brown lichen, is quickly accomplished. Similar terrain to the north-east of Carn Eas allows an easy diversion to the cairned lump of Stob Dubh an Eas Bhig, to be followed by an easy pull to Ben Avon's south-west top. Here, turning to the east, a shallow depression is crossed to reach the summit tor of Leabaidh an Daimh Bhuidhe. This, upon closer inspection, reveals a fracture between two rocky segments, each boasting a small cairn.

Ben Avon's eastern tops

A sweep of the eastern tops of Ben Avon is very time consuming, and is best done on an expedition with that express purpose in mind, preferably on an ascent from Inchrory to the north. From the summit tor of Leabaidh an Daimh Bhuidhe, the dreary summit plateau extends north-eastwards towards another finger of rock at 3625ft on Mullach Lochan nan Gabhar. (Not to be confused with the tor at

3625ft/1136m passed a little to the west).This lies at the junction of three broad spurs. To the north of the approach spur lies the knob of Stob Bac an Fhurain, from which the northern edge of the hill sweeps eastwards to the knots of West Meur Gorm Craig and East Meur Gorm Craig.

The latter can be reached from the north by a stalkers' path, climbing from the Glen Avon track, a little east of Linn of Avon to a col just west of Meall Gaineimh, a rounded hill bared by extensive patches of coarse grits. About 80 yards north-west of this col stands Clach Bhan, the most extensive of Ben Avon's tors, characterized by an extraordinary variety of deep cavities, recesses and passages. To the south of the col a broad, gravelly ridge, flanked on its western side by broken buttresses, provides the access to the plateau. There are more impressive rocky horns to be seen on Clach Bun Rudhtair to the north of Stob Bac an Fhurain. The highest, a 75ft stack at the centre of the group, has a window right through it, and on a round of the tops from Inchrory can be inspected by taking the spur of Da Dhruim Lom for the descent to the Avon.

South of the rock stack (3625ft) on the main ridge another broad ridge supports a second stack of Mullach Lochan nan Gabhar (3662ft/1122m) and the rocky tor known as Clach Choutsaich (Coutt's Stone), which is passed to gain the cairn on the snout of Stuc Gharbh Mhor.

Beinn a' Bhuird

Rather than sweeping up all the outlying tops of Ben Avon the walker may opt for the far more satisfying return over Beinn a' Bhuird. The mountains are linked by 'The Sneck', a convenient ridge on the 3200ft contour. This can also be reached from the corries to the north and south. The ridge is narrow, and the contrast between the easy, grassed sweep of the corrie to the south, and the splendid architecture of the rock buttresses and crags of Garbh Choire to the north, is quite dramatic.

To the west of the gap, Cnap a' Chleirich stands above level ground between the summit and the northern top of Stob an t-Sluichd, whose cairn is reached by crossing a curious arch in the rock. Slopes here fall easily to the turbulent Avon, beyond which the grey walls of Faindouran are seen. A three-quarter mile walk up easy slopes to the south-west along the rim of Coire nan Clach leads to the summit of Beinn a' Bhuird. The ridge to the south top lies on a north-south line but is deeply cut by the eastern corries. In mist route-finding can be tricky here, but in clear conditions the going is easy and provides few problems in the return to Glen Quoich.

Beinn a' Bhuird can also be tackled from the south. Near Allanaquoich, a track (locked gate) runs along the west side of the lower reaches of the Quoich Water to Coire Gorm (not marked on O.S.maps), where a track to the left should be followed to the ugly scar of zig-zags seen on the steep slope of An Diollaid. This track makes the ascent to the 3600ft contour on the south top of Beinn a' Bhuird seem deceptively easy and provides a fast start for those planning to traverse both mountains.

The previously-described Gleann an t-Slugain path can also be used. A branch crosses the Quoich Water to the heather of Carn Fiaclach but it disappears at the 2500ft contour. A stiff grassy pull up the corrie ahead (the Snowy Corrie) finds the level ground on the south top, which is fortunately marked by a fair-sized cairn, as between this point and the north top, the plateau never falls below 3700ft.

The prominent rock of A' Chioch lies near the edge of massive slabs and contorted rock dropping into Coire an Dubh Loch, and in the adjacent recess of Coire nan Clach, more gaunt crags rise to within a few feet of the summit cairn. This pile of stones seems very small for the tenth highest mountain in Britain, but without it the exact top might be difficult to locate.

Beinn a' Bhuird can also be linked to Beinn Bhreac and Beinn a' Chaorruinn to the west, on a round of the Dubh-Ghleann (see Walk 6).

CHAPTER 14   WALK 6

Beinn Bhreac 3051ft/931m
  (west top) 3045ft/927m
Beinn a' Chaorruinn 3553ft/1082m
  Beinn a' Chaorruinn Bheag
  3326ft/1015m

The widely-spaced peaks along the east side of Glen Derry could be added to Walk 4 as a round of Glen Derry, or taken in after an ascent of Beinn a' Bhuird (Walk 5).

Beinn Bhreac

Easy heathery slopes to the north of a large belt of trees, at the entrance to Glen Derry, lead to the two diminutive tops of Beinn Bhreac. A similar slope on the hill's other flank, climbs through the woods at the foot of the Dubh-Ghleann.

Beinn a' Chaorruinn

To the north of these bland summits, the spacious table of the Moine Bhealaidh (Yellow Moss), spreads towards Beinn a'

Chaorruinn. A spongy field after rain, it is perfect when dry, and a speedy crossing is assured to the cairn seen on the western point of the hill, overlooking the watershed at the head of Glen Derry. Several tarns lie in a low depression to the east, where Beinn a' Chaorruinn Bheag looks into the northern drain of the Yellow Moss. The Glas Allt Mor, drawing water from the plateau's western margins, can be followed down to Glen Derry.

If attempting Beinn a' Bhuird from this direction, broken ground by the Allt Cumh na Coinnich should be avoided by a line to the south (line of the old county boundary). Above the eastern edge of the Moine Bhealaidh there are few points of reference and in thick mist the directional flow of the streams on the flank of Beinn a' Bhuird are the only visual aids to direction. If the fold at the head of the Allt Cumh na Coinnich can be located, a line almost due east is the best guide to the summit of Beinn a' Bhuird. Deviations slightly north can be corrected at a tiny lochan lying in a small hollow near the 2850ft contour (080012). From this point a line south-east finds the summit cairn dead ahead.

CHAPTER 15

WEST OF THE DEVIL'S ELBOW

Ten scattered mountains located in the rolling heathery wastes between the Devil's Elbow and Glen Tilt. Although their ascents lack topographical interest and stimulating views they still provide the challenge of working them into logical cross-country expeditions.

AN SOCACH   CARN BHAC   BEINN IUTHARN MHOR   CARN AN RIGH   GLAS TULAICHEAN
A series of awkwardly-distributed, heathery hills in remote countryside with long plods between summits.

THE CAIRNWELL   CARN A'GHEOIDH   CARN AOSDA
Easily reached peaks scarred by skiing impedimenta.

AN SGARSOCH   CARN EALAR
Very isolated peaks offering great solitude and atmosphere, despite an apparent lack of distinction.

CHAPTER 15   WALK 1

An Socach 3073ft/944m
  (east top) 3059ft/938m
Carn Bhac 3098ft/946m
  (south-west top) 3014ft/920m
Beinn Iutharn Mhor 3424ft/1045m
  Beinn Iutharn Bheag 3121ft/953m
  Mam nan Carn 3224ft/986m
Carn an Righ 3377ft/1029m
Glas Tulaichean 3449ft/1051m

These scattered hills west of Glenshee and south of Braemar derive some charm from

their inaccessibility. They are also very inconveniently positioned to link together into one walk, the only chance of doing this being by an approach along Glen Ey (locked gate at Inverey). The best plan is to climb An Socach first, bivouac in the soft grass near the ruins of Altanour Lodge and take in the other hills on the following day.

An Socach

An Socach, also known as Socach Mor, on the eastern side of the glen, promises that its ascent will be a tedious labour, and so it proves, as all the slopes are coarse, clinging heather. The shoulder of Carn

Recommended Valley Base Braemar

Maps O.S. 1:50 000 Sheet 43; Bartholomews 1:100 000 Sheets 51 and 52; O.S. 1:63 360 Sheet *Cairngorms*.

Starting Point/Length and time for main itinerary
Walk 1 Altanour Lodge (082824). 16 miles/5750ft of ascent, 8–12 hours (Inverey to Altanour walk-in 5 miles).
Walk 2 Devil's Elbow (140780). 6 miles/1800ft of ascent, 3–5 hours.
Walk 3 Linn of Dee (061897). 24 miles/3100ft of ascent, 10–15 hours.

Cruinn provides an obvious route to the cairn. The mountain can also be reached from Glen Clunie, where a track to a bridge near Baddoch farm provides the easiest access to Coire Fhearneasg, under the northern edge of the hill. The metric survey reversed the status of the two tops, but on so featureless a ridge it seems hardly relevant, and a brisk walk to the west-south-west soon finds the second cairn of the higher western top.

Carn Bhac

Carn Bhac, to the west of Glen Ey, proves to be even less interesting, as the route along the Alltan Odhar crawls to within a few hundred feet of the depressingly level heather summit, where it is merely a matter of locating the cairns, starting with the highest point on the north-east spur and finishing on Carn a' Bhutha. To compensate for the monotony of the traverse, there are views to the high tops of the Cairngorms to the north.

Beinn Iutharn Mhor

To the south-east of Carn a' Bhutha, the broad ridge crosses a small hillock, to reach a saddle at the foot of a steep northern embankment supporting Beinn Iutharn Mhor. There is more shape to this hill, which reserves its finest walk for ascents by its north-eastern nose. Seen end-on from Altanour, this heather snout climbs to a bare scalp, attaining its highest point at a cairn at the south-western end of a broad, twisting ridge. The smaller mounds of Beinn Iutharn Bheag and Mam nan Carn, though little more than 500ft ascents, involve detours from a round of the five major hills. Mam nan Carn sits between the three highest peaks, each connected to it by a saddle, and on traverses between peaks may be crossed in the passing, or avoided by contouring its easy flanks. It is probably best to contour around it when approaching Carn an Righ.

Carn an Righ

Carn an Righ confronts the rambler with steep heather rising 800ft from the short col connecting it to Mam nan Carn. It is crowned by a tumbledown cairn, hardly a fitting tribute for the 'Cairn of the King'. The stalker's cottage in the green oasis of Fealar, seen to the north, is serviced by a private road to the head of Gleann Fearnach (see Chapter 12, Walk 6) and a land-rover track, which continues across the watershed at the base of the mountain. This track offers an alternative approach to this remote peak as permission may be obtained to take a vehicle to Daldhu. From the bridge on the Allt a' Ghlinne Mhoir, the climb to the summit is a demanding 1000ft, and although it is exceedingly difficult to reach the outlying summits of Carn Bhac and An Socach, the traverse of the three major peaks on a round of Gleann Mor is perfectly feasible in a day using this southerly approach. This would, however, leave the outlying peaks of Carn Bhac and An Socach awkwardly placed for a joint

expedition. They could be climbed on a tedious walk around the head of the glen above Altanour, with An Socach offering the added alternative of an ascent from Glen Clunie as previously described.

Glas Tulaichean

Reaching this peak from Carn an Righ provides the option of crossing Gleann Mor or retracking over Mam nan Carn to the col at the head of Gleann Mor. An ascent of less than 1000ft to the north-east leads to the summit. For a return to Altanour it is best to return down the north-east ridge to skirt or cross the little hillock at its base to gain Loch nan Eun. Beinn Iutharn Bheag could then be picked off before descending to the Allt Beinn Iutharn. The alternative is a descent to Glen Shee which leaves a 14 mile road journey back to Braemar.

Glas Tulaichean is most often ascended from Dalmunzie Hotel, above the Spittal of Glenshee. From the ruins of Glenlochsie Lodge a path on the broad heathery ridge to the east of the Allt Clais Mhor rises to an Ordnance Survey pillar on a summit table of mossy stone, supported by the sweep of a corrie buttressing the eastern edge of the hill. The wide green ridge to the north-east runs to the head of Gleann Mor, where Mam nan Carn can be crossed or contoured to reach the stiff pull to Carn an Righ. A steep descent into Gleann Mor, followed by a sharp rise of about 500ft to a gap in the ridge west of Faire Ghlinne Mhoir, provides the most direct return passage to the upper reaches of the Glen Lochsie Burn.

The Cairnwell 3059ft/933m
Carn a' Gheoidh 3194ft/975m
  Carn Bhinnein 3006ft/917m
  Carn nan Sac 3000ft/920m
Carn Aosda 3003ft/917m

The commercial developments on their slopes make these hills even less inviting than before, and walkers have to contend with a variety of tracks, lifts, and other ski-ing paraphernalia.

The Cairnwell (An Carn Bhalg)

On The Cairnwell's ascent by its north-eastern slope, the rambler has to contend with the presence of a chairlift until he is within a few feet of the summit cairn. This is reached by an obvious, denuded path worn by the countless visitors attracted by the prospect of a view, encouraged by the chairlift ascent. To find the peace and quiet of the tops to the west follow the rough track and snow-fence along the saddle connecting the hill to Carn Aosda, and here, above Loch Vrotachan, a small cairned knoll marks the start of the ridge running out to the flat-topped hillocks of Carn a' Gheoidh.

Carn a' Gheoidh

Carn nan Sac, the first bump encountered along the ridge, might go unnoticed were it not for its cairn. The main summit of Carn a' Gheoidh, further to the west, is a more solid heap, but again the rise to the cairn is not exactly demanding. The broad ridge continues to Carn Bhinnein, a distinctive knob with an attractive view to Glas Tulaichean's broad sweep. There is a convenient descent to Dalmunzie Hotel by the steep corrie of the Allt Aulich, but for a return to the road there is little alternative but to retraverse the ridge to the cairned point above Loch Vrotachan. Here, the broad track is rejoined for the easy amble along the broad ridge to Carn Aosda.

Carn Aosda

Carn Aosda was never a hill of beauty, just another heathery, stone-capped lump which, at one time, enjoyed the modest distinction of being the lowest 3000ft mountain in Munro's lists. Even the mountain's one good view down Glen Clunie is bettered by hills to the east of the pass. The descent to the car park at the foot of the chairlift could hardly be less inspiring.

An Sgarsoch 3300ft/1006m
  Druim Sgarsoch 3100ft/954m
Carn Ealar 3276ft/994m

The major streams draining this unfrequented watershed suggest the most practical routes to the dreary isolation and extreme remoteness of these hills.

Approach from Glen Geldie

The nearest public road is at the Linn of Dee Bridge, a ten-mile walk from the summit of An Sgarsoch. To the north of the river, a track runs to White Bridge, and thence by the north bank of the Geldie to a ford near the ruins of Geldie Lodge. The water runs swift and deep and wading is, more often than not, the only way to cross the swollen stream near this point. To avoid this cross the wire bridge at the Red House, and follow the Glen Tilt path as far as Bynack Lodge, where, keeping to the northern bank of the Bynack Burn, an easy passage can be made to the heathery eastern shoulder of Druim Sgarsoch.

An Sgarsoch

Druim Sgarsoch is a wide platform of moss, broken by bands of crumbling stone supporting two cairns, and although the northernmost pile appears to be on the highest point, the curvature of the ridge is deceptive, so visit both cairns. To the west, the broad crest rises in a lazy curve above the smooth, green sweep of Ghlas Choire, onto the summit of An Sgarsoch.

From Geldie Lodge a track rises to the lower contours of An Sgarsoch, where the Allt Coire an t-Seilich proves to be a useful guide through the peat-hagged moors towards Druim Sgarsoch and thence along the ridge to An Sgarsoch.

Glen Feshie — the northern approach
This could be considered to offer the shortest approach providing that permission is given to take a car to the Glen Feshie roadhead at Carnachuin (see Chapter 13, Walk 3). A pleasant path runs along the deep passage of the River Feshie to a footbridge on the Eidart (see Chapter 13, Walk 3 and Chapter 14, Walk 2). To the east of this stream, the bank of the Feshie should be followed to a point of an acute bend, where the river almost doubles back on itself, whence the rugged cairn of Carn Ealar, at the top of a wide heather spur, is seen directly to the south. The easier contours of An Sgarsoch, to the east, are reached by crossing the Allt a' Chaorruinn to gain the track to Geldie

Lodge, from which the heathery northern flanks of the hill can be tackled at will.

Glen Tilt — the southern approach
The old drove road through Glen Tilt is motorable as far as Forest Lodge (see Chapter 12, Walk 5). Thence it runs to a stable at the foot of the Tarf Water, which is forded to reach the foot of An Sgarsoch. The soft grass on the south bank of the Tarf can just as easily be followed to the angle formed by its course and a tributary, Feith Uaine Mhor. Here stands a semi-derelict shelter known as 'The Tarf Hotel'. This may also be reached by a more direct crossing of Carn a' Chlamain (see Chapter 12, Walk 5).

Hereabouts the streams are wide, and only when the water is low are dry crossings possible on the stony flood debris. Grassy flats run to the foot of the heathery spur of Sron na Macranaich,

which gives an easy climb to An Sgarsoch's smooth, rounded summit, with its huge pointed cairn. To the west, Carn Ealar appears as a long ridge running north-south, at right-angles to the crest of An Sgarsoch, which is seen falling gently to the dip of a wide, boggy saddle between the head of the Allt a' Chaorruinn and the Allt a' Chaorainn.

Carn Ealar
The 1000ft rise to Carn Ealar (also known as Carn an Fhidhleir) is a weary drag of heather and grass. Those returning to the Geldie or Feshie should descend by the wide heathery spur to the north to reach the respective paths. Those returning to the Tarf have to endure a tedious drag through the peat-hagged ground along the Allt a' Chaorainn, which is gained by following a tributary from a source on the heathery nose to the south of the cairn.

CHAPTER 16

LOCHNAGAR AND THE EASTERN GLENS

The broad plateau area that provides the plinth for the fourteen mountains in this group tends to limit their horizons. Small tarns and a number of magnificent crags add character to hidden corries.

CREAG LEACACH GLAS MAOL CAIRN OF CLAISE CARN AN TUIRC
Hills typified by smooth, rounded ridges and heathery hollows providing a pleasant traverse.

TOM BUIDHE TOLMOUNT CAIRN BANNOCH CARN AN T-SAGAIRT MOR
BROAD CAIRN (CARN BRAGHAID)
A walk of an uncanny, eerie quality, across a dead and desolate landscape.

LOCHNAGAR (BEINN CICHEAN): CAC CARN BEAG
THE WHITE MOUNTH (AM MONADH GEAL): CARN A'CHOIRE BHOIDHEACH
Lochnagar holds much promise for climber and rambler alike, and never fails to give an enjoyable day.

DRIESH MAYAR
Twin hills offering interesting walks replete with old fence posts that provide excellent guides in mist.

MOUNT KEEN
A hill ideally suited for a relaxed outing, and enhanced by hints of a past era of graceful living.

CHAPTER 16	WALK 1

Creag Leacach 3238ft/987m
  (south-west top) 3088ft/943m
Glas Maol 3504ft/1068m
  Meall Odhar 3019ft/922m
  Little Glas Maol 3184ft/973m
Cairn of Claise 3484ft/1064m
  Druim Mor 3144ft/961m
Carn an Tuirc 3340ft/1019m

The car-park at the top of the Devil's

traverse of these four hills, though from this quarter Creag Leacach tends to be ignored.

Creag Leacach
If including Creag Leacach in the itinerary, the grassy spur of Meall Gorm, above the foot of the pass, provides a convenient easy clamber to the stony knot of the south-west cairn. Creag Leacach's uneven blocks have been used to build a wall on the east side of the narrow crest, and more lie in the untidy heap of the summit cairn on the opposite edge, above the Braemar road.

Recommended Valley Bases Braemar and Glen Doll

Maps O.S. 1:50 000 Sheets 43 and 44; Bartholomews 1:100 000 Sheets 51 and 52; O.S. 1:63 360 Sheet *Cairngorms*.

Starting Point/Length and time for main itinerary
Walk 1 Rhiedorrach (129744). 13 miles/2300ft of ascent, 5–8 hours.
Walk 2 Braedownie (288757). 18 miles/3900ft of ascent, 8–12 hours.
Walk 3 Spittal of Glenmuick (310852). 18 miles/4700ft of ascent, 8–12 hours.
Walk 4 Braedownie (288757). 8 miles/2700ft of ascent, 4–6 hours.
Walk 5 Glen Tanar House (473957). 16 miles/2500ft of ascent, 7–11 hours.

They also pave the top of an escarpment above Glen Brighty, as far as the nose of Sron Riabhach, where the grassy carpet of a wider ridge runs to a fence starting up the even rise to the broad level crown of Glas Maol.

Glas Maol

If starting from the Devil's Elbow walkers must wade through thick heather on ascents of Meall Odhar. The ski-lift climbs towards the head of the Fionn Choire, above which a broken fence on the old county boundary acts as guide to a junction of the fences running out to Cairn of Claise and Creag Leacach. Looking a little to the east, an Ordnance Survey post and a substantial cairn can be seen on the level moss of the summit.

There is an interesting traverse of this mountain that is worthy of note. In the upper reaches of Glen Isla, a track runs from the roadhead to the ruins at Shielin, in a vast amphitheatre under the eastern wall of the hill. Beyond Tulchan Lodge, a signpost points to the path climbing the grassy ridge of Monega Hill, an old right of way across the hill to the Braemar road. On the top of Monega Hill the path turns west, above the steep precipice falling to the Caenlochan Glen, to reach the flattened hump of Little Glas Maol. A little to the north of the cairn are the remains of a wooden hut. Here the pass contours above the eastern corrie to the broad level ridge between the summits of Glas Maol and Cairn of Claise. The route is obvious until near the end where it becomes very indistinct on the spur of Sron na Gaoithe on the final drop to Glen Clunie (look for minute cairns). The value of this track becomes apparent when, having made a deviation to the south-east to take in Little Glas Maol, the walker has a ready-made contouring route back to the fence on the main ridge.

Cairn of Claise

Here, the fence posts can be followed to the summit of Cairn of Claise (also known as Cairn na Glasha), though visitors to the cairn of Druim Mor must leave it temporarily and cross a broad shoulder above the Caenlochan Glen. Cairn of Claise, whose easy moss gives way to untidy beds of stone, is an expansive hill, which spreads a high tableland towards the mounds of Tolmount and Tom Buidhe.

Carn an Tuirc

On the summit of Cairn of Claise, the fence is replaced by a short stone wall, which should be crossed near the cairn to reach a shallow saddle above Loch Kander. Here, the broad ridge turns to Carn an Tuirc, where Glen Clunie comes into view. Below the cairn uneven stone-beds fall to the heather of the Gharbh Choire where, beside the Allt a' Gharbh Choire, a path carries the walker to the track at the

northern end of the Monega Pass route, which reaches the Glen Clunie road at the Uisge Bhruididh bridge. Alternatively a northern spur of the hill falls to Loch Callater, where a track can be followed to Auchallater two miles south of Braemar.

Carn an Tuirc is seldom climbed from the north, but a route from Loch Callater does have attractions as a start of a traverse of the hills around Glen Callater, which may appeal to someone staying at Braemar (see Walk 2).

CHAPTER 16   WALK 2

Tom Buidhe 3140ft/957m
Tolmount 3143ft/958m
  Crow Craigies 3014ft/920m
Cairn Bannoch 3314ft/1012m
  Fafernie 3274ft/1000m
  Creag Leachdach 3150ft/960m
  Cairn of Gowal 3242ft/983m
  Craig of Gowal 3027ft/927m
Carn an t-Sagairt Mor 3430ft/1047m
Broad Cairn 3268ft/998m
  Creag an Dubh-loch 3200ft/983m

Once visited, these hills will long be remembered for their utter desolation, and one cannot help but feel a regard for the pack-men who once struggled across these eerie wastes. One old trail, Jock's Road, runs from Glen Clunie along Glen Callater to the head of Glen Clova. After skirting the northern side of Loch Callater this climbs to the deep cut of the Allt an Loch and thence steeply up under the humps of Tolmount and Creag Leachdach, to emerge on level ground on the approach to the highest point reached, the summit of Crow Craigies. It then continues over desolate hillsides eventually to link up with a well-trodden path to Glen Doll.

The southern approach offers the best access for a complete round of these tops. From the termination of the Glen Clova road at Braedownie the access track to the Glen Doll Youth Hostel bears left across a bridge on the South Esk where there is a convenient car-park and camping area. Beyond the hostel a track passes through the woods to the waymarked path of Jock's Road at the foot of Glen Doll.

Tolmount and Tom Buidhe

The twin hummocks of Tolmount (also known as Doll Monadh) and Tom Buidhe sit above a wild depression above Glen Doll. Identical, bare, rounded lumps little more than 400ft above the general level of the plateau, they can be reached with little difficulty from Jock's Road. Their summits are good vantage points for viewing the isolation of Jock's Road, a route that has seen its share of tragedy.

Carn an t-Sagairt Mor

From Crow Craigies a long striding ridge runs northwards over Fafernie to Carn an

t-Sagairt Mor. To include Creag Leachdach in this section of the walk calls for the merest of diversions to the north-north-west after the crossing of Jock's Road near the head of its climb from Loch Callater. The summit of Carn an t-Sagairt Mor is very stony, and several larger rocks form a cairn around a section of crashed aircraft. Minor pieces of wreckage lie scattered on the slopes to the west, where the hill falls away towards Glen Callater. On this flank, a twisting stalkers' path climbs towards the summit but avoids the cairn by taking a circuitous route across the plateau to the south, on a route to Lochnagar (Walk 3).

The mountain is well situated for viewing the intricacies of the Lochnagar range around the head of Glen Muick. The mountain can of course be approached from that quarter following the Glas-allt Shiel track to a path into the austere glen of the Allt an Dubh-loch, which disappears near the Dubh Loch. The corridor of the upper glen is confined, and the obvious route lies beside the stream, to a moorland basin below the summit banks of the hill.

Cairn Bannoch

Between Carn an t-Sagairt Mor and Cairn Bannoch (also known as Carn Beannach) is one of the easiest walks on the whole plateau, but requiring very accurate navigation in mist as the slope rises so imperceptibly to the latter's cairn that it could be missed, and become confused with that on the summit of Cairn of Gowal about half a mile to the south-east. At its southern end, this mound dips sharply for about 300ft to a short saddle rising in turn to Craig of Gowal, a heathery bump carrying two cairns, the highest of which lies at the south end, looking across to Loch Esk. If continuing to Bachnagairn, the craggy eastern slopes above the Burn of Gowal should be avoided by following the stream seen in the fold of the hill to west.

Broad Cairn

Broad Cairn (also known as Carn Braghaid) lies almost due east of Cairn of Gowal, and the flat rock at its cairn can fairly claim to be the finest viewpoint on the traverse as it looks along the length of Loch Muick to the distant pimple of Mount Keen. The smaller cairn of Creag an Dubh-loch lies on a hump, where crags above the Dubh Loch give a dramatic edge to the scree-covered hillside hereabouts. Those returning to Glen Callater could either cross the head of Glen Muick to the stalkers' path on Carn an t-Sagairt Mor or work back west by Craig of Gowal and Fafernie to Jock's Road.

Of more interest, if transportation problems can be resolved, is a complete traverse of the range to Braedownie. On Broad Cairn's eastern slope, a stalkers' path is encountered and this can be followed to a pony shed on the wide saddle at the head of a pass from Glen Clova to Glen Muick. Here the track, which falls to Loch Muick, meets the path, which crosses the moor to the south to zig-zags leading to a small bridge across a chasm on the infant River Esk. A wider track is joined near the crumbling wall of Bachnagairn, reputedly haunted by a witch. At the mouth of the gorge downstream, a footbridge crosses to the watermeadows above Moulzie, where the track, crossing a ford further downstream, is rejoined for a return to Braedownie.

Those who enjoy very long cross-country expeditions might also consider the traverse of the whole watershed of high peaks from Lochnagar to the Devil's Elbow, on a ridge which crosses no fewer than six mountains, with easy diversions to another five (see Walks 1 and 3).

CHAPTER 16   WALK 3

Lochnagar (Beinn Cichean):
Cac Carn Beag 3789ft/1155m
  Cac Carn Mor 3768ft/1150m
  Meall Coire na Saobhaidhe 3191ft/974m
  Cuidhe Crom 3552ft/1083m
  Little Pap 3050ft/956m
  Meikle Pap 3211ft/980m
The White Mounth (Am Monadh Geal):
Carn a' Choire Bhoidheach 3650ft/1118m
  Creag a' Ghlas-uillt 3495ft/1068m
  Stob an Dubh Loch 3470ft/1051m
  Carn an t-Sagairt Beag 3424ft/1044m

Lochnagar is the royal mountain: Queen Victoria visited its summit and purchased the Balmoral Estate in which it stands and it has maintained its royal connections ever since. Writers, climbers and travellers have been inspired by 'the steep frowning glories of dark Lochnagar' as Byron described it in his evocative verse, *Lachin y Gair*.

To the north, a track runs from a locked gate near the tiny store at Easter Balmoral to an estate cottage at Gelder Shiel. An adjacent hut, which walkers are allowed to use, can at times be overcrowded, and those seeking a bunk should arrive early. Further west, the Loch Callater track is much favoured by those staying at Braemar, as a useful stalkers' path ascends Carn an t-Sagairt Mor (see Walk 2) to reach the flat, stony crown of The White Mounth. The shortest route is that from the Spittal of Glenmuick (camping allowed), and as most of Lochnagar's tops lie on this side, a variety of excursions can be made across The White Mounth, with the possibility of visiting Carn an t-Sagairt Mor on a round of the Dubh Loch to Broad Cairn (Walk 2).

Lochnagar
The paths from Gelder Shiel and the Spittal meet to the east of Meikle Pap, and

thence cross to the col at the foot of its conical stack. From Gelder Shiel a moorland approach can be made direct to the most northerly top, Meall Coire na Saobhaidhe, following the Allt a' Ghlaschoire. Linked as it is to the opposite end of the plateau, it completes a traverse around the corrie to Meikle Pap, which is a superb excursion with exciting views. This top is, however, inconveniently placed for inclusion in a round from Glen Muick.

The Spittal path is the more popular approach and at the saddle between Meikle Pap (Cioch Mor) and the round shoulder of Cuidhe Crom, the spectacular cliffs of Lochnagar come into view. Several fearsome-looking gullies fall from the plateau, the largest of which, the Black Spout, carries snow well into spring, but in summer provides an easy scrambly route to the top of the cliffs.

Cuidhe Crom is a flat, stony top, falling away to the south-west on to the small hump of Little Pap (Cioch Beag). The path crosses the plateau, keeping a short distance from the edge of the crags, to the cairn of Cac Carn Mor, a top only surpassed by the higher rocks of Cac Carn Beag lying a quarter of a mile to the north, where an Ordnance Survey pillar, beside an indicator, stands at the head of scree-fanned slopes falling to the foot of Meall Coire na Saobhaidhe.

The White Mounth
The tiny tarn of Loch nan Eun can be seen at the foot of crags buttressing The Stuic, a top which highlights what is said to be the highest point of The White Mounth, Carn a' Choire Bhoidheach, at a small cairn to the south. To the west, the plateau runs out beyond The Stuic to Carn an t-Sagairt Beag, whose cairn can be passed to reach the broad hill-slopes of Carn an t-Sagairt Mor (see Walk 2).

Another top, Stob an Dubh Loch (White Mounth 1:25,000 series maps also known as Top of Eagles Rock) lies on a short shoulder on the southern rim of the plateau faced by cliffs overlooking the Dubh Loch. The high point is difficult to locate and even in clear conditions the use of a compass may be required.

The cairn of Creag a' Ghlas-uillt (242842), three quarters of a mile to the east-south-east of The Stuic, is equally difficult to locate visually and accurate compass work will again prove invaluable.

To the south-east of Creag a' Ghlas-uillt, one of the hill's many broad shoulders drops with increasing rapidity to the stream of the Glas Allt. Here a path beside waterfalls adds to the enjoyment of a steep descent to the Glas-allt Shiel, where the track beside Loch Muick is joined for a return to the Spittal.

CHAPTER 16   WALK 4

Driesh 3108ft/947m
Mayar 3043ft/928m

Mayar and Driesh are, by tradition, inseparable twins, and by long association regarded by generations of Dundonians as home territory. They are most directly approached from Glen Clova but a more relaxed ascent can be made from Glen Prosen to the south. Both the Glen Clova and Glen Prosen approaches involve long road journeys to the starts for those already based at Braemar for the other walks in the group, so a two-day expedition combining Walk 2 and a bivouac or a stay in the Glen Doll Youth Hostel may be the best way of capturing these summits.

Driesh
Seen from the head of Glen Clova, the bold thrust of The Scorrie appears well-nigh perpendicular, as this slope of Driesh climbs 1700ft in a half-mile lift from the farm at The Doll to the craggy headwall of the Winter Corrie. A track from Acharn, near the Youth Hostel, crosses the White Water to a forest fence, which can be followed on the first 700ft of the ascent until it parts company with the rib of the hill to contour towards the Burn of Kilbo, in a corrie to the north of the summit. Another 1000ft of persistent climbing finds the top of The Scorrie, where the slopes relent on a long, dragging ascent to a small circular windbreak, just feet below the Ordnance Survey pillar on the summit. An easier route lies through the forest to the north-west, where a track leads to a path beside the fence climbing the crest of the Shank of Drumfollow. This reaches the wide ridge between Driesh and Mayar, both about half an hour's walk away along the fence, which links the two.

Mayar
From Driesh, Mayar can be reached by a straightforward ridge walk of two miles. Mayar's top is not greatly pretentious, but its northern corrie has one of the grandest cirques of crags anywhere in the hills south of the Dee. The track to this grassy bowl leaves Jock's Road about three-quarters of a mile beyond the hostel, and above the treeline there is a pleasant scramble beside the Fee Burn. South of the waterfall at the head of the corrie wall, an easy passage is found to the plateau north of Mayar's summit, a dreadful waste of mossy grass and peat which stretches to Tom Buidhe, three and a half miles away. To the west, this grim moor falls to the Canness Glen, beyond which the broad humps of Glas Maol and Cairn of Claise may be seen. The Fee Burn makes a logical descent to east-west crossing of the peaks.

Approaches from Glen Prosen
Under the southern flanks of the hill, a

track runs from Glen Prosen to the ruin at Kilbo, where a poor path can be seen following the line of a fence as it climbs the easy spur to Cairn Dye and then to the watershed, west of Shank of Drumfollow. Alternatively, walk along the White Glen to the foot of South Craig whose grassy ascent continues around the head of the Mayar Burn to the plateau north of Mayar's cairn. Near Glenprosen Lodge, another forestry track strikes off to the north up the long spur of Lick, at the start of a pleasant walk across the broad folds of the hilltops, to the summit of Driesh.

The most relaxing walks across these mountains are combinations of these routes from Glen Prosen.

CHAPTER 16	WALK 5

Mount Keen 3077ft/939m

Mount Keen (also known as Monadh Caoin), the most easterly Munro, lies above the ancient hill-crossing of Mounth Keen, a right-of-way between Glen Tanar and Glen Mark nearly eight miles south-south-east of Ballater.

A public road from Bridge o' Ess runs to a car-park at Glen Tanar House, where a signpost at a corner of the park points the way through fine woods of juniper and pine which, at a little beyond a rest-shelter called the 'Halfway Hut', give way to the wilder moors of the upper glen. Shiel of Glentana, a shooting lodge, is eventually sighted near the foot of the climb to the Mounth, which is breasted by a bulldozed track towards the older track struggling across the hill to Invermark. All that remains is 550ft of ascent to gain the summit to the east.

This north-eastern approach is quite long as the motorist is denied access to the Shiel of Glentana track by a locked gate at Glen Tanar House. The shorter, southern approach (five miles from Invermark) is therefore the most popular. At Invermark, the track starts beside a small bridge over the Water of Mark (a few yards beyond a convenient car-park (448804) near the roadhead in Glen Esk), and runs beside the river to a clearing of clipped turf, where the ornate canopy of the Queen's Well commemorates a spot where Queen Victoria rested on her travels in 1861. Above Glenmark Cottage, seen across this glade, the ascent of the Mounth begins in earnest, up steep zig-zags appropriately named 'The Ladder'. At the head of the pass a moorland path clambers the last few feet to the Ordnance Survey post at the summit.

LOCH LOCHY, LOCH ARKAIG AND LOCH EIL

A disparate group of mountains all within easy reach of Spean Bridge, with views ranging from a bird's-eye view of the Great Glen to aspects of the western coastline and some of the deepest lochs in Scotland.

SRON A'CHOIRE GHAIRBH MEALL NA TEANGA
Accessible but steep peaks strategically situated beside the Great Glen.

GULVAIN
An intimidatingly steep climb after a long approach slog.

SGURR NAN COIREACHAN SGURR THUILM
A grand ridge links these two attractively-situated hills.

Recommended Valley Base Spean Bridge

Maps O.S. 1:50 000 Sheets 34, 40 and 41; Bartholomews 1:100 000 Sheets 50 and 51.

Starting Point/Length and time for main itinerary
Walk 1 Dark Mile (183887). 11 miles/3800ft of ascent, 5–8 hours.
Walk 2 Drumsallie (960794). 12 miles/3500ft of ascent, 6–9 hours.
Walk 3 Glenfinnan (906808). 13 miles/4000ft of ascent, 6–9 hours.

CHAPTER 17	WALK 1

Sron a' Choire Ghairbh 3066ft/935m
Meall na Teanga 3010ft/917m

Protected by Loch Lochy and a thick pine forest, these mountains have an impressive barrier on their viciously steep eastern flanks. Even the softer contours to the south and west of Meall na Teanga are cloaked in scrub oak and sycamore, with a damp undergrowth of saplings. Ascents of these mountains involve a crossing of a gap linking the two, at the head of the Cam Bhealach, which also provides the logical approach to both peaks.

Approaches to the Cam Bhealach
At the north end of Loch Lochy cross by the Laggan Locks to Kilfinnan, which is also served by a minor, motorable access road to a track continuing through the forest to Clunes. In the woods, a short distance north-east of the ruins at Glas-dhoire, look along the bank above the track for the faint stamp of a footpath, which points to the start of the path on the gruelling climb up a steep mountain wall to the head of the pass. This is certainly the finest scenic route to these summits and if using this approach it is best to climb Meall na Teanga first, return to the col, ascend

Sron a' Choire Ghairbh and then descend its long eastern spur directly to Kilfinnan.

To the south, a track struggles from the 'Dark Mile' (Mile Dorcha) through a thick screen of trees to the grass of Meall Odhar, whose easier slopes climb towards the tops of Meall Coire Lochain and Meall na Teanga. Alternatively, if wishing to tackle Sron a' Choire Ghairbh first, follow the Amhainn Chia-aig path further north, to the Allt Cam Bhealaich. This drains a wide peat-hagged valley, whose bogs must be crossed, to reach a path seen climbing diagonally eastwards on the flank of Sron a' Choire Ghairbh, to the deep notch of the Cam Bhealach.

Sron a' Choire Ghairbh
If approaching from the south it is best to climb this hill first. Above the pass, the zig-zags of a stalkers' path ease the pull to the summit ridge of Sron a' Choire Ghairbh, where it peters out within sight of the cairn in an angle of a wide L-shaped ridge.

Meall na Teanga
On the opposite side of Cam Bhealach's gap, broad heather slopes climb to the western nose of Meall Dubh, which, on its opposite flank, turns the headwall of Coire Leacachain towards the steep pull up onto the point of Meall na Teanga. To avoid the desperate plunge to Loch Lochy, the narrow ridge makes another twist, on a precipitous drop to the south-west, where a short saddle leads to the clipped ridge of Meall Coire Lochain. From this peak, an easy walk westwards across Meall Odhar allows the views to be savoured a while longer on a casual descent to the Amhainn Chia-aig track.

CHAPTER 17   WALK 2

Gulvain 3224ft/987m
(south top) 3155ft/961m

The great whaleback of Gulvain (also known as Gaor Bheinn) lies, isolated from other 3000ft peaks, in the rarely frequented moors between Loch Arkaig and the Fort William to Mallaig road. The most direct route to the hill starts on the Fort William/Mallaig road, near the turn to Strontian. Here a wide track heads north following the stream of the Fionn Lighe to a path near the foot of a towering mountain. Immediately ahead, almost 3000ft of convex slopes lie beneath Gulvain's south top and there is little alternative but to set to work on a grinding and remorseless slog.

More varied but longer routes can be made from the Arkaig direction. There is a long approach starting at the eastern end of the loch. A track follows the shore to Inver Mallie, and thence towards the head of Glen Mallie, where tougher going on a climb to the ridge west of Mullach Coire nan Geur-oirean, leads to the saddle at the foot of Gulvain's long north-eastern ridge. This gives the easiest climb to the dumpy cairn at the summit. This approach is perhaps best left for a traverse of the mountain.

The route from the west end of Loch Arkaig is shorter but more complex. Near Strathan, just west of the end of the loch, a footbridge crosses the River Pean to boggy ground surrounding the derelict cottage at Kinlocharkaig, whence, keeping just above the boggy shore of the loch, continue through rough woodland to the entrance to Gleann Camgharaidh. Here a faint path may be detected on the walk up to the ruined shieling of Glencamgarry. The Allt Camgharaidh is difficult to cross dryshod unless a climb is made towards the head of the glen. Alternatively, a more direct route from Strathan across the slopes of Leac na Carnaich finds a higher crossing of the stream, but here again the walker is confronted by the savage inclines of Gulvain's north-north-east spur. A more attractive approach, avoiding the slabs on this western face of the hill, keeps to the easier folds of Gualann nan Osna, as a step to the final pull to the south top.

CHAPTER 17   WALK 3

Sgurr Thuilm 3164ft/963m
Sgurr nan Coireachan 3136ft/956m

Sgurr nan Coireachan and Sgurr Thuilm, to the west of Loch Arkaig, lie on the boundary of a vast, unfrequented area of peaks which look out across the deep inlets of Scotland's western seaboard.

The southerly approach uses a track leaving the Fort William/Mallaig road (sign Glenfinnan Lodge) which passes through the high concrete arches of the Glenfinnan Viaduct and along a deep forested valley to a bridge over the Allt a' Chaol-ghlinne. Glenfinnan Lodge comes into view on the slopes ahead, with the green banks of Sgurr nan Coireachan rising immediately behind it. The track turns right at the bridge, passing Corryhully and heading towards Loch Arkaig. Near the top of its first rise, a cairn on a rock (left) marks the start of a stalkers' path, which climbs some way up the outcropped slopes of Sgurr a' Choire Riabhaich. Rough grassed terraces then provide a staircase to a short spur which in turn leads to the rough summit of Sgurr nan Coireachan.

Sgurr Thuilm

It may be better to start up this mountain first, leaving the previously described spur for the descent. The track continues along the River Finnan to a ford on the Allt Coir' a' Bheithe, where, looking to the left, the whole length of the ridge between Sgurr Thuilm and Sgurr nan Coireachan is seen above the sweep of Coire Thollaidh. More grassy slopes on Druim Coir' a' Bheithe, immediately ahead, provide the obvious route to Sgurr Thuilm. From the summit there is a good view down the long ridge of Meall an Fhir-eoin which falls to a footbridge across the River Pean. There is a shorter and more popular north-eastern approach directly from Strathan.

Sgurr nan Coireachan

To the west of Sgurr Thuilm's cairn, rusty iron posts lead the walker along a narrow ridge and over the humps of Beinn Gharbh and Meall an Tarmachain to a last rocky clamber to Sgurr nan Coireachan's triangulation pillar for an impressive western view. If returning to Glenfinnan, it will now be necessary to make a careful descent of Sgurr a' Choire Riabhaich. The return to Arkaig follows a boundary fence over rough ground towards a narrow pass at the head of Glen Pean, where the faint band of a path, forced onto the hillside above Lochan Leum an t-Sagairt, leaves walkers to pick their own way to the easier passage above Pean. The face of the hill below the northern wall of Meall an Tarmachain provides an alternative descent to a stream in the head of Coire nan Gall, which can be followed to lower Choire Dhuibh and the ruin of Glenpean, where worn stepping stones cross the river to the shelter at Pean.

KNOYDART AND LOCH QUOICH

Situated in the depths of a remote tract of rugged countryside the expeditions to climb these mountains give some of the most picturesque and strenuous walks in all Scotland.

LADHAR BHEINN
An arresting centrepiece for the region, with walks of commensurate quality.

LUINNE BHEINN   MEALL BUIDHE
Marvellous hills – isolated and unkempt, with long, intriguing approach walks.

SGURR NA CICHE
A magnificent mountain with equally fine satellites. Statuesque and remote.

SGURR NAN COIREACHAN   SGURR MOR
Fine ridge walking giving another version of Knoydart's demanding theme.

GAIRICH
A modest hill with an interesting approach climb and wide summit views.

SGURR A'MHAORAICH
Situated for detailed study of Loch Hourn and the South Cluanie Ridge.

GLEOURAICH   SPIDEAN MIALACH
A stalkers' path speeds access to the ridge linking these fine hills.

Recommended Valley Base Invergarry

Maps O.S. 1:50 000 Sheets 33 and 40; Bartholomews 1:100 000 Sheet 50.

Starting Point/Length and time for main itinerary
Walk 1 Barrisdale (872042). 8 miles/3400ft of ascent, 4–6 hours.
Walk 2 Barrisdale (872042). 12 miles/4300ft of ascent, 6–9 hours.
Walk 3 Strathan (980914). 13 miles/2800ft of ascent, 6–9 hours.
Walk 4 Strathan (980914). 14 miles/5200ft of ascent, 7–11 hours.
Walk 5 Loch Quoich dam (070024). 9 miles/2500ft of ascent, 4–6 hours.
Walk 6 Quoich Bridge (014040). 7 miles/3200ft of ascent, 4–6 hours.
Walk 7 Loch Quoich (029030). 7 miles/3500ft of ascent, 4–6 hours.

CHAPTER 18   **WALK 1**

Ladhar Bheinn 3343ft/1020m
 Stob a' Choire Odhair 3138ft/957m

The long walk along the southern shore of Loch Hourn from Kinloch Hourn is a finer approach to the ascent of Ladhar Bheinn than the western route from Inverie. The rambler will almost certainly opt to camp or seek shelter in the glen, though it is possible to make the ascent and return on a very long day.

The Loch Hourn footpath
The walk from the jetty at Kinloch Hourn is a grand introduction to the scenery yet to come. Hugging the shore, the path slips beneath a precipitous hillslope and, between Skiary and Runival, climbs to the 300ft contour, dips to a tiny bay near some ruins, and rises once more to cross a small knolly promontory. Ladhar Bheinn swings into view when breasting the last rise before a ruined church on Barrisdale Bay. Here a wider track turns a corner by the shore to reach a lodge in a coppiced enclosure, and the stalker's cottage near a ford on the River Barrisdale. Ponies are brought from Inverie for stalking the northern corries of Ladhar Bheinn, and when the stalkers are not using their bothy walkers are, by prior arrangement, permitted to use it.

Coire Dhorrcaill
A bridge nearby crosses to an indistinct path across the saltings, in search of the stalkers' path below Creag Bheithe. The zig-zags at the start of this route may be difficult to locate on the terraced slopes though they may be spotted on the west bank of the largest stream. At the top of the zig-zags, the path rounds the nose of Creag Bheithe and passes through birch and rowan at the turn into Coire Dhorrcaill. Ahead, the whole mountain face above the inner corrie is a masterpiece in rock, dramatised by the airy stances of the path

which, at this point traverses a precipitous slope falling to a deep gorge below. Looking up to the corrie wall, a tower, seen at the end of a short spur, cuts off part of the bowl to form Coire na Cabaig which provides a route to the summit ridge, with a steep exit up the headwall below the Bealach Coire Dhorrcaill (Bealach on the old one inch maps).

An alternative route crosses the Allt Coire Dhorrcail upstream to the equally tantalizing terraces of Druim a' Choire Odhair, crowned by the cragged horn of Stob a' Choire Odhair.

Ladhar Bheinn
This ridge can be attacked more directly on steeper terracing above Inbhir Dhorrcail, at the end of a poor shoreline path from Barrisdale Bay. From Stob a' Choire Odhair a short arête dips down to the foot of a scrambly rise to a cairn on the main ridge of Ladhar Bheinn. In mist, this cairn might be taken for the summit, which is in fact a second cairn a few hundred yards to the west, above a more pronounced lip of Coire Odhar. At the western end of this summit ridge, an Ordnance Survey pillar (3313ft/1010m) looks out across the wide mouth of Loch Hourn.

The main thrust of the mountain runs to the south-east as steep, stony ground along the headwall of Coire Dhorrcaill. It dips steeply down to Bealach Coire Dhorrcaill and continues until interesting double spurs, a sort of T-junction, mark the termination of the hill on the point of Aonach Sgoilte. The knobbly spur leading south-west reaches out to the wider ridge of Sgurr Coire Choineachain, which dips a foot into Loch Nevis near Inverie. The shorter north-west spur terminates in the greasy crags of Stob a' Chearcaill, an impasse to be avoided. The best descent works down slopes to the east of Aonach Sgoilte, towards the ridge of Stob na Muiraidh and thence to the headwaters of Mam Barrisdale and the col beyond, where a footpath descends a wide corrie back to Barrisdale Bay.

Ascent from Inverie
A forestry track crosses the Mam Uidhe to Gleann na Guiserein, where a bridge near the ruin at Folach gives access to a good stalkers' path above the Allt Coire Torr an Asgaill, which peters out in the boggy ground below Bealach Coire Dhorrcaill. On this side of Ladhar Bheinn there is no hint of the magnificence of the northern corries and cliffs, and the immediate impression is of a steep-sided hog's-back, with traces of crag on Aonach Sgoilte, at the head of the glen. The gradual incline of An Diollaid's western ridge gives the easiest climb to the summit, and a return to Inverie across the ridge of Aonach Sgoilte would make the best of the day. A traverse of the mountain starting from

Kinloch Hourn and descending the south-western spur of Aonach Sgoilte would be interesting if the transportation difficulties could be resolved.

CHAPTER 18   WALK 2

Luinne Bheinn 3083ft/939m
  (east top) 3074ft/937m
Meall Buidhe 3107ft/946m
  (south-east top) 3051ft/930m

These are extremely remote summits. Luinne Bheinn is nine miles from the nearest road at Kinloch Hourn, and Meall Buidhe a further three. The long, tedious walk by the heathery shores of Loch Quoich may be longer still if the Amhainn Chosaidh is in spate and a detour up to the head of its glen becomes a necessity. From the south corner of the dam at the head of the loch, a path runs west to Lochan nam Breac, where stepping stones provide a river crossing. The passage is unreliable, for deluges are common in Knoydart, a factor always to be borne in mind when planning expeditions hereabouts.

Luinne Bheinn
The path continues along the foot of Druim a' Chosaidh, in the shadow of Ben Aden, which looks impressive in backward view from the zig-zags below the bealach at the eastern end of Luinne Bheinn. From the top of the pass a narrowing ridge climbs 1000ft to the cairn on the eastern summit, beyond which the narrow crest dips to the knoll of the higher cairn of the main summit.

The best base for this ascent is Barrisdale, reached by the coastal path from Kinloch Hourn (see Walk 1). Behind the old schoolhouse near the foot of Glen Barrisdale, a path climbs a wooded slope to reach the pass by way of the passage of the Allt Gleann Unndalain. Alternatively, take the Inverie path to the head of the Mam Barrisdale. Above the head of this pass the north-west ridge, bounded on its southern edge by crags, lifts in a sharp, even line to a rib below the knob of the summit.

The ascent from the Mam Barrisdale conveniently links the traverse of Ladhar Bheinn (Walk 1) with that of its nearest neighbours to give a fine expedition from a Barrisdale or Inverie base.

Meall Buidhe
At the eastern end of Luinne Bheinn, a steep southern flank falls to a knolly ridge. This undulates to the lump of Druim Leac a' Shith where, turning westwards, the ridge forms the boundary wall of a bare northern corrie. The complex of knots and knolls rises gradually to the grassy table of Meall Buidhe. Of the two cairns found here the most westerly is the higher.

Those returning to the Kinloch Hourn road or Barrisdale should retrace their

steps to the pass at the east end of Luinne Bheinn and return by the route of approach.

If Meall Buidhe is to be ascended first, it is best approached from the south. Here, Inverie provides an ideal base at the start of the track running to the head of Loch an Dubh-Lochain. From this a path running to a footbridge spanning the gorge of the Inverie River eases the start of a climb to the head of the pass of Mam Meadail, just above the 1850ft contour. This path is the easiest access route to the steep grass terraces of the eastern and western ridges of Meall Buidhe, whose only impediments are some minor escarpments above the upper limits of the crossing. These are easily by-passed on convenient terraces found on either hand.

The traverse to Luinne Bheinn follows the ridge previously described with a convenient descent to the Mam Barrisdale by the narrow north-western ridge of Luinne Bheinn. The Mam Barrisdale path then provides a convenient staircase down to the track beside Loch an Dubh-Lochain.

Access from the south-east is by the road to the head of Loch Arkaig, and thence by the Mam na Cloich' Airde path to the head of Loch Nevis (see Walk 3). The path from Sourlies to Carnach follows the shoreline round the promontory west of the hut, to salt-flats at the mouth of the River Carnach. At high tide this lies under water and the rocky headland must be crossed to reach the saltings which, in wet conditions, are best crossed by following the shore and the river bank. A bridge near Carnach, shown on most maps but long defunct, has been replaced by a wire footbridge.

A poor path runs along the west side of the river and through the ravine at its head to provide a link with the Barrisdale/Lochan nam Breac path, at the eastern end of Luinne Bheinn. The alternative is to tackle Meall Buidhe first. From Carnach steep zig-zags climb to the head of the Mam Meadail, from which ascents can be made, similar to those taken on ascents from Inverie. The Ile Coire, a little upstream on the Carnach River, provides a gentler rise, with a convenient exit to the ridge at its head (marked 'Bealach' on the one-inch maps, 'Bealach Ile Coire' on the 1:50,000 series). To the west lie the knolls of the ridge climbing to the summit cairns of Meall Buidhe.

CHAPTER 18   WALK 3

Sgurr na Ciche 3410ft/1040m
  Garbh Chioch Mhor 3365ft/1013m
  Garbh Chioch Bheag 3100ft/968m

Sgurr na Ciche springs straight from the shore of Loch Nevis in a fine upward

sweep of terraces, to a cone of perfect symmetry.

The approach from Loch Nevis
Access to Finiskaig at the head of Loch Nevis involves a long walk along the trackless southern shores of Loch Nevis from the roadhead at Bracorina on the shores of Loch Morar to the west. The traveller passing through this remote, uninhabited region will welcome the single-roomed hut at Sourlies, on the threshold of wildest Knoydart.

The ascent of the mountain is perhaps most conveniently tackled by a path which zig-zags up the hillside to the pass of Mam na Cloich' Airde. This gives an enchanting wild climb in the shadow of Sgurr na h-Aide. Immediately east of the twin lochans near the watershed, the path passes a huge cairn, at the gate in an old boundary fence. From here it is possible to make a direct ascent up steep slopes to the north to the ridge between Sgurr na Ciche and Garbh Chioch Mhor.

The approach from Loch Arkaig
Less romantic, but more direct, is the approach from Loch Arkaig. A track leads from the roadhead near Strathan towards the cottage of Upper Glendessarry. Take a path a few yards up the slope behind the cottage to reach the Allt Coire nan Uth, beyond which a diagonal climb towards the boggy saddle of Bealach nan Gall finds the eastern end of Garbh Chioch Bheag. Here, grassy slopes rise beside a wall, seen thrusting its way up to a rougher, stony mountain crest.

In the grass below the summit of Garbh Chioch Bheag, on an edge above Coire nan Gall, two small pools look along the ridge towards Sgurr na Ciche, which hitherto has hidden behind Garbh Chioch Mhor. The wall continues to two cairns, sitting on either side of it, on the twin hummocks of Garbh Chioch Bheag.

Continue on the south side of the wall for the walk to Garbh Chioch Mhor. Loch Nevis now gradually comes into view below as the rough top of Garbh Chioch Mhor is crossed. The ridge narrows on the descent to the gap of Feadan na Ciche. On the far side, the wall ends on an edge of crag overlooking the desolate glen of Coire nan Gall.

A grassy ramp a little to the west leads to grass ledges, which meander through great blocks to disappear in a thick covering of scree below the summit rib, on which an Ordnance Survey post on a rock platform marks the highest point. Care should be taken on the return to the Feadan gap. In mist, the slabby rock to the east of the summit should be avoided by a slight move to the south a few yards beyond the O.S. pillar, as the ridge, if followed too far to the east, is deceptive and there is a real danger of descending into Coire nan Gall.

The descent back to Mam na Cloich' Airde follows the incipient Allt Coire na Ciche, which rises in the stones on the west side of the Feadan gap. This can be followed down to a curious terrace at the base of a craggy nose on Garbh Chioch Mhor. From it, easy slopes drop towards the remains of the boundary fence running to the gate at the head of the col and the path for the return to Upper Glendessarry.

CHAPTER 18   WALK 4

Sgurr nan Coireachan 3125ft/953m
Sgurr Mor 3290ft/1003m

These peaks, though of similar mould, are more rounded and weathered than the neighbouring Sgurr na Ciche.

Sgurr nan Coireachan

Take the Glen Dessarry/Finiskaig path (see Walk 3) to its crossing of the Allt Coire nan Uth, and then take a direct line up the mountain's southern slopes by grassy steps which climb to a cairned top. The main summit is at a more substantial cairn, decorated with two rusty posts, a little to the north. The steep western face of the hill drops to the gap of the Bealach nan Gall.

The line of an old boundary fence to the north-east of the cairn leads round the head of Coire nan Uth, where steep slabs encroach on the ridge on the dip to a saddle, making it very rocky. Under snow there is excellent sport to be had on the narrower sections of this ridge.

Sgurr Mor

The ridge leads to An Eag which commands a fine view down Glen Kingie. The continuation to Sgurr Mor heads north-east along another ridge which dips to a grassy col, and thence the peak of Sgurr Beag. A stalkers' path climbs grassy tiers on the wall above Glen Kingie to this saddle, and continues its erratic course to the summit of Sgurr Beag. Beyond another small dip in the ridge, the larger Sgurr Mor beckons, and a further 600ft clamber finds the small summit cairn.

If climbed on its own, Sgurr Mor is best approached from Glendessary Lodge, by a path crossing the Feith a' Chicheanais. On the Glen Kingie side of this pass, the path turns east to Kinbreack, and here should be left. In the upper glen beneath An Eag, the main stream of the Kingie can be forded to reach the stalkers' path climbing to the An Eag-Sgurr Beag col, a route often used on returns from Sgurr Mor.

Kinbreack is also an ideal starting point for a westward traverse along ridges taking in all the peaks in Walks 4 and 3 to gain Sgurr na Ciche. In favourable weather the views to the coasts and islands of Knoydart make this one of the most rewarding expeditions in the Western Highlands.

CHAPTER 18   WALK 5

Gairich 3015ft/919m

This attractive little hill (also known as Scour Gairoch) stands isolated in the moors to the south of Loch Quoich, and a look at the map suggests the best approach is one from the eastern end of the loch. Along the southern shore, a short distance from the dam wall, a path found near the water's edge crosses the heather to a grass-grown cart-track along the foot of Druim na Geid Salaich. From the junction of the pathways, an easy stalkers' path climbs to the wide shoulder of the hill, where, looking ahead, the broader ridge of Bac nam Foid leads to steeper grass. Crags now appear at the edge of a high corrie tucked under the eastern corner of the upper hill. Above these, along the actual ridgeline, there is some easy though slightly exposed scrambling for a short distance. This can be avoided on steep, terraced banks climbing between the cliff edge and a deep gully, which appears on the left.

The broad slopes to the north of the summit are much easier, and on a descent allow the westward views to be enjoyed a while longer, but it is best to bear quickly to the north-east and retain height, as the return walk beside the loch is boggy.

The walk in to Glen Kingie by a track from the eastern end of Loch Poulary is too long and tedious to be recommended. If an approach from Loch Arkaig via Kinbreack is used, one must be prepared to wade the River Kingie, which is quite wide at this point, though once across there is a reasonable path to the end of Gairich's western ridge, a steady plodding route to the summit.

CHAPTER 18   WALK 6

Sgurr a' Mhaoraich 3365ft/1027m
    Sgurr a' Mhaoraich Beag 3101ft/948m

Sgurr a' Mhaoraich is a bulky, grassy hill which stands in a commanding position above the head of Loch Hourn.

The quickest line of ascent follows a stalkers' path (roadside cairn) up Bac nan Canaichean, whose ridge runs north and then west across Sgurr Coire nan Eiricheallach towards the summit, where mild scrambles can be enjoyed on the narrower, rockier knots above the sweeps of two wild corries.

From the cairn of Sgurr a' Mhaoraich a short walk of half-a-mile to the north and west finds the smaller cairn of Sgurr a' Mhaoraich Beag, a slightly better view-point overlooking Loch Hourn. Ladhar Bheinn is seen from a particularly interesting angle and, to the south, Sgurr na Ciche asserts its mastery over a complex of ragged ridges that exemplify Knoydart.

Turning to the north, Am Bathaich's tiny cairn beckons across a rock strewn gap which dips 600ft below the cairns of Sgurr a' Mhaoraich. At the eastern end of its narrow ridge, the slopes plunging to Glen Quoich are fretted with the zig-zags of a stalkers' path, a useful line of ascent, which as a return route to the Quoich Bridge track provides a pleasant descent.

CHAPTER 18   WALK 7

Gleouraich 3395ft/1035m
    Craig Coire na Fiar Bhealaich
        3291ft/1006m
Spidean Mialach 3268ft/996m

The view of these peaks from across Glen Loyne does not do them full justice, though the graceful fall of their northern faces hints at their finest features, a series of steep corrie walls buttressing a high linking ridge.

Gleouraich

The finest approach to Gleouraich is a stalkers' path rising almost to the summit from the south, which, to the west of the Allt Coire Peitireach, starts as a faint scuff in the grass. Above the 1000ft contour, it moves on to a broad grassy spur, with airy views of Glen Quoich, and then zig-zags up a steady incline until turning under the southern flank of the hill to terminate as a small, flat, pony stance. The ascent continues for a further 600ft, reaching the rocky crest high above one of the deep northern corries. The wide, stony ridge heads east, bounded on the north by a high-walled corrie, with steep slopes of grass on the other hand falling to the shore of Loch Quoich. The eastern extremity of the hill which Munro noted as Gleouraich east top, marked by a simple cairn, pokes a finger out to the north, and in mist care should be taken not to follow this spur, whose eastern edge is buttressed by broken cliffs above Coire na Fiar Bhealaich. A path follows the edge of this, on a descent to a crude staircase of slabs in the boulders leading to the pass.

Spidean Mialach

Spidean Mialach is a lump of coarse, weathered stone, with splintered buttresses at its north-west corner. The rise from the bare saddle is a steady pull of 800ft through a stonefield which, on the level crown, gives way to a thin carpet of delicate, mossy grass supporting a small cairn. The easy tussocks of the mountain's southern slopes make for a pleasant descent, across the open folds of Coire Mheil.

SOUTH GLEN SHIEL AND CLUANIE FOREST

Ten mountains that conveniently separate into three diverse and interesting walks: one of the steepest climbs in all Scotland; one of the finest scrambling routes in the west; and a grand ridge walk which is a peak-bagger's delight.

BEINN SGRITHEALL
3000ft of sustained climbing in less than a mile.

THE SADDLE   SGURR NA SGINE
The rocky ridges of The Saddle when combined with Sgurr na Sgine provide a most enthralling expedition.

CREAG A'MHAIM   DRUIM SHIONNACH   AONACH AIR CHRITH   MAOL CHINN-DEARG
SGURR AN DOIRE LEATHAIN   SGURR AN LOCHAIN   CREAG NAN DAMH
Seven peaks in seven miles makes the elevated Cluanie Ridge one of the best traverses in Scotland.

CHAPTER 19   **WALK 1**

Beinn Sgritheall 3196ft/974m
(north-west top) 3039ft/928m

Imagine a 3000ft scree curtain on a sea-wall, and there you have some impression of Beinn Sgritheall (also known as Ben Sgriol).

The road along the shore of Loch Hourn makes a southerly approach to the ascent of the mountain an obvious choice. An old right-of-way crossing the hill from a high point on the road one mile west of Arnisdale is rather obscured at its start. However, it is just as convenient to make directly for a break seen in the rocky escarpment high on the western ridge of the hill.

Turning above the crags, the line of the ridge up on to Ben Sgriol is obvious, and ahead the hill appears as a well defined turret. Approaching the foot of the tower, a wide grassy rake appears to the left to ease the scramble to the summit. The views from the pink cairn perched on its western end are breathtaking.

A small pile of stones, seen a quarter of a mile to the north-north-west of the summit, marks a second top, at the end of a short stony height between two barren corries to the north and east.

A grassier nose to the east of the summit falls sharply to a green ridge where the ground appears to disappear at your feet, and this airy promenade extends to the Bealach Arnasdail. To the south, a stream runs through boulders, and this is the most useful guide to a precipitate descent to Arnisdale. On an ascent, this is a laboured climb on scree slides at their most intense,

for here Beinn Sgritheall offers no compromise.

It is also possible to climb the mountain from Gleann Beag to the north by way of Rosdail and Bealach Arnasdail. This is a longer route and more remote and has less proximity to the sea than the Arnisdale approach.

CHAPTER 19   **WALK 2**

The Saddle 3317ft/1010m
(Trig point) 3314ft/1010m
(west top) 3196ft/974m
(east top) 3143ft/958m
Sgurr nan Forcan 3100ft/958m
Sgurr Leac nan Each 3013ft/919m
Spidean Dhomhuill Bhric 3082ft/940m
Sgurr na Sgine 3098ft/945m
(north-west top) 3097ft/944m

The high notch of The Saddle is a familiar landmark to the traveller passing through Glenshiel in Kintail.

The finest and quickest line of ascent starts near Achnangart, a little to the north-west of the bridge on the Allt Coire Mhalagain. Here a stalkers' path, detected in the heather, runs to the more obvious zig-zags seen on the rough nose of Meallan Odhar. The path continues across the face of the hill to several cairns on the level saddle to the south of the long ridge of A' Mhuing, traversed by those ascending from Shiel Bridge, which is probably the best starting point if a full round of the peaks of The Saddle is planned. Small cairns on the easy rise to the south indicate the way to the foot of the high tower of Sgurr nan Forcan, now seen above a deep corrie to the right. It is possible to avoid the

Recommended Valley Base Shiel Bridge

Maps O.S. 1:50 000 Sheet 33; Bartholomews 1:100 000 Sheets 50 and 54.

Starting Point/Length and time for main itinerary
Walk 1 Eilean Rarsaidh (815120). 6 miles/3500ft of ascent, 4–6 hours.
Walk 2 Achnangart (968142). 11 miles/4725ft of ascent, 5–8 hours.
Walk 3 Cluanie Inn (077117). 14 miles/5800ft of ascent, 8–12 hours.

Forcan Ridge by a move to the left, under the edge of the slabs which buttress the narrow rib above. Here a drystone wall climbs the steep grass from the Bealach Coire Mhalagain, to guide the walker to the upper slopes above the rocky section.

Sgurr nan Forcan
At the start of the climb up the Forcan Ridge a rough, grassy rake avoids small, rocky outcrops to left and right. A path is soon encountered on the narrow rock bands atop the gigantic slabs which fall away to the left, and although the slopes on the right seem less fearsome, there is little room for manoeuvre on the narrowing ridge once a small top is passed. From here, the summit tower of Sgurr nan Forcan seems impregnable, as the only way to it lies across the knife-edge of a short arête which, with a deep corrie on its right, crosses the top of the massive slabs, again much in evidence to the left. A rocky gendarme is then turned along a slab to its right, where a careful move is required on a couple of short steps to regain the spine of the ridge. Here, where an impressive little horn of rock sticks out over the abyss, a rib of airily-balanced blocks carries the ridge to easier terraces above. A path of sorts outflanks the continuation of this rocky staircase on the right by keeping to

the terraces above the mountain's western wall followed by a short scramble of easier rock leading to a shelf with the tiny cairn of Sgurr nan Forcan.

The route from this shattered point to the peak of The Saddle ahead looks very difficult. The short, narrow ridge-line continues to a gap cutting across the hill, where a wall appears to bar the descent, but steep clefts revealed to the left and right of the wall make possible scrambly descents to both sides of the gap ahead, the rake to the right being the easier of the two, leading down to a slab and gully which leads up to an earthy gap across the ridge.

The Saddle

At the head of the gully, keep to the left of the ridge-line until the rocky outcrops immediately below the summit. These are turned on the right to gain a rib at the cairn of the east top. Seen a little to the west is a rounded triangulation pillar, which might reasonably be supposed to mark the highest point of the mountain. However this is said to be a small lump on the rib mid-way between the other points (936131).

The western tops

There is also a pool lying in a shallow cup immediately below The Saddle's Ordnance Survey pillar. The stony ridge turns above this pond to the cairn on the west top, where high crags above Loch a' Choir' Uaine appear on the right. The narrow crest follows a line of iron posts along the top of these cliffs to Spidean Dhomhuill Bhric. Here a sharp dip to the north-west turns the ridge to a wider crest, leading to the green mossy table of Sgurr Leac nan Each.

Beyond this cairn, an easy ridge heads north then north-east to a tarn lying in a shallow fold. Ahead, the grassy knolls of Sgurr a' Gharg Gharaidh are crossed to gain a col by Loch Coire nan Crogachan with a path linking Glenmore to Glen Shiel. Those seeking an easier line of descent to the path in the glen might discover the traces of a stalkers' path above the Allt a' Choir' Uaine; a tiny footbridge across the Allt Undalain lies on the final stages of the descent to Shiel Bridge.

Sgurr na Sgine

Although close to the main ridge the ascent of this peak involves an inconvenient deviation or retracing of steps from The Saddle's western tops. Some may opt to leave its ascent for another visit or (for the ultra-energetic) add it to a traverse of the South Cluanie Ridge. Steep grassy slopes fall from the summit of The Saddle to the drystone wall, which crosses the Bealach Coire Mhalagain, at the foot of the Sgurr nan Forcan slabs. Above the lochan on this col, broad slopes of scree drift up to the wide ridge linking the summit cairns of Faochag and Sgurr na Sgine. The walk between these tops looks out across the glen to Sgurr na Ciste Duibhe and the high tops above Glen Shiel. The descent from Faochag, however, seems less dramatic than might be imagined, considering the steep angle of the walls as seen from below.

CHAPTER 19	WALK 3

Creag a' Mhaim 3102ft/947m
Druim Shionnach 3222ft//987m
Aonach air Chrith 3342ft/1021m
Maol Chinn-dearg 3214ft/981m
Sgurr an Doire Leathain 3272ft/1010m
Sgurr an Lochain 3282ft/1004m
Creag nan Damh 3012ft/918m

On its south side, the Cluanie ridge presents a severe rampart to Glen Quoich and the River Loyne. This, combined with the absence of a motorable road, is sufficient deterrent, and the mountains are seldom, if ever, tackled from this direction. The northern face of the ridge is equally steep, buttressed by a series of craggy escarpments at the head of the many corries between spurs to the tops.

At the western end of the ridge a faint path climbs under Faochag, to reach the steep zig-zags of the Bealach Duibh Leac. Most ramblers, however, prefer to use the old road from Cluanie Inn to Glen Loyne, which crosses a high pass to the east of Creag a' Mhaim. This peak can be reached by following streams up to Coirean an Eich Bhric or by using a stalkers' path up its south-east spur beyond the head of the pass.

Looking beyond the bare crest running to Druim Shionnach, the many ups and downs of the ridge promise a fine traverse as the day progresses. A dip to more level ground is followed by a gradual rise along the edge of a northern escarpment to the levelled hump of the second Munro of the day. On a turn west-south-west, the ridge then strides towards the more pronounced hummock of Aonach air Chrith, buttressed by minor crags seen in the south-west corner of a corrie wall. These are turned on the left on the approach to the cairn, which is the highest point on the ridge.

The narrowest section of the ridge now follows. With precipitous slopes on either hand, an airy path crosses several knolls astride a narrow grassy blade.

On the northern spur of Maol Chinn-dearg, a stalkers' path leads up from Coire Chuil Droma Bhig, to the centre of the ridge. This would provide a convenient break for those wishing to split the traverse.

Sgurr Coire na Feinne follows and then the short table of Sgurr an Doire Leathain. This is a low mound, with a poor cairn, 10ft above the general level of the hilltop, and a little to the north of it. For the sixth time, the ridge dips to confront another rise, to Sgurr an Lochain which is followed by the tramp to Sgurr Beag (2926ft/896m), a similar summit buttressed by the crumbling headwall of Choire Reidh. This second hill can be contoured on its grassy southern slope to reach the col east of Creag nan Damh. The broken crags of a southern face, and its stony crown, make this the roughest hill in the group. For descent a fence leads from it to the Bealach Duibh Leac and the stalkers' path to Glen Shiel. Alternatively broken rock leads down north to the head of the corrie of Sgurr a' Chuilinn, from which it is possible to make a more direct descent. The slopes of Sgurr na Ciste Duibhe, opposite, emphasize the incline of these slopes which at times seem almost vertical. The north-east spur of Sgurr a' Chuilinn may avoid the deep stream gullies below Creag nan Damh, but not the leg-jarring descent on the plunge to the road.

NORTH GLEN SHIEL AND GLEN CLUANIE

The great peaks of Kintail are a closely-knit collection of mountains, defended by remorselessly steep lower slopes.
Once their high tops are gained, long, linking ridges offer some of the best traversing expeditions in the north.

SGURR NA CISTE DUIBHE   SGURR FHUARAN
The celebrated Five Sisters ridge provides a picturesque walk – a Scottish classic.

SAILEAG   SGURR A'BHEALAICH DHEIRG   AONACH MEADHOIN   CISTE DHUBH
A worthy extension to the Five Sisters ridge, ending in the intriguing crags of Ciste Dhubh.

BEINN FHADA (BEN ATTOW)
Unrelenting slopes of merciless proportions give access to a spacious summit plateau.

A'GHLAS-BHEINN
This small green hill refuses to be up-staged by the higher peaks of Kintail.

MULLACH FRAOCH-CHOIRE   A'CHRALAIG   SGURR NAN CONBHAIREAN   CARN GHLUASAID
TIGH MOR NA SEILGE
The Cluanie Horseshoe of stark hills are notable for their barren isolation, and bare windswept tops.

CHAPTER 20	WALK 1

Sgurr na Ciste Duibhe 3370ft/1027m
Sgurr nan Spainteach 3129ft/990m
Sgurr Fhuaran 3505ft/1068m
Sgurr nan Saighead 3050ft/929m
Sgurr na Carnach 3270ft/1002m

There can be few people who have not seen a picture postcard, photograph, or illustration, depicting the 'Five Sisters of Kintail'. Purchased for the National Trust by the late P.J.H.Unna, a one-time president of the Scottish Mountaineering Club, they rank high on any list of mountains.

Near Shiel Bridge, two routes give immediate access to the hill; above the cottages at the bridge, the rough slopes of Sgurr an t-Searraich provide a rocky scramble to the crown of Sgurr nan Saighead, and above the causeway at the head of Loch Duich, banks of grassy terraces step up to Sgurr na Moraich (2870ft/876m), the lowest of the 'Five Sisters'.

The route from the eastern end of the range is probably a better way, even though it is steeper at the start. Once on the ridge you are rewarded with views of the peaks around Loch Duich in a magnificent westerly aspect. Above Glenshiel Bridge, the grassy staircase of Sgurr na Ciste Duibhe, set at an angle of 40 degrees, gives the longest continuous slope of this angle in the whole of Scotland,

matching Beinn Sgritheall in the severity of its ascent. Rocky outcrops to the west of the bridge are best avoided by following a stream at the forest boundary, which indicates a more straightforward climb to the ridge, which can be gained near Sgurr nan Spainteach.

Sgurr na Ciste Duibhe
Reaching the cairn of Sgurr nan Spainteach, the full magnificence of Sgurr Fhuaran across Coire Dhomhain is revealed. The deep trench of the corrie dramatizes the narrow prow pushing out to the east in front of Gleann Lichd with Beinn Fhada beyond. Turning westwards the narrow ridge dips to the foot of the grassy rise to Sgurr na Ciste Duibhe along an edge overlooking Coire Dhomhain, here rimmed with crags. A sizeable cairn marks the summit.

Hereabouts, care should be taken, especially in mist, to avoid a false ridge slightly to the north of the peak, and enclosing a rocky hollow between it and the steep northern wall of Sgurr nan Spainteach.

Sgurr Fhuaran
A gradual dip by the true ridge leads to Bealach na Craoibhe, and the turn north over Sgurr na Carnach to the V-shaped gap of Bealach na Carnach. Here the walker is confronted by a short, sharp ascent of 600ft to Sgurr Fhuaran's cairn, perched on a narrow table at right angles to the spine of the ridge. Running east from this airy stance is a knife-edge ridge which provides

Recommended Valley Base Shiel Bridge

Maps O.S. 1:50 000 Sheets 33 and 34; Bartholomews 1:100 000 Sheets 50 and 54.

Starting Point/Length and time for main itinerary
Walk 1 Glenshiel Bridge (992132). 10 miles/ 5200ft of ascent, 6–9 hours.
Walk 2 Glenlicht House (005172). 11 miles/ 5500ft of ascent, 6–9 hours. (Croe Bridge to Glenlicht House walk in 4 miles.)
Walk 3 Croe Bridge (958210). 11 miles/3800ft of ascent, 6–9 hours.
Walk 4 Strath Croe (977222). 8 miles/3 000ft of ascent, 4–6 hours.
Walk 5 Alltbeithe (080202). 19 miles/6300ft of ascent, 9–14 hours. (Shiel Bridge to Alltbeithe walk in 11 miles.)

a dramatic ascent route from Glenlicht House.

To the north of the cairn, crags support the main ridge as it steps down to the Bealach Bhuidhe, 800ft below. The ridge can be quitted here by very steep descents to the west and south-west but most people will wish to complete the full traverse.

The western tops
West of the Bealach Bhuidhe, Sgurr nan Saighead lifts a triple-headed peak clear of massive slabs. These crags provide a line that can be followed west then north, to another saddle at the head of Coire na Criche, where easier grass falls to the road beside Loch Duich. The ridge continues to Sgurr na Moraich, which can be quitted by steep grassy terraces to the west of the summit which give a swift descent to Loch Duich, thus completing the traverse of the 'Five Sisters'.

CHAPTER 20   WALK 2

Saileag 3124ft/959m
Sgurr a' Bhealaich Dheirg 3378ft/1038m
Aonach Meadhoin 3284ft/1003m
   Sgurr an Fhuarail 3241ft/988m
Ciste Dhubh 3218ft/982m

Climbs from the the head of Gleann Lichd are more strenuous and, with a variety of approaches, less uniform than the steady pulls from the road to the south. The gorge of the Allt Granda and Gleann Lichd are also well worth visiting for their own sake.

Saileag

From the junction of the Allt an Lapain and the Allt Granda, at the head of Gleann Lichd, the grassy wall of Meall a' Charra climbs to the long, graceful line of a spur, seen rising to the hump of Saileag. An alternative route follows the Allt an Lapain to reach a high saddle to the east of Sgurr nan Spainteach, where a continuation of the 'Five Sisters' ridge (Walk 1) rises to the cairn of Saileag.

Sgurr a' Bhealaich Dheirg

Further to the east the hill-top dips to another saddle on a traverse of the heights above the Fraoch-choire, whose streams tumble to the Allt Granda, now seen far below. An upward sweep in the ridge then leads to the cairn of Sgurr a' Bhealaich Dheirg, a broad top supported by narrow grassy spurs, enclosing A' Ghlas-choire. The summit cairn lies 50 yards to the north of the main ridgeline on an exposed knot of rocks.

Aonach Meadhoin

Another sharp dip carries the grassy crest above yet another high-walled corrie. On the southern side of the ridge the steep banks of a broad spur nudge regiments of conifers into line. More grassy banks push the ridge up on to Aonach Meadhoin (cairn) and the short, narrow crest to a second cairn on Sgurr an Fhuarail.

The broad spur leading down south-east to the Cluanie Inn is frequently used on ascents to gain the peaks at the eastern continuation of the 'Five Sisters' ridge, as Saileag is protected on this side by the Glenshiel Forest. A wider ridge to the north of the cairn dips to the mossy hill-crossing between the An Caorunn Beag and Fionngleann.

Ciste Dhubh

Above the pass a steep, narrow ridge runs north to the cairn on the edge of the slabby cliff of Ciste Dhubh's north-eastern face. The eastern edge of the hill, below the summit, is broken and rough, with grassy pinnacles peering over a rough scarp. In thick mist it is advisable to keep to the convex grass on the western slopes as a broken cliff cuts back into the ridge on the final approach to the cairn. The best return to Gleann Lichd descends the north-

western slopes and crosses the Allt Cam-ban, which sometimes involves a wade of waist-deep proportions. To avoid this it will be necessary to arrange transport to allow a crossing of the peaks with a finish at Cluanie.

The whole of this walk can be combined with that of the 'Five Sisters', (Walk 1) on an exceptionally long and strenuous expedition starting at Cluanie and leaving Ciste Dhubh for a short day. This peak is often taken as a short expedition from Cluanie Inn, as the grassy walk up An Caorunn Beag to the Bealach a' Choinich gives an easy ascent to the 2000ft contour.

CHAPTER 20   WALK 3

Beinn Fhada (Ben Attow) 3385ft/1032m
   Ceum na h-Aon Choise 3150ft/956m
   Sgurr a' Dubh Doire 3100ft/963m

Seen from the head of Loch Duich, Beinn Fhada (also known as Ben Attow) appears a daunting hill, a formidable seven-mile barrier between Croe Bridge in the west and Gleann Gniomhaidh to the east.

The quickest way to the top is a direct ascent up the viciously steep southern slope above Gleann Lichd. At the foot of this mountain fortress, the path from Loch Duich to Glen Affric crosses a rickety bridge over the infant River Croe, at the start of a steep, narrow path through the gorge of the Allt Granda, to Fionnleann. If this direct assault is chosen, the overpowering slopes above Glenlicht House offer no alternative, and only one respite halfway, where a curious level gallery is encountered. Once the summit ridge is gained a detour to the east will be required to take in the tops.

More steep terraces climb from the Fionnleann above Glen Affric, and here Camban is ideally placed for an attack on the broad ridge which overlooks Coire'n t-Siosalaich. Starting by this route the mountain can be traversed from east to west in a logical manner. Sgurr a' Dubh Doire, an enlarged undulation on the ridge, is often confused with a higher, cairned top, a third of a mile south-south-east of the summit (O.S. Pillar).

West of the summit lies the high alp of Plaide Mhor, which is drained by the Allt Coir' an Sgairne, beside which a stalkers' path (unmarked on the map) climbs from a path in the depths of Gleann Choinneachain — a way that would also serve for an ascent. If a direct descent towards Bealach an Sgairne is chosen, to link up with an ascent of A' Ghlas-bheinn (Walk 4), care should be taken on the blunt snout at the end of the ridge above the pass.

Most walkers prefer to continue west along the crest leading to Ceum na h-Aon Choise, also known as Meall an Fhuarain

Mhoir, where rocky tors give an interesting, though easy, scramble over a series of broad knolls perched above steep patches of scree in the northern corries. This top's southern slopes are the steepest on the mountain, and the whole hillside is scored by the deep channels of streams. The western point of the ridge, above Sgurr a' Choire Ghairbh, looks directly onto Loch Duich, and on this end of the hill nimble footwork will be needed on a careful descent to the crofts of Morvich, beside the Croe.

CHAPTER 20   WALK 4

A' Ghlas-bheinn 3006ft/918m

At the head of Loch Duich a narrow road slips away from the ancient highway rounding the bay at its north-eastern corner, into the woods of the Inverinate Forest and a car-park at a junction of tracks near Dorusduain. Above these dark pines, A' Ghlas-bheinn climbs to a knobbly skyline.

A forest track climbs steadily to the steeper path across the Bealach na Sroine, where the open slopes of Meall Dubh provide a convenient staircase to the upper hill, on the easiest route to the summit. Another path drops from the car-park at the junction to a footbridge over the Amhainn Chonaig, and thence to the footpath at the start of the long climb up Gleann Choinneachain. This path pulls clear of the stream, across the lower slopes of Ben Attow, to steep zig-zags above the confluence of the Allt a' Choire Chaoil and the Allt Coir' an Sgairne, above which it squeezes through a narrow defile bounded by rocky tiers. Several parts of the slopes to the north can be decidedly tricky, especially in wet weather, and on the ascent to the rough, grass knolls of the hill-crest, a route from the head of the pass gives the safest passage. The ridge ahead has the appearance of a green switchback, but there is no need to cross all the bumps, as they can be contoured without difficulty to reach the highest one, which is cairned.

The hill has a third spur, running to the west. This ends above the Inverinate Forest, looking out across the tiny bay at the head of Loch Duich. This might be used for a direct descent although it is very steep.

The mountain is roughly triangular in shape, bounded on all sides by high mountain passes. On the eastern flank is the deep trench of Gleann Gaorsaic linking Glen Affric with Glen Elchaig. Glen Elchaig has a private road which provides the shortest route to the Falls of Glomach, the second highest cascade in Scotland. The access path, which scrambles high above the deep gorge of the Allt a'

Ghlomaich, runs to a platform looking straight at the centre of the waterfall.

It would be convenient to combine a visit to the Falls with an ascent of this mountain. If the Glen Elchaig approach is used it is normal to return by the same route. However an approach from Loch Duich via the Bealach na Sroine or the Bealach an Sgairne is better, as this allows different routes to be taken to and from the mountain.

CHAPTER 20   WALK 5

Mullach Fraoch-choire 3614ft/1102m
   (north-east top) 3435ft/1047m
   (south top) 3295ft/1008m
A' Chralaig 3673ft/1120m
   A' Chioch 3050ft/948m
Sgurr nan Conbhairean 3635ft/1110m
   Drochaid an Tuill Easaich 3300ft/1000m
   Creag a' Chaoruinn 3260ft/999m
Carn Ghluasaid 3140ft/957m
Tigh Mor na Seilge 3285ft/1002m
   (centre top) 3276ft/1001m
   (north-north-east top) 3045ft/929m
   Sail Chaoruinn 3025ft/921m

The 'Cluanie Horseshoe' is a crescent of high peaks to the north of Cluanie, clustered around Gleann na Ciche, whose streams spill into the head of Loch Affric. As both points of the horseshoe overlook Glen Affric, the complete round is best tackled from the Youth Hostel at Alltbeithe. This is lengthy expedition and at various points involves deviation, but the rise and fall between the peaks is not great and the going straightforward. A complete traverse allows 13 peaks and tops to be bagged at one go.

A bridge over the River Affric gives a direct access to the base of the northern spur of Mullach Fraoch-choire, a very, steep, convex, grassy slope which relents, temporarily, above the 2500ft contour.

Mullach Fraoch-choire
To the north-east of the summit, a smaller cairn adorns the blunt end of another, similar, spur whose eastern edge peers into Gleann na Ciche. An interesting, knobbly ridge with several pinnacles pushes south from the main top above two steep walls. Coire na Geurdain, to the east, is a jumble of broken crags and vertical grass; the opposite side of the ridge is the reddish scree-slide of upper Coire Odhar. The crumbling pinnacles are passed on the right (west), where a lofty parapet eases on to a grassy bank running to the small hummock of the south top (also known as Stob Coire na Cralaig).

A' Chralaig
Beyond this untidy cairn, the ridge crosses a shallow dip to the foot of a steady climb to the larger cairn of A' Chralaig (also known as Garbh Leac). A narrow nose of a hill pushes on to an unnamed top, which throws out a ridge further to the south. This spur gives a laboured ascent from the A87 by Loch Cluanie, and is often chosen by those who prefer to split the walk into two halves. The long hog's-back of A' Chioch to the north-east pushes out to a central cairn, from which there are unrivalled views of the eastern corries of A' Chralaig. To the east, the Bealach Coir' a' Chait (2381ft), at the point of the horseshoe, marks the lowest point of the walk. The ridge beyond the gap, rises to a cairn on Drochaid an Tuill Easaich.

Carn Ghluasaid
The corrie wall to the south of Sgurr nan Conbhairean is easily contoured to reach the bare col of Glas Bhealach above the eastern corries. The cairn of Creag a' Chaoruinn, a few hundred yards to the east, lies near the craggy lip of Coire Sgreumh, whose rim turns south-east to the stony cap of Carn Ghluasaid.

A stalkers' path climbs from the old military road, a little to the west of the site of Lundie cottage, of which only two concrete foundations remain below a bend in the road. The path climbs up a drab heather hillside, twisting round numerous outcrops to reach the level plateau of Carn Ghluasaid.

Sgurr nan Conbhairean
The southern slopes of Sgurr nan Conbhairean are open heather, and any ascent from the road is steep. The Carn Ghluasaid path eases the pull towards the cairn of Creag a' Chaoruinn and the barren slopes beyond it, which rise to a mound of flat stones on the summit of Sgurr nan Conbhairean.

Tigh Mor na Seilge
To the north, the bare crest of a ridge, pinched between Gleann na Ciche and the rough corrie to the east, gives an easy walk out to the cairn on the highest point of Tigh Mor na Seilge. Across a small depression on the ridge, and beyond the cairned mound of the centre top, (also known as Carn na Coire Mheadhoin) the two undulations of the north-north-east top are found to be without cairns. A short, easy dip a little south of the main summit leads to the cairn of Sail Chaoruinn, lying on a prominent point above the rough couloir of Coire Mheadhoin.

Anyone returning to the road beside Loch Cluanie needs to be mindful of the re-ascent of Sgurr nan Conbhairean. Those completing the horseshoe will find the broad, grassy flanks to the north-west give a leg-jarring descent to Gleann na Ciche.

GLEN AFFRIC, CANNICH AND STRATH FARRAR

Sixteen remote mountains that give long challenging ridge walks above deep glens, to provide some of the most rewarding cross-country traverses in all Scotland. Judicious use of the bothies in the region will help reduce the effort needed to reach the peaks.

AN SOCACH   SGURR NAN CEATHREAMHNAN   CREAG A'CHOIR'AIRD
A choice of interesting approach walks of deceptive length lead to this fine group of peaks.

TOLL CREAGACH   TOM A'CHOINICH   CARN EIGE(EIGHE)   BEINN FHIONNLAIDH
MAM SODHAIL(MAM SOUL)
With their satellites, the two highest peaks north of the Great Glen give a long day above 3000ft.

CARN NAN GOBHAR   SGURR NA LAPAICH   AN RIABHACHAN   AN SOCACH
A chain of peaks extending deep into the deserted territory between Lochs Monar and Mullardoch.

SGURR FHUAR-THUILL   SGURR A'CHOIRE GHLAIS   CARN NAN GOBHAR   SGURR NA RUAIDHE
An entertaining switchback. The key to its enjoyment is that required to unlock the gate at Struy.

Recommended Valley Base Cannich

Maps O.S. 1:50 000 Sheets 25 and 33;
Bartholomews 1:100 000 Sheets 54 and 55.

Starting Point/Length and time for main itinerary
Walk 1 Alltbeithe (080202). 16 miles/5560ft of
ascent, 8–12 hours. (Loch Beinn a' Mheadhoin
to Alltbeithe walk-in 10 miles.)
Walk 2 Glen Affric (215242). 23 miles/7800ft of
ascent, 12–18 hours.
Walk 3 Loch Mullardoch dam (220316). 20
miles/6300ft of ascent, 10–15 hours.
Walk 4 Braulen Lodge (237387). 14 miles/5100ft
of ascent, 7–11 hours.

CHAPTER 21	WALK 1

An Socach 3017ft/920m
Sgurr nan Ceathreamhnan 3771ft/1151m
  (west top) 3736ft/1143m
  (east top) 3150ft/960m
  Stob Coire nan Dearcag 3089ft/940m
  Stuc Mor 3496ft/1074m
  Stuc Bheag 3250ft/1043m
  Creag nan Clachan Geala 3282ft/998m
Creag a' Choir' Aird 3210ft/982m
  (east top) 3058ft/932m
  Mullach Sithidh 3188ft/973m
  Carn na Con Dhu 3176ft/968m

These mountains situated between the head of Glen Affric and the remote corners at the head of Loch Mullardoch are difficult to reach. Sgurr nan Ceathreamhnan, the highest peak, has several tops on ridges which radiate from the summit, and expeditions taking in all the tops are further complicated by the outlying peaks of An Socach and Creag a' Choir' Aird.

It is still possible, however to take in An Socach and the main summits of Sgurr nan Ceathreamhnan and Creag a' Choir Aird in a long day's outing from the car-park near the head of Loch Beinn a' Mheadhoin in Glen Affric. The Glen Affric footpath provides a useful route to the base of the first peak but even so, on such an itinerary the walker must be prepared to travel light and fast and it should, therefore, only be attempted by those with experience. If contemplating such an expedition there is an alternative approach — a shorter access path from Cluanie, to the south, by way of the An Caorunn Mor. Either of these approaches could be split by using the open Youth Hostel at Alltbeithe (for use in emergency) which is strategically placed at the head of Glen Affric.

An Socach
From two miles west of Loch Affric a faded track leads up out of Glen Affric to Bealach Coire Ghadheil, where a short, sharp rise south along a grassy crest to the south-west leads to the small hump of An Socach (not named on the metric map). This hill is dominated by Sgurr nan Ceathreamhnan at the end of the ridge to the west, and the great heap of Mam Sodhail to the east. From Alltbeithe a path up Allt na Faing provides a more direct route to gain the ridge just to the west of An Socach.

Sgurr nan Ceathreamhnan
The ridge running west is narrow enough to be distinctive, so that even in mist the route is obvious as it curves above Coire na Cloiche. For about half-a-mile, the crest hovers on the 2700ft contour, then grassy terraces lead up to the cairned top of Stob Coire nan Dearcag. Another gentle rise carries the ridge to the east top (calculated by Munro as 3150ft) of Sgurr nan Ceathreamhnan, beyond which the summit is attained by a laboured clamber over the stones. The western top of the hill lies beyond a well-defined saddle, and its cairn is at a point where four ridges diverge. A short spur to the north-west runs out to the rather insignificant bump of Creag nan Clachan Geala. If attempting a traverse of the tops it is best to reach this first and return to the western summit of Sgurr nan Ceathreamhnan before tackling the ridge to the north. This crosses the two hummocks of Stuc Mor and Stuc Bheag, where it broadens on the fall to the terminal point of Creag Ghlas, above the hidden valley of Srath Duilleach. From Stuc Bheag the walker must either retrace his steps to the main summit of Sgurr nan Ceathreamhnan, or attempt the alternative descent of steep slopes to the east and then work back along the grassy contours pas˙ An Gorm-lochan to gain the spur of Creag a' Choir' Aird.

Creag a' Choir' Aird
Uneven blocks to the north-east of Sgurr nan Ceathreamhnan's main summit lead down to a sharp rib above An Gorm-lochan. The wide ridge of Creag a' Choir' Aird provides a carefree promenade over a cairned top (073242) to another cairn, which lies about half a mile south of the survey point set at 3188ft on the one-inch maps. The new metric maps show the summit cairn (081259), but strangely enough give the hill a new name, Mullach na Dheiragain. To the north-east of the

survey point (3188ft/973m) on the north top, which is now titled Mullach Sithidh, another cairn marks the east top. The aforementioned cairn (073242) three-quarters of a mile south of the summit adds to the confusion of changed names and deletions by entering the current list (seventh edition of Munro's Tables) as Carn na Con Dhu. After re-crossing this, the return to Glen Affric does not require a re-ascent of Sgurr nan Ceathreamhnan, as above Loch Coire nan Dearcag a pleasant grassy ascent can be made to a dip in the ridge to the east of Stob Coire nan Dearcag. Here a stalkers' path tumbles down Coire na Cloiche to the Hostel and the Glen Affric footpath.

Approach from the north

The northern access involves a circuitous approach from the west by way of Dornie and Glen Elchaig. Enquiry also has to be made at Killilan House for permission to proceed to the Falls of Glomach car park at the south-west end of Loch na Leitreach. Here a route starts from the A.E. Robertson memorial bridge, tackling the western peaks by easy slopes above the Falls of Glomach. These climb beside the Allt Coire-lochain to the steeper flanks of the northern ridge of Sgurr nan Ceathreamhnan, or more directly to the snout below Creag nan Clachan Geala.

A rough unmetalled track continues beyond the car-park to Iron Lodge where a stalkers' path struggles up the hill behind the cottage towards the lonely western reaches of Loch Mullardoch. From this a steep climb on grassy slopes to the west of the Allt Cam leads to Mullach Sithidh (973m) and the ridge of Creag a' Choir' Aird. This is a useful start to a round of Gleann Sithidh, glen of the fairies, which takes in the western and northern tops, and the summit of Sgurr nan Ceathreamhnan. Those wishing to include An Socach and the eastern ridge of Sgurr nan Ceathreamhnan in the round should cross the hollow of Loch Coire nan Dearcag and make for the dip in the ridge to the east of Stob Coire nan Dearcag. A short diversion to An Socach is then followed by a traverse of the tops and summits of Sgurr nan Ceathreamhnan as previously described. From Stuc Bheag a descent to Glen Elchaig can then be made by a stalkers' path from the end of the ridge below Creag Ghlas. An alternative path to Carnach can also be found near Loch Lon Mhurchaidh, at the foot of slopes falling from the centre of the ridge. For a more direct return to the Falls of Glomach car-park, a descent to the falls by the Allt Coire-lochain completes the day by the more interesting path through the gorge of the Allt a' Ghlomaich.

Approach from the west

The larger peaks can also be attempted from the west by way of the Bealach an

Sgairne, on another long day's expedition from Dorusduain in Strath Croe (see Chapter 20, Walk 4), or that route can be used for a return, the expedition having started from the Falls of Glomach.

CHAPTER 21   WALK 2

Toll Creagach 3455ft/1053m
    (west top) 3149ft/952m
Tom a' Choinich 3646ft/1111m
    Tom a' Choinich Beag 3450ft/1029m
    An Leth-chreag 3443ft/1044m
Carn Eige (Eighe) 3880ft/1183m
    Stob Coire Lochan 3006ft/917m
    Stob a' Choire Dhomhain 3766ft/1148m
    Creag na h-Eige 3753ft/1147m
    Stob Coire Dhomhnuill 3725ft/1137m
    Sron Garbh 3705ft/1132m
Beinn Fhionnlaidh 3294ft/1005m
Mam Sodhail (Mam Soul) 3862ft/1181m
    Creag a' Chaoruinn 3462ft/1056m
    Carn Coulavie 3508ft/1069m
    Ciste Dhubh 3606ft/1109m
    An Tudair 3500ft/1074m
    Mullach Cadha Rainich 3262ft/993m
    Sgurr na Lapaich 3401ft/1036m

The twin peaks of Mam Sodhail and Carn Eige, the highest peaks north of the Caledonian Canal are the twelfth and thirteenth highest mountains in Britain. They are synonymous with Glen Affric, regarded by many as the finest glen in Scotland. The peaks have two eastern and one northern satellite and the complete chain of five summits and fourteen tops is best tackled by an east/west ridge traverse that is nearly all above the 3000ft contour. Several of the tops are inconveniently situated on outlying spurs, and will involve long detours and re-ascents back to the main ridge if they are included in the traverse. It soon becomes apparent that distances are vast, for both lie seven miles from the road. The complete traverse of the five major summits alone is at least 20 miles which, combined with total ascents in the region of 6550ft, makes for a particularly long day.

Toll Creagach

A path running into Gleann nam Fiadh from the car-park near the head of Loch Beinn a' Mheadhoin is frequently used as an access route to the eastern hills of this group. It turns north along the side of the Allt Toll Easa, rising as a grassy staircase to the Bealach Toll Easa. Toll Creagach can be reached by a direct climb up its southern slopes from Beinn Eun. From the summit triangulation pillar small outcrops look down on Loch Mullardoch and the woods of Cannich. To the west, a broad ridge falls to the smooth cap of the second top, which in turn drifts to the Bealach Toll Easa.

Tom a' Choinich

A line of broken fence-posts clambers up the grassy neck of the hill to the west of the pass, crosses the flat, mossy summit of Tom a' Choinich (cairn), and continues as guide to the first twist in an obvious ridge, which turns south-west, and narrows to the hummocky tors of Tom a' Choinich Beag and An Leth-chreag.

Carn Eige

The deep notch of the Garbh-bhealach is now encountered and this, at 3159ft, is the lowest part of the ridge. Ahead, Sron Garbh is all rock and uneasy scree, but on the climb are the remains of an old stone staircase built to ease the path of Victorian sportsmen through a maze of tumbled rock. The slope levels on to the curve of a broad ridge around the head of Coire Domhain, as an escarpment to Stob Coire Dhomhnuill, and thence to support several small needles of rock, which are easily turned on the left (south side). More grassy banks lead easily up to Creag na h-Eige, which throws out a broad spur to the north as one arm of Coire Lochan. At this point, the long spur connecting Carn Eige and Beinn Fhionnlaidh is seen clearly for the first time. A 1000ft sweep accentuates the majesty of Carn Eige, which presents itself as a great dome above the V-notch of the bealach. Ahead, Mam Sodhail also asserts itself to the south-west. At Carn Eige's summit (triangulation pillar) a green slope falls westwards to the floor of Gleann a' Choilich, 2000ft below; this grassy embankment is common to the neighbouring peaks of Mam Sodhail, Ciste Dhubh, Carn Coulavie and Beinn Fhionnlaidh away to the north.

Beinn Fhionnlaidh

This mountain and Stob Coire Lochan are most inconveniently situated near the foot of the long north ridge of Carn Eige. To reach it involves a descent of 1000ft to a col with a 300ft climb beyond. Only the most energetic will include it on a traverse of these peaks, but as access by any other route is an even more daunting prospect it is better to include it if you can. The only other sure alternative is to climb it by itself on a long expedition from Alltbeithe (Glen Affric) by crossing the Bealach Coire Ghaidheil with an ascent from Gleann a' Choilich. Although it is possible to reach the mountain from Iron Lodge (Glen Elchaig) there will almost certainly be problems with the crossing of the Amhainn a' Choilich. A route from the east, along the shores of Loch Mullardoch, is too masochistic even to contemplate.

Mam Sodhail

If Beinn Fhionnlaidh is included, the 1000ft re-ascent back to the summit of Carn Eige can be avoided by a traverse line up the west slopes to the pass between Carn Eige and Mam Sodhail. The latter summit can be seen beyond Carn Eige's slopes during this traverse, and acts as a guide. Standing in the gap, the rambler finds himself confronted with a short, sharp pull of a little over 400ft to a fort-like structure, built around an Ordnance Survey pillar on the summit.

To the south-west of the main summit, broad slopes of grass and scree fan out to the flattened top of Ciste Dhubh above Coire Leachavie, which overlooks the head of another corrie to the west of An Tudair's spur. This corrie's western wall is a wide, level ridge, which curves in a lazy arc over the rounded shoulders of Carn Coulavie, to link the high point of Ciste Dhubh with the broad spur of Creag a' Chaoruinn (also known as Creag Coire nan Each). Munro gave the name Stob Coire Coulavie (Carn Coulavie) to the first top, and adopted the name of a small knot of crags at the end of the ridge for that of the second cairn. Steps are retraced to Mam Sodhail, where steep slopes immediately below the summit can be contoured to gain the broad crest of the mountain's south-eastern ridge. The small hump of Mullach Cadha Rainich, at its centre, is crossed to reach the 400ft of easy ascent to the cairn of Sgurr na Lapaich. Munro originally classified this peak as a 'mountain', later revising its status to that of a 'top'. Distanced as it is from the parent Mam Sodhail, with crags guarding the eastern end of the ridge below its cairn, the peak certainly does not lack character and many were disappointed to find that its original status was not restored in the seventh edition of Munro's Tables. The edge of the crags to the south-east of the summit lead to steep heather slopes above the Glen Affric footpath. To the east, easier slopes dip to the Allt na Faing, beyond which a footpath to the Affric Lodge track is found on the lower slopes of Am Meallan.

Mam Sodhail from the south

If time and energy do not permit a complete traverse, the south-western tops of Mam Sodhail can conveniently be left for a separate expedition. This could also include An Socach, if it had been missed on a traverse of Sgurr nan Ceathreamhnan (Walk 1).

The two rogue spurs can be tackled from two convenient paths climbing from the Glen Affric footpath. A stalkers' path up Coire Leachavie climbs to the ridge between Mam Sodhail and Ciste Dhubh. An alternative climb to Mam Sodhail starts up a steep grass slope behind a ruined shieling to gain the south-eastern ridge by Mullach Cadha Rainich. On the opposite wall of the basin steep heather terraces climb to An Tudair (also known as Saoiter Mor).

The slopes dropping to the Bealach Coire Ghaidheil, to the west of Carn Coulavie are exceptionally steep and if starting the walk from this end it is certainly better to take the path to the pass, but even then, the slopes must be contested sooner or later and the long drag from the summit of the pass to the cairn of Carn Coulavie rises 1150ft in three-quarters of a mile. On these traverses, whether it be east-west or vice versa, the Bealach Coire Ghaidheil holds the key to the easy diversion westwards to the peak of An Socach (Walk 1).

CHAPTER 21   WALK 3

Carn nan Gobhar 3251ft/992m
　Creag Dhubh 3102ft/946m
Sgurr na Lapaich 3775ft/1150m
　Rudha na Spreidhe 3484ft/1057m
　Sgurr nan Clachan Geala 3591ft/1095m
　Creag a' Chaoruinn 3195ft/972m
　Braigh a' Choire Bhig 3317ft/1011m
An Riabhachan 3696ft/1129m
　(north-east top) 3664ft/1117m
　(south-west top) 3559ft/1086m
　(west top) 3406ft/1040m
An Socach 3508ft/1069m

This is an extremely remote chain of mountains most awkwardly placed for a one-day expedition with a return to the starting point. Strathfarrar is a possible base but access to this valley is restricted (locked gate at Struy) and the route is still very extended. Most walkers will choose Glen Cannich for a starting point and thereby have to face the tiresome choice of a long approach or return along the shores of Loch Mullardoch. The best itinerary, if transport can be arranged is a traverse from Glen Cannich to Glen Elchaig. Another possibility is a multi-day round of all the peaks of Loch Mullardoch (see Walks 1 and 2 and a long chapter in *Memorable Munros* by Richard Gilbert). Such an expedition would, of course, involve camping or bivouacking. The peaks might also be tackled piecemeal from either end, though once on the ridge the walker will probably wish to bag as many summits and tops as possible in one expedition. The route described is the east – west traverse with a return along the loch, but in good conditions this route taken in the opposite direction might be preferable, for once the summit of Sgurr na Lapaich is attained, the hummocks of Carn nan Gobhar and Creag Dhubh seem effortless, and almost downhill. The road through Glen Cannich to the Mullardoch dam has the advantage of a closer approach to the eastern tops, though the barrier of Loch Mullardoch makes the tops of An Riabhachan and An Socach seem especially remote.

Carn nan Gobhar

From a boathouse near the dam wall, the path climbs above the Clan Chisholm monument, and across the hillside sweeping towards the Allt Mullardoch, whose eastern bank carries a stalkers' path up into the heathery basin of Coire an t-Sith. Ahead, the broad flanks of Carn nan Gobhar and Creag Dhubh rise steeply to rounded tops, marked by cairns sitting slightly to the north of a broad, connecting ridge.

Sgurr na Lapaich

The broad ridge to the north-west of the goats' cairn crosses a wide grassy saddle, beyond which a steep rib leads upwards to Sgurr na Lapaich's summit. This gives an entertaining, easy scramble above the rough wall of the Garbh-choire, joining the head of an easier scree-rake seen on the left, to climb by a shattered ridge to the Ordnance Survey pillar on the summit.

The northern top, Rudha na Spreidhe, lies out at the end of a short, stony crest above crags at the head of a long spur above the wooded glen of the Uisge Misgeach. Sgurr na Lapaich also has three southern tops. From the summit the slope is followed in a southerly direction for about half-a-mile to a broad, stony saddle. If choosing to ignore the tops, and adopting a westerly course, be sure to avoid the precipitous western face above Loch Mor by a similar move towards this saddle before tackling the steep 1000ft tumble of grassy banks to the col at the end of An Riabhachan. A broad ridge continues south above cliffs on the east flank to the three southern tops.

There are white quartzite blocks which are convenient landmarks on the south side of Sgurr nan Clachan Geala, the highest top at the junction of two spurs. The edge of one follows a line of shattered crags down 500ft to the east, to the foot of Creag a' Chaoruinn. To take this in will involve a re-ascent to regain the other spur which heads south-west to the cairn on Braigh a' Choire Bhig. From this point it is possible to work down and across slopes to the north to gain the col at the foot of the ridge leading to An Riabhachan. It is also a good place to terminate a shorter expedition and follow the long ridge above Choire Bhig to the Allt Taige for the return to the dam.

An Riabhachan

The haul out to An Riabhachan takes the walker further into the remote corner to the north-west of Loch Mullardoch, and high above the boggy plain to the south of Loch Monar. A rough, rock-strewn ridge rising from the deep gap under the western flank of Sgurr na Lapaich follows a precipitous edge above the rocky basins of Loch Mor and Loch Beag. The north-east cairn of the hill heralds the easy, level walk across the summit to the cairn of the south-west top (3559ft/1086m), above a spur falling towards the Allt Socrach. Here the main ridge turns north-west, running for a third-of-a-mile to the west top (not spot-heighted on the map), where another twist leads to a narrow rib on the fall to a rough gap to the south-west.

An Socach

Ahead, the ridge climbs to the Ordnance Survey pillar on the flat crown of An Socach. The cross-country walker can amble down open slopes to the west to reach a track in the glen of the Allt Coire nan Each, where the bothy at Maolbhuidhe (053359) can be attained, or the path followed to Iron Lodge. Those returning to Glen Cannich will take the broad southern sweep of the hill in an easterly curve around Coire Mhaim, on a descent to a hut and sheep pen on the Allt Socrach.

After a long day on the tops, the return walk beside Loch Mullardoch is uninviting. The path is indistinct and one diversion, above several outcrops at the water's edge, is particularly trying.

CHAPTER 21   WALK 4

Sgurr Fhuar-thuill 3439ft/1049m
  Sgurr na Fearstaig 3326ft/1015m
  Creag Ghorm a' Bhealaich 3378ft/1030m
Sgurr a' Choire Ghlais 3554ft/1083m
Carn nan Gobhar 3251ft/992m
Sgurr na Ruaidhe 3254ft/993m

These four mountains are difficult to get at because the only road running anywhere near them, that in Glen Strathfarrar, has a locked gate at Struy (restricted access — permission to use must be obtained at the cottage beside the gate, Tel: Struy 260). In

its lower reaches there are woods of naturally-seeded oak, beech and sycamore, which, beyond two small lochs gracing the middle glen, give way to moors as the mountains close in upon the road.

Sgurr Fhuar-thuill

As the cluster of ruined buildings at Broulin (Braulen) Lodge is passed, the nose of Beinn na Muice is seen thrusting into the glen. A stalkers' path along the west bank of the Allt Toll a' Mhuic leads to a hidden corrie beneath broken cliffs. Struggling through the hollow of Loch Toll a' Mhuic, the path labours up the steeper slopes of the upper hill to peter out just below the crest of Sgurr na Fearstaig, the most westerly top in the range.

Throughout most of this approach the fine panorama down Loch Monar is hidden. Another approach, taking a moorland path along the Allt Coire na Faochaige, affords a clearer view. Sgurr na Fearstaig and the similar humps of Sgurr Fhuar-thuill, and Creag Ghorm a' Bhealaich all boast small cairns. Sgurr Fhuar-thuill, the central and highest of the three, is linked to its 'tops' by the shallow undulations of a broad ridge which, above Loch an Fhuar-thuill Mhoir, is ringed with small crags, so that the crest is easily navigated even in mist.

Sgurr a' Choire Ghlais

The ridge continues eastwards to a narrow saddle linked to Sgurr a' Choire Ghlais. This summit, a little to the east-south-east of the main ridge, is a short platform, which has a triangulation pillar and a large cairn set above a wide corrie sweeping down to Glen Strathfarrar. In thick mist,

the lead off this table to the east can be a little confusing, as a small false ridge lies slightly to the north of the main crest, which here falls to a saddle at the foot of Carn nan Gobhar.

Carn nan Gobhar

An easy 400ft ascent leads to the stony wastes of this great barrow, with a glum, grey cairn to mark the summit at its northern end. To the east, stony fans line the headwall of a spacious corrie on the south face of the hill, and in poor weather careful navigation is needed on the crossing towards the heathery Sgurr na Ruaidhe, passing the saddle of Bealach nam Bogan (unnamed on maps) to the south-west.

Sgurr na Ruaidhe

Sgurr na Ruaidhe rises to a broad, flat dome whose squat cairn lies some 700ft above the saddle. Open slopes dipping to the Allt Coire Mhuillidh give an easy return to the loch in the valley.

The approach from the north

The many streams to the north of the range feed the Orrin, which can be approached from a minor road in Strath Conon. A track climbing south-east through the woods above Inverchoran gives easy access to a stalkers' path, which crosses a pass on the 1500ft/440m contour to reach Glen Orrin. A footbridge crosses the Orrin below Creag a' Ghlastail followed by a lengthy walk up spongy and boggy moors to reach the peaks. This combination of obstacles tends to discourage attempts on the peaks from this direction, and anyway the views from the Glen Strathfarrar approach are finer.

STRATHCARRON AND ACHNASHEEN

Peaks that straddle a geological frontier, where crumpled mica schists and granulites meet beds of layered sandstone. High ridges above vast deer forests to the south, contrast with the vertiginous sandstone towers to the north, providing a varied selection of outings.

MAOILE LUNNDAIDH SGURR A'CHAORACHAIN SGURR CHOINNICH
Seemingly uninteresting peaks that prove fascinatingly complex on closer inspection.

BIDEIN A'CHOIRE SHEASGAICH LURG MHOR
Two very inaccessible peaks that may require an overnight camp. Craggy and intricate.

MORUISG SGURR NAN CEANNAICHEAN
It is difficult to be complimentary about Moruisg, but Sgurr nan Ceannaichean improves the walk.

BEINN LIATH MHOR SGORR RUADH
Evocative sandstone peaks of distinctive character.

MAOL CHEAN-DEARG
Another isolated sandstone knoll which can be combined with the previous duo into a demanding outing.

FIONN BHEINN
A diminutive hill, offering interesting aspects of the Fannichs and the distant Torridon giants.

Recommended Valley Base Achnasheen.

Maps O.S. 1:50 000 Sheets 20 and 25; Bartholomews 1:100 000 Sheets 54 and 55.

Starting Point/Length and time for main itinerary
Walk 1 Craig (040492). 20 miles/5 590ft of ascent, 9 – 14 hours.
Walk 2 Bearnais (021431). 10 miles/3 000ft of ascent, 5 – 8 hours (Strathcarron to Bearnais walk-in by Achintee path 5 miles/1 600ft of ascent).
Walk 3 Craig (040492). 11 miles/3 600ft of ascent, 5 – 8 hours.
Walk 4 Achnashellach (005484). 9 miles/3 850ft of ascent, 5 – 8 hours.
Walk 5 Coulags (963452). 8 miles/3 000ft of ascent, 4 – 6 hours.
Walk 6 Achnasheen (162586). 4 miles/3 000ft of ascent, 3 – 5 hours.

CHAPTER 22   WALK 1

Maoile Lunndaidh 3304ft/1007m
  Creag Toll a' Choin 3295ft/1006m*
  Carn nam Fiaclan 3266ft/996m
Sgurr a' Chaorachain 3455ft/1053m
  Bidean an Eoin Deirg 3430ft/1046m
Sgurr Choinnich 3276ft/999m

This remote group of mountains is situated north of Loch Monar and south of Gleann Fhiodhaig. As Loch Monar and its moors all but prevent access from the south and east, the only feasible approach to these hills is that to the north and west. Here, a forest track through the plantations along the Allt a' Chonais provides the access from the Strath Carron road.

Creag Toll a' Choin and Maoile Lunndaidh
Near the watershed, about a mile west of Glenuaig Lodge, an east-flowing stream can be crossed to boggy heather beneath Sron na Frianich. Below the waterfalls of the An Crom-allt, large boulders can be used as stepping stones to the convex slopes climbing above the Fuar-tholl Mor on to the high plateau of Carn nam Fiaclan. Alternatively, a second stream from Fuar-tholl Mor can be forded to reach the heathery terraces below the steep northern slopes of Maoile Lunndaidh. This allows the mountains to be traversed in order from east to west, but the greater interest of the former route and the ease of movement on the level summit make this easterly diversion hardly necessary.

In the climb to Carn nam Fiaclan, heather gives way to moss and stones, and from the eastern edge of the hillside the first tiny tarn of Fuar-tholl Mor may be seen at the foot of near-vertical rock which lines the corrie rim. The edge of broken crags curves round where the hill towards the flat brow of Creag Toll a' Choin, and should be left where the main slope of the open ridge broadens to the mound of Carn nam Fiaclan's summit. From the cairn the going is flat to the cairn of Creag Toll a' Choin, on the edge of the precipitous wall encircling Toll a' Choin, which at this point almost meets the rim of Fuar-tholl Mor.

The summit of Maoile Lunndaidh is broad and featureless, broken only by the pillar of stones which marks its highest elevation and is now considered to be the summit of this mountain.

After returning to Carn nam Fiaclan, scree patches are crossed on the broad spur to the west and small outcrops break the slopes overlooking its southern flanks, which plunge to the Amhainn Srath Mhuilich. Broad, convex, heather slopes also drop to the An Crom-allt. The nose of the spur turns to the south-west down a steep rib leading to a saddle below the towering wall of Bidean an Eoin Deirg. Here a small tarn provides a useful landmark in misty weather.

Sgurr a' Chaorachain
The face of Bidean an Eoin Deirg, scarred with broken crag and steep gullies, will involve scrambling with a degree of seriousness. It may be easier to work across steep ground to the mountain's east ridge. All this can be avoided by an extensive detour to the west. From the tarn, cut across the green corrie of the An Crom-allt to Lochan Gaineamhach, above which a steep slope merges into the scrambly rise of Sgurr a' Chaorachain's northern spur. A short, stiff 800ft pull up this finds the Ordnance Survey pillar and an attendant cairn on the mossy summit.

A wide ridge above the Allt Toll a' Chaorachain and the northern corrie's craggy rim can be followed to blocks which push the path away from the edge on the descent to the col at the foot of Bidean an Eoin Deirg. The summit of this barren hill is at a cairn perched on the edge of an escarpment falling to Srath Mhuilich, over 1000ft below. To reach this summit by the described route involves a two-mile detour and 600ft of ascent. The ascent from the saddle below is far more direct. If tackling the peaks in the opposite direction the loose north-eastern slopes of Bidean an Eoin Deirg are best avoided.

Sgurr Choinnich
To the west of Sgurr a' Chaorachain's top, a narrow ridge, almost an arête, drops to a saddle with rough, broken ground under its northern edge. Slabs and scree slant to the left of the arête which climbs to the grassy ridge of Sgurr Choinnich. This heads up along an edge of vegetated cliffs to a cairn on a grassy knot, beyond which grassy terraces and small outcrops add interest to the descent to the Bealach Bhearnais. Here, cross to the north side of the stream heading east, where a stalkers' path speeds the descent to the Allt a' Chonais. In dry weather this stream can be forded, but when impassable follow the bank downstream to a clump of trees. These signpost a waterfall, obscured by a heathery mound, where a tiny footbridge will be found to regain the Strath Carron track.

CHAPTER 22   WALK 2

Bidein a' Choire Sheasgaich 3102ft/945m
Lurg Mhor 3234ft/986m
Meall Mor 3190ft/974m

These mountains are very isolated, the nearest being at least five miles as the crow flies from the nearest road. They are hidden from view behind a long range of hills to the south of Strath Carron.

The easiest route to them leaves the Strath Carron road near Attadale House, where a track follows the River Attadale and a twisting route on to Bendronaig Lodge. If using this approach and returning to Attadale, the traverse of the three tops involves approximately 4000ft of ascent and some 23 miles of walking in one of the least frequented areas of the Highlands. Even in summer this is a particularly long and exhausting outing.

Several other paths from Strath Carron cross higher passes to meet near the tiny one-roomed cottage of Bearnais (021430). The lowest of these, though not the shortest, is the 'Achintee Path', through a glen above Strathcarron Station. A climb above the Eas an Teampuill leads to a steep bealach at the western end of Creag a' Chaoruinn Eagan.

From a bridge over the River Carron (979458), near Balnacra, a second path

reaches the wild moors by way of a desperate scrabbly scarp, which climbs over 1000ft in half-a-mile. The indistinct path then crosses the heather and scrambles up the rough slopes of Creag a' Chaoruinn Eagan, to disappear on a flattened ridge above Bearnais.

The third path, which toils up the hill from Achnashellach, in common with the shattering climb from Balnacra, enjoys excellent views. Zig-zags carry the path across the 1000ft contour on the first mile of the journey, towards a line of crags which appear to bar further progress. Here, a laboured ascent leads to a flat bealach by a series of stony zig-zags on the craggy edge of Coire na h-Eilde, before a pleasant, easy descent to Bearnais.

To the north-east of the cottage, another track climbs from the Allt a' Chonais to the Bealach Bhearnais (see Walk 1). The west side of the pass lacks any path, and the Amhainn Bhearnais is the best guide through the peat-hagged moors.

Bidein a' Choire Sheasgaich
The Amhainn Bhearnais can become quite boisterous after rain, and in such conditions the rambler must be prepared for a detour upstream to ensure a safe, dry crossing. An ageing path, seen below Beinn Tharsuinn, gives a level walk to the foot of Coire Seasgach.

To the east, Bidein a' Choire Sheasgaich guards its cairn with a series of precipices high above Loch Monar. Should anyone be foolish enough to contemplate the long, desperate walk across these moors, these battlements are likely to repulse any attempt on the summit. To the north of the cairn, another craggy bastion thrusts out above Bealach an Sgoltaidh. This provides stiff but entertaining scrambling. Minor bluffs also block routes out of the head of Coire Seasgach. On the climb from this corrie, all these obstructions are avoided by taking to the spur of Sail Riabach, which squeezes on to the narrow summit table, crowned by a poor cairn at its western end.

Lurg Mhor
Following the line of the eastern crags, a rough, narrow ridge steps down across a short col, to a rise which sweeps up to the cairn on the flat moss of Lurg Mhor. Further to the east, the ridge-crest crosses slabs of puckered rock. Greasy when wet, and precariously near to the hill's craggy face, these delicate steps creep down to a gully cutting across the lowest point of the ridge.

Beyond this gap, grassy knobs rise to Meall Mor, an insignificant cairn looking down Loch Monar; from here also, above the marshy Loch Cruoshie, it is possible to make out the small, white cottage of Maol-bhuidhe.

The descent from Meall Mor should present little difficulty, as the southern

flanks of Lurg Mhor are grassy and a diagonal line is easily taken to reach the path near Loch Calavie for the return to Bendronaig Lodge. A faint path above the Black Water avoids the worst of the marshy ground near Loch an Laoigh, on a return to Bearnais.

CHAPTER 22   WALK 3

Moruisg 3026ft/928m
Sgurr nan Ceannaichean 2986ft/915m

Moruisg
Moruisg on its own is an unexciting hill; there seems little that can be said about it, except that it tops 3000ft. Most ascents were made from the footbridge (082520) over the River Carron, and, once across the railway, a 2500ft plod brought the walker directly to the bare earth and stones of the summit.

As the views from the cairn are uninspiring, the return was usually a quick dash down the hill in the reverse direction. The Ordnance Survey has changed all this, for their re-survey lifted the neighbouring peak of Sgurr nan Ceannaichean above the magic 3000ft.

Sgurr nan Ceannaichean
Near Craig, a forestry road crosses the railway line and the River Carron, and climbs through the Strathcarron Forest to emerge from the trees near the foot of the first of two deep gullies, which split the western face of the mountain.

This resolute prow of Sgurr nan Ceannaichean can be turned by following the track around the base of the hill to a stalkers' path, seen beside the debris of a stream on an easier southern flank. The path twists and turns, in parts loose and broken where sections have been washed away, breaking free to the upper slopes at the end of a long diagonal traverse above a small hanging corrie. The path peters out on the walk up to the cairn, found at the south end of a short grassed escarpment. At its northern end, this embankment drops to an obvious narrow ridge, falling away to corries on either hand. At its foot, a broader ridge turns the craggy head of Coire Toll nam Bian, to a small, level top at 2794ft/854m. In a dip beyond this un-named point, a shallow channel lies athwart the line of ascent to the broader back of Moruisg.

A direct descent from the summit to the bridge over the River Carron avoids the worst of the peat-hags on the path from Coire Toll nam Bian. The road walk back to Craig is a pleasant downhill stroll.

CHAPTER 22   WALK 4

Beinn Liath Mhor 3034ft/925m
Sgorr Ruadh 3142ft/960m

These are two of the highest summits in a chain of interesting rocky peaks in the wild country between Strath Carron and Glen Torridon. Maol Chean-dearg is the third 3000ft peak in the group, and although they are closely grouped the three peaks are curiously inconvenient to link up, as craggy walls frequently impede the route, requiring complex diversions. In many ways the peaks are better climbed on two separate expeditions from various points in Glen Torridon and Strath Carron. These smaller projects would allow the lower satellite peaks, which are no less interesting, to be included. We are primarily concerned with the 3000ft peaks, however, so the most logical and interesting way of linking the third peak is described in Walk 5. Here we concentrate on the two most easily traversed in a single expedition of moderate duration.

To the west of Achnashellach station a path climbs through twisted pines, above the gorge of the River Lair, to a heathery hillside beneath the craggy snout of Beinn Liath Mhor. Here the path divides. One branch crosses to the Easan Dorcha; the other heads up into wild and desolate Coire Lair, flanked by the grey ridge of Beinn Liath Mhor and the russet cliffs of Sgorr Ruadh.

Beinn Liath Mhor

Above Loch Coire Lair the south slope of Beinn Liath Mhor is rough and loose, but worn sandstone terraces which break through the scree on the lower slopes aid progress. The upper slopes are devoid of vegetation and on such a stony peak the summit cairn, at the western end of the ridge, is not surprisingly a very substantial affair. This is an excellent point from which to observe the full extent of Liathach's range of peaks, possibly as an appetizer to a later conquest.

On the descent to the Bealach Coire Lair, a broken edge on the slope south-west of the cairn, and a rocky tower above the head of the pass must be turned. This is achieved by a flanking movement towards a tiny lochan 400ft below and to the west of the summit cairn (958520). It is then possible to work south to gain the path at the head of the pass.

Sgorr Ruadh

Above another tarn at the foot of the tower, stone slides break through the craggy escarpments which elsewhere bar the way to Sgorr Ruadh. These rakes give a steep scree-scramble to a wide, stony ridge which rises south-eastwards to a large cairn looking out across Loch Torridon.

Sgorr Ruadh can also be climbed directly from the River Lair (ford) by a path up the heathery slopes to the north of Fuar Tholl. This reaches a cluster of lochans nestling in a broad corrie. The largest of these lies below the saddle of the Bhealaich Mhoir which is the lowest point on the broad ridge linking Fuar Tholl and Sgorr Ruadh. This pass is a fine viewpoint from which to observe the impressive cliffs of Fuar Tholl and the great dome of Maol Chean-dearg across Coire Fionnaraich. From here Sgorr Ruadh is gained by a steep climb, broken briefly by a short level terrace halfway to the top. This route in reverse affords the easiest descent to the Coire Lair path for the return to Achnashellach.

Although not a 'Munro', Fuar Tholl is an attractive hill, and many prefer to add it to their itinerary during a circuit of Coire Lair. There are massive slabs on its eastern face and care should be exercised in the choice of descent. If caught in mist near the cairn, a slightly westerly bearing will avoid the worst of any difficulties on the steep fall to the woods lining the road near Loch Dughaill.

Ascent from the north

The shortest and most practical route from Glen Torridon starts at the Ling Hut (957564), reached by an access path by the eastern shore of Lochan an Iasgaich. This continues southwards for a time before disappearing in the moors at the foot of Sgorr an Lochan Uaine. Here, streams provide a guide to the wide saddle of Lochan Uaine where, turning south, easy beds of scree climb to the summit of Beinn Liath Mhor.

CHAPTER 22   WALK 5

Maol Chean-dearg 3060ft/933m

This bald hill completes the trio of rocky 3000ft peaks between Strath Carron and Glen Torridon. Though in reasonable proximity to Sgorr Ruadh, and Beinn Liath Mhor, the complexity of routes between the peaks makes the longer traverse of all three less frequented than it might otherwise be. Consequently Maol Chean-dearg is most often climbed on its own from points further to the west of Strath Carron or Glen Torridon.

A path from Coulags in Strath Carron (A890) follows the east bank of the Fionn-amhainn to a bridge and stepping stones beneath a terraced bank of Meall nan Ceapairean. These stepped slopes give immediate access to an easy-angled ridge running north-west to a summit cairn. From this point the dome of Maol Chean-dearg is seen beyond a short col, which is gained by following an escarped edge to the north-west of the cairn.

Maol Chean-dearg

The col lies at a junction where Meall nan Ceapairean's ridge meets those of An Ruadh-stac, an impressive rock tower seen to the south-west, and Maol Chean-dearg to the north-west.

Above the col a path twists through jumbles of quartzite rubble on the climb to a cairn perched above the steep western face of the hill. Continuing across a shallow dip, the path all but disappears on a slope of unsteady blocks supporting the broad stonefield of Maol Chean-dearg's summit dome. At its northern edge, this boasts a huge cairn, possibly the largest encountered on any Scottish peak.

Walkers approaching by the moorland path from Annat on Loch Torridon find that cliffs above Loch an Eoin prevent access from that quarter, and they should look for an obvious line of ascent on the north-western corner of the hill. A long fringe of crags similarly guards the eastern face of the mountain above Coire Fionnaraich. A break in these eastern bluffs, south-east of the summit cairn, allows an easterly descent by a stony ridge to a rough terrace along the top of a lower band of east-facing craggy slabs. Edging under a higher cliff the terrace runs towards Bealach na Lice, with a descent to the path by a broad eastern gully, for a return by Coire Fionnaraich, or Loch an Eoin if returning to Torridon. This complex route calls for skilful navigation and is best attempted in clear weather. Any uncertainty is best avoided by retracing steps to the foot of Meall nan Ceapairean with a descent from the col as later described; or a path by way of Loch Coire an Ruadh-staic if returning to Torridon. The complex north-eastern route provides a way on for those combining a traverse of Maol Chean-dearg with Sgorr Ruadh and Beinn Liath Mhor.

The traverse of three Munros

The traverse of Maol Chean-dearg can be used as a beginning or end to an expedition across all three Munros in Walks 4 and 5. If done in an east-west direction, Walk 4 is taken to the summit of Sgorr Ruadh. It will then be necessary to return to Bealach Coire Lair thereby avoiding the crags barring a direct descent to the Bealach Ban. The Coire Lair path continues around the northern end of the mountain and across the Bealach Ban to the head of Coire Fionnaraich, where it joins the Coulags path on the Bealach na Lice. The north-east route of Maol Chean-dearg provides a direct climb to the summit, its slabby buttresses being more easily turned in ascent than descent. From the summit descend to the col at the foot of Meall nan Ceapairean and follow the path beside the stream which falls to join the Fionn-amhainn in Coire Fionnaraich. Here, the

Coulags path is regained for the walk down to the Strath Carron road.

Those attempting the major traverse of the peaks in Walks 4 and 5 should bear in mind that the distance is approximately 16 miles, with combined ascents of about 5600ft. This is an exceptionally time-consuming expedition and it is best to try and shorten it by avoiding the three mile return walk to Achnashellach by arranging transport at Coulags at the end of the day.

CHAPTER 22   WALK 6

Fionn Bheinn 3062ft/933m

Fionn Bheinn, a broad, grassy mountain to the north of Achnasheen, possesses no really distinctive features, excepting a minor precipiced slope above the boggy hollow of Toll Mor, north-east of the summit. More noteworthy is the prediction of Kenneth MacKenzie, the Brahan Seer, that 'the day will come when a raven, attired in plaid and bonnet, will drink his fill of human blood on Fionn Bheinn, three times a day, for three successive days', a prophecy as yet unfulfilled.

The Allt Achadh na Sine is a useful guide, but any of the streams draining the slopes can be followed to the upper hill which, steepening to the west, requires only a steady walk to the easier eastern ridge. From the flat summit, with its Ordnance Survey pillar, the most impressive view lies to the west. It is an even easier run down the hill on the return to Achnasheen.

CHAPTER 23

KINLOCHEWE AND TORRIDON

The celebrated Torridon peaks provide every delectation the rambler could desire: deep corries, imposing buttresses, airy pinnacles and magnificent views.

BEINN ALLIGIN: SGURR MHOR
An exquisitely sculpted mountain of great beauty.

LIATHACH: SPIDEAN A'CHOIRE LEITH
The traverse of this majestic mountain is one of the finest in Scotland.

BEINN DEARG
An unique belvedere with magnificent aspects of the other Torridon giants.

BEINN EIGHE: RUADH-STAC MOR
Shattered quartzite ridges and wild corries typify this complex range.

SLIOCH
An imposing fortress standing guard over a lonely glaciated wilderness.

CHAPTER 23   WALK 1

Beinn Alligin:
Sgurr Mhor 3232ft/985m
Tom na Gruagaich 3024ft/922m

Beinn Alligin, the mountain of beauty, is best seen from the south side of Loch Torridon, or the path through Coire Mhic Nobuil, which gives a fine perspective of the steep-walled cirque around the moor-land basin of Toll a' Mhadaidh, hole of the fox. An almost perpendicular cleft scars the face of the main peak, and the eastern end of the hill is no less interesting for here the knobbly 'Rathains' or 'Horns of Alligin' line the crest of a rugged, terraced spur.

Recommended Valley Base Kinlochewe

Maps O.S. 1:50 000 Sheets 19, 24 and 25; Bartholomews 1:100 000 Sheet 54; O.S. 1:25 000 Sheet *The Cuillin and Torridon Hills.*

Starting Point/Length and time for main itinerary
Walk 1 Coire Mhic Nobuil bridge car-park (869576). 6 miles/4000ft of ascent, 4–6 hours.
Walk 2 Coire Dubh car-park (957568). 9 miles/4700ft of ascent, 5–8 hours.
Walk 3 Coire Mhic Nobuil bridge car-park (869576). 8 miles/3100ft of ascent, 4–6 hours.
Walk 4 Cromasaig (024608). 12 miles/5530ft of ascent, 7–11 hours.
Walk 5 Kinlochewe (034619). 12 miles/3600ft of ascent, 6–9 hours.

Tom na Gruagaich

The finest approach starts at the road linking Glen Torridon and the tiny village of Diabaig, near the mouth of Loch Torridon. A small car-park at the Amhainn Coire Mhic Nobuil bridge lies conveniently near the start of a cairned, and in places indistinct, path crossing the sandstone pavements in the direction of a high-walled cove in the face of Tom na Gruagaich. A stream tumbles from it, falling beside the path which struggles upwards to the headwall of its shadowy recess. Sun-seekers can try a modest scramble on the west wall of the hollow, to join the path at a dip between two hummocks, the highest of which, that to the east, proves to be the summit of Tom na Gruagaich. Here a cairn sits on a worn platform of sandstone at the edge of a face plunging to Toll a' Mhadaidh. Across this intimidating void, Sgurr Mhor meets the eye, with the 'Horns of Alligin' to its right.

Slightly to the left of the cairn, a path continues to sandstone steps on the lip of Toll a' Mhadaidh. At one point, a large terrace across the ridge forms a big step almost on the edge of the precipice. Although exposed the difficulty here is slight, and anyway the awkward move can be avoided on the left.

Sgurr Mhor

Beyond a short saddle the path shuffles over a grassy hummock, drops briefly, and then begins the laboured climb to the north-east to the summit of Sgurr Mhor, passing the edge of the huge cleft, or slash, previously seen from below. This appears as a 'window' in the cliffs to the right, with an enclosed view to the corrie below. The path keeps away from the edge on the climb to the cairn. The summit view looks over the cliffs and across the pit of a deeper corrie, backed by the 'Horns', with Beinn Dearg beyond.

'The Horns of Alligin'

A path follows the dipping ridgeline of the arête leading north-east which, veering eastwards to a rocky col, confronts the highest of the thrusting tors. Twisting up and around broken ledges the path searches out a route to the knobbly crest, and the crossing of the 'Horns'. The route along the tops of the three humps is a well marked modest scramble, which can be by-passed on the steep grassy slopes on the south side if needs be. There is a scrambly route along the south-east edge of the most easterly peak but easy alternative lines of descent are to be found on the Toll a' Mhadaidh slopes with, here and there, an indistinct path marking out a route through the worn terraces. At the foot of steep slopes by the Allt a' Bhealaich, a path crosses the moor to a bridge across the Amhainn Coire Mhic Nobuil. This provides a delightful return walk close to the waterfalls over sandstone shelves, which disappear into a chasm shielded by the trees bordering the road.

The mountain can also be climbed from a point above the village of Inveralligin.

The grassy slopes hereabouts offer only token resistance on an ascent that lacks the variety and interest of the approach up Coire Mhic Nobuil. Routes from the north are long and tedious.

CHAPTER 23   WALK 2

Liathach:
Spidean a' Choire Leith 3456ft/1054m
    Bidean Toll a' Mhuic 3200ft/975m
    Am Fasarinen 3050ft/927m
    Mullach an Rathain 3358ft/1023m
    Meall Dearg 3150ft/960m

Travellers heading west along Glen Torridon are suddenly confronted by Liathach's overpowering bulk. The name Liathach, the grey one, embraces a whole range of peaks, connected by a five-mile-long ridge running as a high wall along the north side of the glen.

Those wishing to climb the mountain will first have to decide a strategy. A complete traverse is best — taking in all the tops — but it is very long and if time or energy are in short supply the walker may elect to climb the eastern tops on one expedition and the western ones on another. The mountain can be traversed equally well from either direction, though the eastern approaches seem most favoured, probably because of the seaward aspect and the easier descent at the western end.

The eastern tops

The eastern top, Stuc a' Choire Dhuibh Bhig, can be climbed directly from near the road. A path rises into Coire Dubh from a car-park by the bridge over the Allt a' Choire Dhuibh Mhoir. After following this for a short distance heather slopes on the left lead to the base of the rocky upper tiers of the peak. They steepen considerably on the climb to a point beneath the highest line of cliffs, seen under the eastern peak. At the base of these crags a faint path may be detected, providing 50ft of scrambling to quartzite blocks above. The climb to the eastern top, Stuc a' Choire Dhuibh Bhig, is then a straightforward scrambly path.*

Another less steep and more frequently used route starts further down the road to the west. An easy natural line moves obliquely across the worn terraces to a dip in the ridge, just to the west of Stuc a' Choire Dhuibh Bhig.

The immediate view westwards from this peak is completely dominated by great walls of tiered sandstone supporting the bold quartzite peaks of Bidean Toll a' Mhuic (also known as Stob a' Coire Liath Mhor) and Spidean a' Choire Leith. Most impressive is the great prow of a short, level ridge, terminating in a gigantic

*Stuc a' Choire Dhuibh Bhig (3050ft) was a Munro top until 1974 when re-mapping fixed its height at 913m.

plunge of cliff, which abuts the pointed cap of Spidean a' Choire Leith.

The stony ridge ahead presents no difficulty though care should be exercised on the steep clamber to the eastern point of Bidean Toll a' Mhuic, where loose angular blocks and scree are encountered above the northern cliffs. The ridge across Bidean Toll a' Mhuic's twin humps is again well-defined, but on their southern slopes screes shower over an edge of crumbling crags. In thick mist, to those making a traverse in the reverse direction, this slide may look deceptively like an easy route to the road. It should always be borne in mind that any descent from the ridge at the eastern end of the mountain requires great care, especially in bad visibility or under winter conditions, and the access routes previously described are the best. Only one direct descent from Spidean a' Choire Leith is possible and is here described as a route of ascent.

Spidean a' Choire Leith

Those wishing to miss out the eastern tops and climb directly to Spidean a' Choire Leith should take a cairned path beginning at the foot of the lower corrie immediately east of the summit prow. This climbs to the hanging hollow of Coire Leith, by a route skirting the base of a short, false ridge. More cairns mark the zig-zags clambering to a grassy break in a rock band crossing the face of the mountain. From here a prominent cairn seen on the rock band above and to the west points the way to the steep scramble to Coire Leith where, on the left, easy zig-zags lead up to the ridge between Bidean Toll a' Mhuic and the summit boulder-field. Large angular blocks encumber the final climb to the cairn of Spidean a' Choire Leith. Care is needed on the west to east traverse when descending this section to the notch at the head of Coire Leith, as the blocks are large enough to complicate direction finding in mist. If taken too far south, the route leads out on to the short false ridge, hemmed in by steep crags.

The centre of the ridge

From the bulky cairn of Spidean a' Choire Leith, the view to the west exposes the magnificence of Coire na Caime on the north (the crooked corrie) and the attendant peaks of Mullach an Rathain and Meall Dearg. The tiny lochans of this great hollow are overshadowed by a gigantic headwall buttressing the pinnacles of Am Fasarinen. Even in summer the traverse of these pinnacles provides a heady scramble, and although the holds are good, the degree of exposure is quite sensational, especially when peering down into Coire na Caime. Those unsure of the difficulties can opt for a narrow path along the south side of the ridge. In mist, difficulty may be

experienced when attempting to locate the route towards the pinnacles from below the summit of Spidean a' Choire Leith. Several people have become confused in such conditions and found themselves contouring round the upper cone of the summit, after losing the indistinct path in the boulder-field. A grassy ridge runs from the foot of the boulder-field, crossing two small knots to reach the eastern end of the pinnacles. Here a path steps down from the ridge on to the level of one of the sandstone terraces to skirt the base of the towers. This gives an exhilarating walk along a high gallery 3000ft above the Torridon road. The path eases its way towards the western end of the stacks to emerge on a wide grassy ridge.

Mullach an Rathain

This ridge provides a straightforward route to the Ordnance Survey pillar on the summit of Mullach an Rathain, a peak now accorded the status of a 'mountain'. This is debatable, and many traditionalists argue that Liathach is the mountain, with a summit called Spidean a' Choire Leith, the designation adopted by Munro. To the north a short, stony arête runs out to the highest of the northern pinnacles and the lower peak of Meall Dearg. The pinnacles are best left to those with climbing experience (see 'Ascents from the north'). A line of cairns along the ridge to the west leads to the head of a large stone chute dropping to Torridon village. Slightly to the west and south of the summit pillar, a narrow ridge drops towards a broadening slope of easy, worn terraces for a more direct descent to Glen Torridon (see 'Routes to the western tops').

Routes to the western tops

A small belt of trees beside the road at the western end of the mountain helps to locate the Allt an Tuill Bhain, which can be followed to a wide, grassy corrie on the upper slopes of Mullach an Rathain. Several bands of turf cut into the scree leading to the ridge, but contouring to the left gains the rocky rib of the south-west ridge. There are airy views across Upper Loch Torridon and out to sea, and shattered rock needles visible below the summit of Mullach an Rathain have to be by-passed on easier slopes to the right. The masochistic ascent of the great scree-fan which reaches the ridge to the west of this summit is best avoided, though a tolerable scree-run is possible on the descent.

The ridge can be gained at its extreme western extremity. Here the bluffs on the south face of Sgorr a' Chadail can be turned most easily by using the path along the Amhainn Coire Mhic Nobuil, which gives access to the northern corries. Above this path the heather slopes of Sgorr a' Chadail sweep up to a narrow ridge, where a line of cairns at the head of the scree-fan leads to the top.

Ascents from the north

At the eastern end of Liathach, a path along the Allt a' Choire Dhuibh Mhoir leads into Coire Dubh. Rounding the base of the terminal crags on Stuc a' Choire Dhuibh Bhig, Coireag Dubh Beag can be seen immediately below the peaks of Bidean Toll a' Mhuic and its eastern neighbour. The higher, broken terraces on this side of the mountain can be negotiated, but a stiff scramble is still needed to reach the corrie. Scree leads up from it to the dip between the two eastern tops and the level stonefield of the ridge.

A long, continuous scree-slope rises from the floor of Coire na Caime almost to the foot of the north-west spur of Spidean a' Choire Leith, which offers a moderate rock-climb to those taking the most direct line of ascent. On the western wall of this great hollow, the ridge of Meall Dearg (the northern pinnacles) is not a walking route but a climb, which starts at the base of the crags to the west of a small watercourse. The route lies up a steep, narrow shelf rising diagonally from right to left in the centre of the rocky face, and this gives a moderate climb for 600ft. The five pinnacles lining the crest, being very shattered, are covered in unstable blocks, and the first to be encountered is climbed by a narrow gully on its north-western side. The last finger of rock is met head on, a small slab just below the top leading to the point of its crumbly spire, which in turn leads to a loose scramble over less exposed rock on the rise to the top of Mullach an Rathain. The difficulties on all flanks of Meall Dearg qualify it for consideration as the most difficult top in the British Isles, challenged only by the Inaccessible Pinnacle of Sgurr Dearg.

CHAPTER 23 WALK 3

Beinn Dearg 2995ft/914m

This mountain is the most controversial of the 'high' peaks, since the one-inch map height of 2995ft has been replaced on the 1:50,000 series maps by a height of 914m, which is either marginally above or below 3000ft. Whatever the height an ascent of this peak is most worthwhile for its splendid views of the northern corries of Liathach and its equally fine vantage point between Beinn Alligin and Beinn Eighe.

From the small car-park at the Amhainn Coire Mhic Nobuil bridge on the Torridon/Diabaig road, the path along the south bank of the stream should be followed to the second bridge across it (882589).

Continuing beside the Allt a' Bhealaich the path lifts to the Bealach a' Chomhla

where, looking at the steep, terraced slopes to the right, a buttress falling south-west from the summit will be seen. Here the steepness of the ground and the massive rock-steps to be threaded are the only impediment, though a descent by the same route might prove a more difficult proposition. It would appear to be possible to ascend the mountain anywhere on its easier western flank, but everywhere will be steep and sandstone terraces will usually require circumnavigation at some point or other. As the top of the south-west buttress is reached, the gradient eases and a short walk is all that lies between this point and the summit cairn. This is about five feet high, as its constructors were determined to ensure that the highest point of the mountain attained the magical 3000ft. The natural line of the ridge eastwards from the cairn leads on to the top of a buttress, and it is necessary to get off this false ridge by a move to the north (left) across a pinnacle. The turn at approximately 896607 directs the route along the line of the National Trust boundary, as shown on the map. The ridge is narrow at this point with precipitous slopes on both sides, and a 20ft scramble on the eastern side of the pinnacle adds to the interest of the traverse to the broader ridge to Carn na Feola (761m), at the eastern end of the mountain.

On the descent from the crest a little to the south of this point, there is a temptation to move across the face of the hill to the west, but this leads to problems on the difficult rock terraces. The easiest descent follows a line to the south-east. An indistinct path in the marshy moors around Loch Grobaig follows the stream to the more obvious passage at the foot of Coire Mhic Nobuil, where steps are retraced to the road.

An attractive alternative route to and from the eastern end of the mountain is that through Coire Dubh Mor (see Walk 4), and this could also be used for the return journey for the described walk, if the transport problems could be resolved.

CHAPTER 23 WALK 4

Beinn Eighe:
Ruadh-stac Mor 3309ft/1010m
Sail Mhor 3217ft/981m
A' Choinneach Mhor 3130ft/954m
Spidean Coire nan Clach 3188ft/972m
Sgurr Ban 3288ft/971m
Sgurr an Fhir Duibhe 3160ft/963m
Creag Dubh 3050ft/929m

Liathach's sandstone terraces climb vertically from the road, whereas the tilt of Beinn Eighe's bedrock has resulted in greater weathering, with easier-angled slopes covered in a protective shield of quartzite. On the walls of the hidden

northern corries, the terraces are much more in evidence, culminating in the towers above Coire Mhic Fhearchair.

Coire Mhic Fhearchair

A path rises into Coire Dubh from a small bridge over the Allt a' Choire Dhuibh Mhoir (small car-park to the west), climbing steadily to the heather wastes between Sail Mhor and the high buttress of Liathach. Rough stepping stones cross the stream to a parting of the ways near Lochan a' Choire Dhuibh, where a well-cairned path to the right should be followed beneath Sail Mhor, whose northern buttresses are turned beside the Allt Coire Mhic Fhearchair. Breasting the final rise to a sandstone pavement, the grandeur of one of the finest corries in Britain is exposed to full view.

The western tops

The buttressed end of Sail Mhor is split by several scree gullies which, from below, appear steep and unstable and are best avoided. However, wide scree fans behind the lochan climb to the ridge along the southern slopes of the corrie and reach up to the rock-strewn crest a short distance south and a few hundred feet below Sail Mhor's cairn. This arm of the mountain runs east to A' Choinneach Mhor, which has a scrambly section to reach its summit with an ugly step, Ceum Grannda, which overlooks an exposed drop to the corrie floor. Here a few remains of a Manchester bomber which crashed into the Triple Buttress can still be found. When approached from above, the line of the scrambling route is not very obvious, and the airy stances above the broken rock face do little to dispel a feeling of insecurity. There are good holds however and with care this awkward section is soon passed.

The main ridge

A' Choinneach Mhor is an almost level field of moss which, to the north of the cairn, dips sharply to the narrow col at the head of Coire Mhic Fhearchair (the end of the Triple Buttress acting as guide), beyond which an easy rise leads out north along a spur to the pink-stoned cairn of Ruadh-stac Mor, the highest point of the massif. A diversion is required to take in this peak, and re-tracking is necessary to regain the main ridge.

To the east of A' Choinneach Mhor, a stony arête runs on to the point of Spidean Coire nan Clach. This peak, which, although not the highest summit is geographically the pivotal centre point of the mountain, is graced by a theodolite plinth. Its height is now firmly fixed at 3188ft/972m by the Ordnance Survey, proving that Munro's original estimate of approximately 3220ft was not wildly exaggerated. To the north-east, the landscape is a wilderness of bleached scree which attains its highest point on

Ruadh-stac Beag. Continuing eastwards the ridge dips to its lowest point where screes fall evenly towards the Torridon road.

The next point, Sgurr Ban, looks across a bare couloir to the jagged needles on the crest between Sgurr an Fhir Duibhe and Creag Dubh. Broken crags, seamed by long gullies full of scree, buttress the northern edge of the ridge between Sgurr Ban and Sgurr an Fhir Duibhe. The southern side offers wide scree fans.

Continuing beyond Sgurr an Fhir Duibhe, the first obstacle on the pinnacled ridge leading north to Creag Dubh is a 30ft section of exposed scrambling. This is an awkward descent and to avoid it keep to the south side of the ridge below the cairn and look for a faint path which contours round the summit to a chockstone at the head of a gully below the 30ft pitch. This route through the pinnacles is described later (see 'The eastern tops').

This section of the route is normally tackled on the east – west traverse as the start of the path is much more obvious. Those seeking to include Sail Mhor in the round can then tackle it from Coire Mhic Fhearchair after a diversion to the main summit of Ruadh-stac Mor, returning to the corrie for the walk out to the Torridon road. The only alternative is to get more rock climbing practice and tackle the bad step, with a return to A' Choinneach Mhor for the walk out to Ruadh-stac Mor, which would then be descended to the corrie.

The eastern tops

Sgurr an Fhir Duibhe and Creag Dubh are the tops most obviously seen from Kinlochewe and the best starting point to reach them is by the small bridge near the cottage at Cromasaig on the Torridon road. The path from Cromasaig (Cairn Shiel on the 1:25,000 Outdoor Leisure map) is a popular approach to the eastern end of the range and is easily followed along the east bank of the Allt a' Chuirn towards a grey quartzite ridge of Creag Dubh, seen ahead. Reaching the steeper scree, it is best to aim for the ridge to the left, where a cairn sits

on a commanding viewpoint below another cairn on the main crest above, which is found to be several yards to the east of the summit of Creag Dubh.

Looking along this ridge, the shattered pinnacles of the 'Black Men' or 'Black Carls' are seen, with the summit of Sgurr an Fhir Duibhe immediately beyond. A path along the crest is easily followed across the first tor of broken rock. The large blocks of the second stack are turned on a rough staircase on the splintered face overlooking the northern corrie. Regaining the centre of the ridge, the path crosses to its southern side where it follows a series of ledges to the head of a gully. A chockstone which abuts the ridge lies at the foot of the 30ft pitch below the cairn of Sgurr an Fhir Duibhe. This can be avoided by keeping to the south side of the rock-wall, where ledges provide an easier route to the cairn.

CHAPTER 23   WALK 5

Slioch 3217ft/980m
  (north top) 3215ft/980m
  Sgurr an Tuill Bhain 3058ft/933m

Looking to Slioch from Talladale or Bridge of Grudie, on the southern side of Loch Maree, there seems little possibility of breaching its western bastions. Closer inspection reveals the mountain to be less invincible than may at first be supposed for Meall Each and Sgurr an Tuill Bhain are less well-defended. Here, the western ramparts and vertical southern flank can be avoided by intruding into the deer sanctuary of Coire Tuill Bhain (Coire na Sleaghaich on the 1:25,000 maps), a hollow above Gleann Bianasdail.

The traditional route to the summit

A narrow road across the river to the east of Kinlochewe serves a cluster of cottages (Incheril) at the start of the path, which, beyond the meadows of Culaneilan, follows the boulder-strewn estuary of the Kinlochewe River.

Through fronds of silver birch at the water's edge, Slioch's buttressed walls

come into view, and above the path the high brows of crag on Beinn a' Mhuinidh mark the turn into Gleann Bianasdail, a deep U-trough drained by the Amhainn an Fhasaigh. Immediately beyond a foot-bridge spanning this stream the path divides, with the right branch beginning its steady pull towards the glen, which follows a fault line linking Loch Maree and Lochan Fada. Passing through the glen, the path reaches the 1000ft contour below the eastern outcrops of Sgurr an Tuill Bhain, before dipping to the shores of Lochan Fada. Before reaching this point the walker heading for Slioch will need to leave the main path and climb firstly a faint path and then steep heather slopes to gain the flattened crown of Sgurr Dubh (Meall Each on the one-inch maps), high above Loch Maree. More leisurely routes of ascent follow the stream into the upper basin of Coire Tuill Bhain (Coire na Sleaghaigh) or climb the easier terraces on the northern perimeter of this hollow.

From the summit of Sgurr Dubh, the vertical walls of sandstone are seen end-on, and a path can be seen scrambling up a narrow ridgeline, above a small tarn a little to the north-west of the cairn. The upper slopes of the mountain ease perceptibly on the pull to the summit triangulation pillar and the northern cairn (004691), which peers down on to the western cliffs.

Slioch's eastern spur is an earthy ridge studded with worn, rounded rocks, which runs out towards a grassier Sgurr an Tuill Bhain. Tumbling heather slopes then make for a speedy descent to the corrie, and the easy walk down to the Gleann Bianasdail path for a return to Kinlochewe.

Those with time to spare should follow the path to the eastern end of Lochan Fada, as the views along the loch and to the adjacent peaks show wild country at its best. An easy moorland crossing between the tarns of Loch an Sgeireach and Loch Gleann na Muice quickly finds a path falling to the track in Gleann na Muice, which, reaching the Heights of Kinlochewe, follows the river to Kinlochewe.

DUNDONNELL AND THE FISHERFIELD FOREST

Seven peaks lying deep in the last great wilderness in Britain, demanding long approach treks. These high tops are some of the finest viewpoints, if not the finest, in all Scotland and a visit to their summits on a clear day is an unforgettable experience.

RUADH STAC MOR   A'MHAIGHDEAN
Outstanding vantage points in the heart of the wild Fisherfield Forest.

BEINN A'CHLAIDHEIMH   SGURR BAN   MULLACH COIRE MHIC FHEARCHAIR   BEINN TARSUINN
A sterile and eerie top combined with a curious high-level table overlooking a remote sanctuary.

AN TEALLACH: BIDEIN A'GHLAS THUILL
This castellated mountain citadel offers an expedition of outstanding excitement and interest.

CHAPTER 24   **WALK 1**

Ruadh Stac Mor 3014ft/918m
A' Mhaighdean 3173ft/967m

A'Mhaighdean is considered to be the most remote Munro, as the nearest roads at Kinlochewe, Poolewe and Dundonnell, are all about nine miles distant. These mountains also enjoy the distinction of lying at the heart of an area considered to be the last great wilderness in Britain, with some of the most spectacular and rugged mountain scenery in these islands.

Without doubt the finest base for an ascent of these remote peaks is Shenavall, reached by a path from Dundonnell. The old one inch maps of the Ordnance Survey were not noted for their accuracy, for at the time of the original survey the owner of the ground was anxious to have as little disturbance as possible. Bad weather also played a part, with the result that several contours on A' Mhaighdean were omitted. Ruadh Stac Mor and Beinn a' Chlaidheimh also suffered similar fates, their narrow ridges appearing as flattened tops, which is certainly not the case, and it was therefore left to the re-survey to sketch in the detail and belatedly add these hills to the list of 3000ft peaks.

The crossing of the Abhainn Srath na Sealga below Shenavall in time of spate can be a difficult wade, often of thigh-deep proportions. In drier conditions a shallow crossing can be made near a clump of thorns below the cottage pastures. South of the river, heathery flats, punctured by deep runnels and small, oozy holes, are best avoided by following the river bank to the Abhainn Gleann na Muice. This stream is wide and full of large boulders,

and a passage should be sought several yards downstream from Larachantivore, as the bridge to the south of the cottage is now virtually non-existent. A path along the west bank of the stream joins a tributary for the climb into Gleann na Muice Beag, where a series of zig-zags carries the pass to a summit near Lochan Feith Mhic'-illean.

Ruadh Stac Mor
Hereabouts, turn across the moors and follow a stream to the plateau to the north of Ruadh Stac Mor, now dominant on the skyline ahead. Above two lochans a passage should be sought through a broken rock band mid-way up the hill, to reach screes below the summit, where a magnificent panorama of mountain walls, moors and lochans unfolds.

Several yards to the east of the summit Ordnance Survey post gaps may be found in the miniature crags on the southern face of the hill. A mass of stones falls to another band of crags above the drop to a saddle, where the pink sandstone meets the grey gneiss of A'Mhaighdean. Two scree-chutes break through the terraces, allowing a descent to just west of a saddle. If descending too far to the east, a grassy patch acts as guide to a way down through the lowest band of crag at the eastern edge of the saddle. A stalkers' path from the Carnmore path reaches the gap on an easier climb by way of Fuar Loch Mor.

A'Mhaighdean
On the opposite side of the gap, plates of rock lead up to mossy steps which, in turn, rise to the gravel of a flattened crown to the north of the summit tor. The tiny cairn of A' Mhaighdean lies at the edge of a wall which falls without interruption almost to the barren valley above the Dubh Loch, seen 3000ft below. The southern face of

Recommended Valley Base Dundonnell

Maps O.S. 1:50 000 Sheet 19; Bartholomews 1:100 000 Sheets 54 and 58.

Starting Point/Length and time for main itinerary
Walk 1 Shenavall (066810). 13 miles/3600ft of ascent, 6–9 hours.
Walk 2 Shenavall (066810). 13 miles/5810ft of ascent, 7–11 hours. (Dundonnell to Shenavall walk-in 4 miles/1100ft of ascent.)
Walk 3 Dundonnell (114850). 13 miles/5315ft of ascent, 7–11 hours.

the mountain is no less spectacular, for here too are shattered faces of plunging rock, with unsurpassed views.

An easy line of descent through a rocky corrie beneath Ruadh Stac Mor's eastern crags comes upon a moorland path near the head of Gleann na Muice, and this gives a pleasant walk beside the stream on the return to Shenavall.

Alternative approaches
Ruadh Stac Mor can be ascended by its eastern flank, but here the heathery slopes are steep and tiresome, and the views less interesting than those on the route previously described. The approach to A' Mhaighdean from Kinlochewe involves a time-consuming eleven-mile walk, aggravated by peat-hags once the track peters out at the eastern end of Lochan Fada. This walk is softened by the fine views along the loch, but the possibility of including Ruadh Stac Mor in the round holds less attraction if returning by the same route. From Carnmore, there is an entertaining scramble up and around the broken pinnacles straddling A' Mhaighdean's western ridge. With care these can be avoided by taking to the screes above Fuar Loch Mor, though snow may be found here often as late as May or June, and in such conditions the route can be a

little intimidating, especially if further difficulties are encountered on rocks greased by rain.

CHAPTER 24   WALK 2

Beinn a' Chlaidheimh 3000ft/914m
Sgurr Ban 3194ft/989m
Mullach Coire Mhic Fhearchair
   3326ft/1019m
   (east top) 3218ft/981m
Sgurr Dubh 3011ft/918m
Beinn Tarsuinn 3070ft/936m

Shenavall also provides the ideal base for a traverse of these peaks, the crossing of the Abhainn Srath na Sealga to the foot of the first of them providing the only serious obstacle (see Walk 1).

Beinn a' Chlaidheimh
The northern face of Beinn a' Chlaidheimh is of intimidating steepness, its lower bands of overgrown sandstone terraces providing a stiff ascent to the narrow quartzite ridge leading to the summit. The mountain provides uninterrupted panoramas of Ruadh Stac Mor and A' Mhaighdean. There are three cairns, sitting on the high points of undulations which appear to be of equal height. The southerly top claims to be the summit, now said to exceed 3000ft by the merest margin.

Scree is much in evidence on the long slide to the saddle east of Loch a' Bhrisidh.

Sgurr Ban
The northern slopes of Sgurr Ban plunge into this hollow, and a line just to the east of the corrie rim is the best aid to navigation, two tiny pools on the level ground there providing useful reference points should mist descend upon the col. Flat and totally devoid of vegetation, the summit covers several desolate acres where only the cairn at its centre has any significance for the wanderer. The quartzite screes are no less dense on the eastern slopes of the hill, where they fall to huge slabs above Loch an Nid.

Mullach Coire Mhic Fhearchair
From a short, barren col to the south of Sgurr Ban's cairn there is another stiff clamber to the distinctive top of Mullach Coire Mhic Fhearchair, crowned by a large cairn at a craggy edge overlooking upper Gleann na Muice. Long before Munro's Tables were revised it had been argued that this mountain possessed a second 'top' at the end of an escarped ridge running south-east from the summit. Identified as Sgurr Dubh (061729), the peak most probably took its name from the face of black slabs to be found at the eastern end of the ridge. Between it and the main summit there are some easy pinnacles and another point (056734) has been classified as the 'east top'. A small prominent knob, at the point of the angle where the

mountain's short south ridge turns westwards to Beinn Tarsuinn, can be passed on easier slopes to the east and south.

Beinn Tarsuinn
A short, mossy platform at the east end of Beinn Tarsuinn was for many years considered to be in excess of 3000ft, though never unreservedly accorded such status until re-survey in the 1970's. There is another curious table at the west end of the summit ridge, beyond which the narrower western end of the hill dips to a deep gully and crags in the defile at the head of Gleann na Muice. This is an obstacle in the way of those heading west to A' Mhaighdean which must be skirted to the south-west. Those returning to Shenavall should take an oblique line across the northern slopes to gain the path in Gleann na Muice.

The addition of A' Mhaighdean and Ruadh Stac Mor to complete the circuit of Gleann na Muice (see Walk 1) is feasible, but very time consuming and arduous.

Approach from Kinlochewe
It is possible to reach the easy southern slopes of Mullach Coire Mhic Fhearchair and Beinn Tarsuinn by a track from Kinlochewe, but other hills in the group are less easily reached, as any route including these tops will almost certainly require a traverse of the screes above Loch an Nid on a lengthy return to base; hence the continuing popularity of the Shenavall approach. A Kinlochewe/Shenavall traverse is an attractive expedition, but transport problems are likely to be too complex.

CHAPTER 24   WALK 3

An Teallach:
   Sgurr Fiona 3474ft/1059m
   Sgurr Creag an Eich 3335ft/1017m
   Lord Berkeley's Seat 3436ft/1047m
   Corrag Bhuidhe 3425ft/1036m
   Corrag Bhuidhe Buttress 3075ft/929m
   Stob Cadha Gobhlach 3145ft/959m
   Sail Liath 3129ft/954m
Bidein a' Ghlas Thuill 3484ft/1062m
   Glas Mheall Mor 3217ft/981m
   Glas Mheall Liath 3156ft/962m

The name An Teallach, some say, is derived from the travelling tinkers who worked their forges in its corries. It is more probable that the rock, seen at sunset giving off a reddish glow, was thought by the local inhabitants to resemble the embers of the smiddy forge which they patronised in the tiny hamlet of Dundonnell close by.

The Torridon sandstone has weathered to form turrets and towers set above the deep hollow of Loch Toll an Lochain, and the mountain can boast no fewer than ten

tops over 3000ft, to give one of the most spectacular traverses in the North-West Highlands. Munro gave it one main summit and numerous tops, presumably to underscore its identity as a single mountain massif. Logically, and when compared with his practice elsewhere, it should be regarded as a massif with two principal summits, each with related tops. All of this is an area of interminable controversy with a choice between tradition and logic — either way one is going to climb both the main heights on any valid ascent of the mountain. The traverse of the ridge can be made in a north-south or a south-north direction. The latter route is chosen here, so that after a long approach walk the dramatic section of the traverse begins at once, leaving a descent back to Dundonnell directly down the easy slopes of Glas Mheall Mor. This way also leaves the outlying spurs to be tackled after the traverse of Sgurr Fiona, according to weather, strength and taste.

Sail Liath
The Dundonnell to Shenavall track provides the access to the broad base of Sail Liath, and above the head of the pass worn sandstone terraces give an easy start to the day. Fans of quartzite covering the higher shoulders of this spur show a path along the lip of the northern corrie, and at the cairn ahead there are the first tantalising glimpses of the peaks yet to come.

Stob Cadha Gobhlach
Descending towards the next top, crumbling pillars line a crest to the head of the first of the two gullies of Cadha Gobhlach, the forked pass. A small rock stack, lying in an angle between these two gullies, provides an easy diversion to a fine viewpoint above the loch in the northern corrie. Beyond the second fork of the pass, there is an easy rise to the heathery top of Stob Cadha Gobhlach, whose flattened crown is crossed to a narrow neck at the head of another gully falling to Toll an Lochain.

Corrag Bhuidhe Buttress
A path on the hill-crest crosses a small lump to reach the towering wall at the end of the Corrag Bhuidhe Buttress. High on the face ahead, a short, difficult 'bad step' guards the exit to the pinnacles of Corrag Bhuidhe. Any apprehension about this exposed clamber can be discounted by rounding the foot of the wall to a path along a sandstone terrace on the western flank, which can be followed to the face below Sgurr Fiona and the western end of Corrag Bhuidhe, for a safer climb back to the ridge.

Corrag Bhuidhe
The pinnacled spine of Corrag Bhuidhe is unquestionably the most dramatic and awe-inspiring feature of this grand mountain cirque, a feeling heightened on

the 'bad step' at the end of the southern buttress. This pitch of 30ft, graded Difficult, can be turned by a move out on to airy stances directly above the void of Toll an Lochain. Three towers top the narrow ridge of Corrag Bhuidhe, which plunges 1700ft to this corrie floor, though here the worst of the exposure can be avoided on the terraces above Strath na Sealga.

Coming in the opposite direction, from Sgurr Fiona, the summit of Corrag Bhuidhe can be reached by a path under the western edge of the tors lining the edge of the northern cliffs. Only in the immediate vicinity of the summit's narrow platform is there any sensational drop. A tiny cairn distinguishes this knob from the others, several of which give modest scrambles to more airy viewpoints overlooking the pit of Toll an Lochain, and the untamed mountains of Letterewe and Fisherfield to the south.

Lord Berkeley's Seat

Between Corrag Bhuidhe and Sgurr Fiona, Lord Berkeley's Seat leans out from the ridge, buttressed by a short, sharp precipice. A move on the edge of this colossal drop reaches an exhilarating perch from which to inspect the grim walls of Corrag Bhuidhe.

Sgurr Fiona

Sgurr Fiona is a stony peak surmounted by a blunt pencil of stone, a perfect example of the mason's art, which says much for the affection in which this particular stack is held, for there are many who feel that this would be a more fitting crown to An Teallach than Bidein a' Ghlas Thuill, which it fails to surpass by the narrow margin of 9ft. There is some measure of compensation as, since 1981, the summit has enjoyed 'mountain' status.

Sgurr Creag an Eich

The spur of Sgurr Creag an Eich to the north-west of Sgurr Fiona is sandwiched between a small escarpment above Coire Mor an Teallaich and the lip of the mountain's south-west corrie.

Those who are based on Shenavall might well choose the southern slopes of this top for a descent. It is worth noting that the scree-filled corrie here can be treacherous as the larger stones are unsuitable for scree-running. A stream rising high on Sgurr Fiona drains this basin, and near the lower lip waterfalls drop into a small chasm, and then a larger gorge. The stream should therefore be crossed in the corrie when heading back to Shenavall.

Bidein a' Ghlas Thuill

Continuing along the main crest of the mountain from Sgurr Fiona, take a slightly northerly course and look for a path in the screes above Coire Mor an Teallaich. This avoids the rib of a false ridge pushing a crag out towards Coire Toll an Lochain, lying a little east of the true line of descent to the col. Bidein a' Ghlas Thuill can be reached by a 400ft climb from the gap (triangulation pillar).

Glas Mheall Liath

To the east, slopes fall steeply to a narrow neck on the ridge of Glas Mheall Liath. This spur separates the tarned hollow of Toll an Lochain from the deep heather basin of Coire a' Ghlas Thuill to the north. A staircase of large terraces at the eastern end of this spur drops to the corridor of Coir' a' Ghiubhsachain which, on its eastern wall, is fringed by a line of awkward crags. It is therefore simpler to leave the massif from the final top, Glas Mheall Mor.

Glas Mheall Mor

This is reached by an easy descent to the north of Bidein a' Ghlas Thuill followed by a pleasant walk along the near-level ridge heading north-east. From the cairn steep slopes lead down to the east to the 2000ft contour by the burn draining Coire a' Ghlas Thuill. From here, easy-angled heather terraces lead back to the starting point by Dundonnell House.

THE FANNICHS AND THE ULLAPOOL ROAD

Contrasting mountains on either side of the main road to the north-west – the Fannichs provide a homogeneous group of rounded peaks; Ben Wyvis, a large Cairngorm-like plateau; the Beinn Dearg group offers craggy tops amidst desolate moorland – some easily accessible, others less so.

AN COILEACHAN   MEALL GORM   SGURR MOR   BEINN LIATH MHOR FANNAICH
MEALL A'CHRASGAIDH   SGURR NAN CLACH GEALA   SGURR NAN EACH
Smooth, grassy tops that provide a very strenuous walk, but with unexceptional views.

A'CHAILLEACH   SGURR BREAC
Views of An Teallach and the Fisherfield Forest add interest to the traverse of two unassuming hills.

BEN WYVIS: GLAS LEATHAD MOR
A vast, characterless, sprawling massif which may well discourage anything but the briefest visit.

AM FAOCHAGACH
Although the views from the summit are worthwhile the walk itself is tedious in the extreme.

EIDIDH NAN CLACH GEALA   MEALL NAN CEAPRAICHEAN   CONA'MHEALL   BEINN DEARG
An intricate knot of mountains that can be conveniently penetrated by long easy-angled corries.

SEANA BHRAIGH
Four alternative approaches give access to this isolated, crag-rimmed mountain.

CHAPTER 25   WALK 1

An Coileachan 3015ft/923m
Meall Gorm 3174ft/949m
  (south-east top) 3026ft/922m
Sgurr Mor 3637ft/1110m
  Carn na Criche 3148ft/961m
  Meall nam Peithirean 3196ft/974m
Beinn Liath Mhor Fannaich 3129ft/954m
Meall a' Chrasgaidh 3062ft/934m
Sgurr nan Clach Geala 3581ft/1093m
Sgurr nan Each 3026ft/923m

These mountains, collectively known as the Fannichs, are a tightly-knit group of summits situated south of Braemore at the junction of the Ullapool and Dundonnell roads.

The peaks can be climbed piecemeal by using various approaches from the north, but the complete traverse of the seven mountains is best attempted from the south where the spurs at the other end of the range come close to a private road to Fannich Lodge. A locked gate at Grudie Bridge (on the A832 at the west end of Loch Luichart) prevents indiscriminate use of this road, but by prior arrangement access can be obtained (see introductory notes).

An Coileachan
Crags on the headwall of Garbh Choire Mor are seen on the way to Fannich

Lodge, and smaller crags scar the slopes above Loch nan Eun, lying to the north of An Coileachan's cairn. The steep spur to the south of Garbh Choire Mor provides a magnificent view of the crags, but an easier way to the summit is by its southern slopes above Loch Fannich. To the north-west, a broad ridge stretches to Meall Gorm.

Meall Gorm (Meallan Rairigidh)
Meall Gorm's two tops are little more than high spots on a broad back, the highest of which, Meallan Rairigidh, is recognized by a windbreak shelter near its summit cairn. The main ridge-crest rolls westwards to the start of a long drag to Meall nam Peithirean, an insignificant cairned point at the head of the spur of Druim Reidh. This ridge displays the longest wall of crag in the Fannichs, and the peaty Allt a' Choire Mhoir and Allt a' Choire Bhig, guarding its approaches, detract from it as a direct southerly route to Sgurr Mor.

Sgurr Mor
The highest cairn of the Fannichs sits near the lip of a deep corrie whose crags break up a short distance to the south-east, where a long steep slope leads to the wide ridge running north-east to the hump of Beinn Liath Mhor Fannaich.

Beinn Liath Mhor Fannaich
This summit is awkwardly placed, distanced from the main ridge, and those

Recommended Valley Base Garve.
Maps O.S. 1:50 000 Sheets 19 and 20; Bartholomews 1:100 000 Sheets 54, 55 and 58.
Starting Point/Length and time for main itinerary
Walk 1 Fannich Lodge (218660) 15 miles/6 650ft of ascent, 8 – 12 hours. (Grudie Bridge to Fannich Lodge walk-in 7 miles – permission to take car by prior arrangement with estates or Hydro Board, Grudie Power Station – Tel. Garve 209.)
Walk 2 A832 near Loch a'Bhraoin (162760). 10 miles/3 850ft of ascent, 5 – 8 hours.
Walk 3 Garbat (413679). 14 miles/4 350ft of ascent, 7 – 11 hours.
Walk 4 Loch Vaich dam (345749). 9 miles/2 450ft of ascent, 4 – 6 hours.
Walk 5 Inverlael (182852). 15 miles/5 100ft of ascent, 8 – 12 hours.
Walk 6 Coiremor (305888). 4 miles/2 100ft of ascent, 2 – 3 hours. (Oykel Bridge to Coiremor walk-in 10 miles/620ft of ascent.)

attempting to complete the major traverse must retrace their steps to Sgurr Mor. It is conveniently placed for a quick ascent from Loch Droma however, and could therefore be left to be 'tidied up' later. Those energetic enough to include it will be able to enjoy a good 800ft of stiff re-ascent to regain the ridge, which turns slightly west beyond Sgurr Mor's cairn towards the flattened mound of Carn na Criche.

Meall a' Chrasgaidh
From Carn na Criche another detour, down the wide slope to the north-west, leads to the lump of Meall a' Chrasgaidh.

Sgurr nan Clach Geala

Heading back south the first landmark is the saddle Am Biachdaich, a lush, grassy scoop replete with a tiny lochan tucked under the northern flank of Sgurr nan Clach Geala. The sharp rise to Sgurr nan Clach Geala is distinctive enough, though in mist the depressions round the head of Am Biachdaich may be slightly confusing when attempting to find the ridge above the precipitous slope of Choire Mhoir. Sgurr nan Clach Geala is the only summit in the group with an Ordnance Survey post, here commanding a small top above a craggy eastern face.

Sgurr nan Each

The long spur to the south deflects the ridge from its westerly course, and here the little horn of Sgurr nan Each can be seen beyond a col where there is an easy descent to the Allt a' Choire Mhoir. This is not recommended as easier slopes of heather fan out to the south of Sgurr nan Each's cairn, descending to the track from Nest Cottage, thereby avoiding the bogs in the moor which, if descending Choire Mhoir, would have to be crossed on the return to Fannich Lodge.

Approaches from the north

Several faded paths run from the Ullapool and Dundonnell roads to the lower slopes of the western tops. To the east of the narrow stone bridge carrying the A832 Dundonnell road over the Abhainn Cuileig, a path crosses the moor to the Allt an Eas Bhig, to disappear in a large corrie beneath Meall a' Chrasgaidh. At the first bend immediately west of Braemore, on the Dundonnell road, another path crosses towards the broad spur of Creag Raineach Mor, where a line of cairns can be followed to a more distinct path climbing to a cairn just below the level of the saddle between Meall a' Chrasgaidh and Carn na Criche.

A mile to the west of Loch Droma, the path following the east bank of the Allt a' Mhadaidh is so faint that a course along either bank is just as convenient. The ground to the north of Loch a' Mhadaidh is very rough and boggy, and the pool, overshadowed by the crags of Carn na Criche, can be passed on its eastern shore on a steep climb to the northern spur of Sgurr Mor. There is a more reliable track from Loch Droma along an aqueduct pipe to the Allt a' Mhadaidh. Still further east, the Abhainn an Torrain Duibh and its tributaries can be followed to the small tarns at the foot of Meall Gorm, but again the boggy heath is a poor introduction to the long walk along the ridge.

CHAPTER 25   **WALK 2**

A' Chailleach 3276ft/999m
Sgurr Breac 3281ft/1000m
    Toman Coinich 3040ft/937m

These peaks are collectively known as the West Fannich Group. From the A832 ('Destitution road') near Loch a' Bhraoin, they appear as one massive hill rising above the stunted trees of a lower slope. A track runs to a footbridge on the Abhainn Cuileig below the loch and continues south for about half a mile to an awkward stream-crossing at the start of the pass running below the foot of a precipitous eastern wall of Sgurr Breac. A' Chailleach's summit is similarly defended by rocky bluffs on the snout of Sron na Coibhre at the end of a northern ridge, seen above Loch a' Bhraoin.

The easiest route to the summits uses the spur of Druim Reidh, which thrusts out towards Loch a' Bhraoin. The ease of this ascent compensates for the inconvenience on the summit ridge of having to re-track to take in both the main summits. The small crags which punctuate its eastern slope are easily avoided on grassy terraces to the right, and once on the broad ridge above, easier ground rises to the cairn of Toman Coinich.

A' Chailleach

Toman Coinich lies in the centre of a broad ridge linking the larger mounds of A' Chailleach and Sgurr Breac. The steep wall of the hill's southern face curves under the narrower summit ridge of A' Chailleach, turning south-east to the point of An Sguman to create the amphitheatre of the Nest of Fannich. To reach the mountain involves a 300ft descent and a 500ft ascent. On the return the southern slopes of Toman Coinich can be traversed to gain the col to its east below the ridge leading to Sgurr Breac. In winter conditions it would be best to keep to the ridge, however, and it is worth noting that in winter the northern escarpments are particularly prone to cornicing.

Sgurr Breac

Sgurr Breac had its height enhanced by some 40ft on the re-survey, and its cairn is now calculated to be higher than that of its twin. Its great hump rises from the head of Druim Reidh, to a summit field set above a craggy northern face, which fringes a broad ridge to the pass at the mountain's east end. This pass is reached by a descent that first heads due east to avoid the steep north-east corrie, then gains the south-east ridge. In mist this will require precise route finding. Facing this line of descent, the Fannichs are seen as a series of rolling ridges dominated by Sgurr Mor. From the head of the pass a grassy path is followed down to the Loch a' Bhraoin track with the

---

aforementioned stream-crossing south of the loch.

CHAPTER 25   **WALK 3**

Ben Wyvis:
Glas Leathad Mor 3433ft/1046m
    An Cabar 3106ft/950m
    Tom a' Choinnich 3134ft/955m
    Glas Leathad Beag 3044ft/928m
    Fiaclach 3018ft/919m

Travellers approaching Inverness on the A9 and looking north from Drumossie Muir, can see Ben Wyvis in the distance across the Beauly Firth.

Above the Garve to Ullapool road, its broad western flank provides the shortest route to the summit, involving a steep 2500ft climb. A gate in a forest fence behind Garbat Cottage identifies the start of a track through the forest, which leads to a squelchy path following the old drove route across the Bealach Mor. Above the pass, a line of rocky outcrops on the face of An Cabar supports a steep ramp of heather, climbing to the mountain's level crest. This runs in a straight line north-east to the summit of Glas Leathad Mor.

The Allt a' Bhealaich Mhoir curves round the eastern flank of the hill, where the wide, heathery hollow of Coire Feithriabhach is easily crossed to a spur rising to another broad-backed ridge above Coire na Feola. A fence along this crest meets the broad shoulder of An Cabar on the mountain's plateau a little to the south of its highest point, Glas Leathad Mor, which has an Ordnance Survey post surrounded by a low wall.

A steep descent leads north to a col, followed by a short rise to the cairn of Tom a' Choinnich. This top commands a fine view across the great north-west slope also called Glas Leathad Mor. A pony track zig-zags down the north-west nose of Tom a' Choinnich to the spur of Carn Gorm, whose heather slopes are easily crossed to rejoin the track leading down through the Garbat woods. The two remaining tops at the north-eastern end of the plateau can be reached by a straightforward walk from Tom a' Choinnich, but they are widely spread and might be better taken in during a traverse of the peak, with a descent to the valley of the River Glass if transport can be organized.

The eastern approach

At the bridge over the River Glass, in the centre of Evanton, a road (signposted 'Assynt') can be followed as far as a locked gate at Eileanach. Lower in the glen, a track leaves the road near Redburn (near a phone box) and runs towards the confluence of the Allt Coire Misirich and the Allt nan Caorach. Upward progress is greatly impeded by extensive afforestation along the whole of the mountain's eastern flanks. The one good access, a stalkers' path (not shown on O.S. maps) climbing the snout of Fiachlach from the lodge track (507727) is also obstructed by a forest fence. These obstacles are factors which further commend the Garbat approach.

CHAPTER 25   WALK 4

Am Faochagach 3120ft/954m

Am Faochagach, seen as a broad heather slope to the north of Loch Glascarnoch, has few attractions, its only asset being a westward view from the summit to the impressive hollow of Coire Ghranda.

To the east of the Aultguish Inn, at Black Bridge, a road runs up Strath Vaich to the Loch Vaich dam. Here, to avoid a direct assault on the steep hillside above the woods, follow the shore to the Allt Glas Toll Mor, where a glimpse of a fine waterfall relieves the monotony of the moorland tramp. The long ridge to the north of this stream, in common with all the spurs on this great heap, is a cheerless plod to the untidy pile of stones which serves as a summit cairn on the west side of the plateau.

The peak can also be attempted from the Dirrie More at the western end of Loch Glascarnoch, but this approach is impeded by deep rivers that present major problems or extensive diversions in spate. From the south end of Loch Coire Lair, slopes climb steeply to a jumble of boulders below the summit. In drought conditions it would be a suitable route but there is no saving in terms of distance from the Strath Vaich route.

CHAPTER 25   WALK 5

Beinn Dearg 3547ft/1084m
Cona' Mheall 3214ft/980m
Meall nan Ceapraichean 3205ft/977m
  Ceann Garbh 3075ft/967m
Eididh nan Clach Geala 3039ft/928m

From Ullapool, looking to the head of Loch Broom, Beinn Dearg and the lesser tops to the north are the broad humps which fill the skyline. They are best tackled as a round of Gleann na Sguaib or in a traverse from the Dirrie More to Gleann na Sguaib, during which the energetic might feel able to add Seana Bhraigh (see Walk 6) to the itinerary. Another possibility is to take in all the peaks except Eididh nan Clach Geala in a round of Coire Lair starting from the Dirrie More. This itinerary could then take in Am Faochagach. Such a grouping would then leave Eididh nan Clach Geala to be climbed during an expedition to Seana Bhraigh starting from Inverlael. On

balance, the three walks described seem to offer the least arduous and most varied ways of tackling the mountains.

Approach from Inverlael
As most of the hills in this group form a crescent around the head of Gleann na Sguaib, their traverse in a single expedition is best attempted from Inverlael, at the head of Loch Broom. A track above Inverlael Lodge crosses the River Lael in the middle of the woods, and runs to the boundary fence (the third turn-off to the left finds the bridge, beyond which follow the track to the right for Gleann na Sguaib). Here, a well-worn path continues to the head of the glen below long lines of crag on Beinn Dearg's western spur. At the waterfall (Eas Fionn) a branch track (left) works up to the slopes below Lochan a' Chnapaich. From this position Eididh nan Clach Geala's stony summit can be gained by a route up its west spur, passing a tiny lochan studded into the crest of the ridge. The descent to another tiny pool, on the saddle above Lochan a' Chnapaich is straightforward and is followed by a steep pull to the east ridge of Meall nan Ceapraichean which can then be followed, over a subsidiary top, to its summit. This subsidiary top, Ceann Garbh, throws out a broad eastern ridge towards the bald hill of Cnap Coire Loch Tuath which is crossed for the turn south to the bland slopes of Am Faochagach, when doing the round of Coire Lair.

An easier route to a high level continues up Gleann na Sguaib to pools on the dip (Bealach Coire Ghranda) between Meall nan Ceapraichean and Beinn Dearg, and within easy striking distance of the former peak. From these pools it will also be necessary to make a diversion to the east to take in Cona' Mheall.

Cona' Mheall
Cona' Mheall is a flat-topped ridge supported by broken crags, which form one wall of Coire Ghranda. The peak is a good vantage point for viewing Beinn Dearg's imposing east face, a bank of 1500ft crags rimming the other side of the corrie. Cona' Mheall used to be one of the few mountains in Scotland which did not possess a cairn, but such a blight has now appeared on the north-eastern corner of the ridge. The south-eastern end of the ridge is steep and rocky, and requires care if it is used for a descent past the entrance of Coire Ghranda to Coire Lair. The boggy ground of this corrie and the difficulty of crossing the lower reaches of the Allt a' Gharbhrain in spate conditions should also be borne in mind if using this route to quit the mountain.

Beinn Dearg
After re-tracing one's steps around the head of Coire Ghranda to the tarns on the bealach (there is a convenient route into the

corrie beside the stream which tumbles to the loch from the saddle), the rough slope to Beinn Dearg must be tackled. Here a wall can be followed to the 3400ft contour, where, turning to the west, it runs down the long escarped spur above Gleann na Sguaib. The summit lies about 300 yards to the south of this turn. The wall continues to provide a guideline on the long, gradual descent to the forest above Inverlael, with views to Loch Broom and the Summer Isles to add the final touch to the day.

Approach from the Dirrie More
From the A835, near the eastern end of Loch Droma, a moorland path can be followed until it peters out near the Allt a' Gharbhrain, whose stream must be crossed, preferably further up the glen, to reach the broad heathery shoulders of Beinn Dearg. The easiest slope is that to the west of a wide south-facing corrie, leading to a grassy level on the 2750ft contour, a short distance below the final 500ft to the summit cairn.

If Cona' Mheall is chosen as the first peak, take into account the soft going in Glen Lair and the sodden moors around Loch a' Gharbhrain. After rain, the Allt a' Gharbhrain can be in terrifying spate, and a formidable hazard on a demanding moorland crossing.

CHAPTER 25   WALK 6

Seana Bhraigh 3040ft/927m

This peak is situated in an isolated position to the north of the Beinn Dearg group at a distance that makes its inclusion in a Beinn Dearg traverse a little impractical. Taking it as a separate expedition allows the walker (with motor transport) the choice of four different approaches: from Inverlael or Glen Achall on the Ullapool side; from Strath Mulzie to the north; and from Gleann Beag to the east. Each involves a considerable walk, on balance the Inverlael route is best as, although slightly longer, it avoids a long approach up remote valley tracks and allows the option of including Eididh nan Clach Geala (see Walk 5) in the itinerary.

Approach from Inverlael
Follow the route described in Walk 5 to Glensguaib and then take a path up through the forest to the spur of Druim na Saobhaidhe. The path continues across the basin of the Allt Gleann a Mhadaidh towards the broad slopes to the west of Eididh nan Clach Geala. A faint path rounding the hill's northern edge turns into the gap of Coir' an Lochain Sgeirich, on a gradual climb to a flat saddle, where, looking north, the expansive flank of Seana Bhraigh is seen across Gleann a' Chadha Dheirg. This crag-fringed trough bars immediate access to the mountain's

summit, which must be approached on a diversion to the north-east across the green folds of a broad ridge around the head of the glen. This is a nondescript trek, but persevere, for the northern precipices of Seana Bhraigh fall suddenly and dramatically, 1300ft to the crater of Loch Luchd Choire, whose walls sweep round to a craggy Creag an Duine, above an even deeper loch-basin to the north, to make this one of the most impressive corries in the Highlands.

Approach from Oykel Bridge

To the north, a minor road runs from Oykel Bridge to Duag Bridge, whence a track up Strath Mulzie is motorable as far as Corriemulzie Lodge (seek parking permission at the shepherd's cottage). Beyond this point, the track runs through bare, green hills, becoming progressively more rugged as the hills close in, with the impressive wall of Seana Bhraigh appearing in bold profile above the river-crossing,

as the turn is made into the narrow corridor of Loch a' Choire Mhoir.

For many travellers, and especially the cross-country backpacker, the initial objective might well be the lonely cottage by the loch. Above the outfall to the tarn a blunt snout of steep grass, broken by outcrops (turned on the right), sees the start of a stiff clamber to the summit of Seana Bhraigh by a ridge overlooking the spectacular hollow of the Luchd Choire.

Approach from Glen Achall

Above Ullapool, a road passing the Ullapool Quarry leads to an estate track (seek permission from West Rhidorroch Estate) running through Glen Achall. At the head of the glen a wooden suspension bridge spans the river, giving access to Rhidorroch Old Lodge (East Rhidorroch Lodge) and a path which continues into the hills to reach lower Glen Douchary. Alternatively, continue along the main track to Loch an Daimh, where another

path runs up into Glen Douchary. At a waterfall, break up the slopes of Meall nam Bradhan on the left (east). This allows a gradual climb that gives access to a grassy saddle at the foot of the west ridge of Seana Bhraigh, which provides a straightforward climb to the top.

Approach from Gleann Beag

Gleann Beag, to the east, can be reached by taking the road which runs up Strath Carron from Ardgay, the small village to the south of Bonar Bridge. At the head of Strath Carron, a track (unsuitable for cars) turns off to Deanich Lodge, which is also served by a similar track from Strath Vaich to the south. These two routes meet a little to the south of the lodge, and continue west into Gleann Beag as far as a bridge about a mile east of Glenbeg cottage. The stream of the Abhainn a' Ghlinne Bhig affords a natural route into the hills, and is easily followed to Loch a' Chadha Dheirg on the ridge to the south of Seana Bhraigh.

CHAPTER 26

ASSYNT AND THE FAR NORTH

Isolated mountains which though close to roads are difficult to reach by public transport. They command extensive panoramas embracing the barren heartland of Caithness and Sutherland.

BEN HOPE
This lone sentinel can be climbed quickly, leaving time for Ben Klibreck later in the day.

BEN KLIBRECK: MEALL NAN CON
A plain hill with a summit conveniently near the road. Moorland views predominate.

CONIVAL   BEN MORE ASSYNT
Mountains built on ancient beds of Lewisian Gneiss. The resulting screes give uncompromising ascents, culminating in a grand traverse above an unearthly landscape of lochan-studded moors.

CHAPTER 26	WALK 1

Ben Hope 3042ft/927m

Ben Hope, the most northerly of the 3000ft peaks of Britain, lies beside the lonely road between Altnaharra and Hope Lodge.

The traditional route to the summit starts at the cottages at Altnacaillich, near the ruined broch of Dun Dornaigil, where a path climbing beside the waterfalls of the Allt na Caillich can be followed to the grassy slope of Leitir Mhuiseil, a gentle rise giving way to a steeper incline leading to the summit. By striking up the hill from a cowshed to the north of Altnacaillich (finger-post 'Ben Hope way up'), a break in the western crags provides a more direct

line to the wide terrace above the escarpment. This ascent is steep but perfectly straightforward, pushing purposefully up the first 1000ft. Turning to the north, the edge of cliffs buttressing the mountain's summit can be followed, and higher on the hill a series of cairns near this drop confirms the correct line of ascent.

In poor visibility, a large cairn near the upper limit of the crags may be mistaken for the highest point, which is actually a few steps to the north-east, at an Ordnance Survey post on a grassy level guarded on three sides by crags, with more steep, broken ground falling away to the north.

If the mountain is approached from the north, a path rising from the head of Loch Hope can be followed for a short distance

Recommended Valley Bases Lairg or Altnaharra and Inchnadamph

Maps O.S. 1:50 000 Sheets 9, 15 and 16; Bartholomews 1:100 000 Sheets 58, 59 and 60.

Starting Point/Length and time for main itinerary
Walk 1 Altnacaillich (461477). 4 miles/3000ft of ascent, 3–5 hours.
Walk 2 Crask Inn (524246). 12 miles/2950ft of ascent, 5–8 hours.
Walk 3 Inchnadamph (251218). 11 miles/3700ft of ascent, 5–8 hours.

in the direction of Dubh-loch na Beinne, a tarn lying on the terrace at the foot of the mountain's north-western corner. Above the lochan an ascent can be made to the narrow northern ridge, where a 30ft section of steep rock gives spectacular scrambling. The difficulty can be avoided by moving left (east) under the cliffs to regain the ridge higher up via an obvious gully. This ridge is by far the best route up Ben Hope, and gives the walker grand views of the northern cliffs.

CHAPTER 26   WALK 2

Ben Klibreck:
Meall nan Con 3154ft/961m

Ben Klibreck (also known as Beinn Cleith Bric), a bland hill overlooking the tiny hamlet of Altnaharra, seventeen miles north of Lairg, lies in the heart of the great open moors that stretch across the old county of Sutherland.

The mountain is most frequently climbed from its western side by one of several possible routes from the A836 between Altnaharra and the Crask Inn. Heather slopes rise above the head of a small pass to the lowly top of Cnoc Sgriodain, where an easy ridge to the short prow of Meall nan Con is seen. Those making the ascent from Altnaharra may opt to follow the road half-a-mile south, to find the track leading to Klibreck farm. Here the tiny Klibreck Burn can be joined for an easy walk to Loch nan Uan, a small tarn at the foot of the steep north-western flank of the hill. This can, of course, be reached more directly from the A836 near Vagastie. A short, stiff pull leads to a pleasant, grassy col lying a little west of the summit's nose, which is gained by a steep final pull. Striding high above Loch Naver, seen almost 3000ft below, the broad, grassy ridge is a fine promenade to the spur of Meall Ailein, where a cairn commemorates some aviators who lost

their lives on the mountain. From here, those who started at Klibreck can return by steep, easy, grassy slopes to the north. For those returning to Crask Inn, a descent down either Meall Ailein or the spur of Meall an Eoin leads to a path beside Loch Choire and Loch a' Bhealaich, which passes several picturesque cascades in the gap of the Bealach Easach. Reaching the open moor of Srath a' Chraisg the roof of the Crask Inn appears ahead to welcome the traveller back to the road.

CHAPTER 26   WALK 3

Ben More Assynt 3273ft/998m
  (south top) 3200ft/975m
Conival 3234ft/987m

Ben More Assynt and Conival are the highest mountains in Sutherland, but Conival (also known as Cona-mheall) is the only one of the two visible from Inchnadamph, from which most ascents are made. A little to the north of the Inchnadamph Hotel, a rough track to Glenbain in Gleann Dubh continues as a path to a ford on the River Traligill (near Nature Conservancy sign).

Conival

At the sign keep to the northern bank of the stream, as far as the head of the glen. From here a tortuous 2000ft climb is needed to gain the saddle between Beinn an Fhurain and Conival avoiding, as far as possible, the rough ground beside the stream. Near the head of the saddle a cairn marks the start of a sharp, quartzite ridge to Conival's summit O.S. triangulation

pillar. Great blocks of quartzite also cover the steeper faces of the mountain above Gleann Dubh and an eastern flank directly below the summit, so that climbs by these routes are particularly savage.

Ben More Assynt

The backbone of the massif turns eastwards from the summit of Conival to provide a linking ridge to Ben More Assynt. One side of the spine falls precipitously to Dubh Loch Mor, and the other drops sharply to moors covered in myriads of lochans. Care is needed on the rocky knots of the ridge, especially in the wet when the quartzite is very slippery.

From the shattered summit of Ben More Assynt, an arête runs south-east above steep, gully-seamed walls falling away to Dubh Loch Mor. Slabs cutting across the narrowest part of the crest shape several bad steps, which must be negotiated to reach the cairn of the south top. Until this is reached, plates of gneiss lining the face of the hill make descents to the corrie exceedingly hazardous, but a little to the south of the cairn a broad gully provides a route to the boggy hollow. Dubh Loch Mor is passed to reach an obvious defile between Conival and the craggy shoulder of Breabag Tarsuinn.

A stalkers' path gives an alternative route from the corrie along the infant River Oykel to Benmore Lodge, whence a track crosses the moors to reach the road about nine miles south-east of Inchnadamph. As an approach route, this eight-mile-walk to the summit of Ben More Assynt compares unfavourably with the five miles from Inchnadamph.

CHAPTER 27

THE BLACK CUILLIN OF SKYE

The most adventurous range of mountains in Britain, whose proximity to the sea causes fickle weather conditions. All but one of the peaks lie on a narrow ridge (approximately seven miles long and rarely below 3000ft), characterised by rocky towers and pinnacles with considerable exposure.

SGURR DUBH MOR   SGURR NAN EAG
Jagged peaks gained by Coir' a' Ghrunnda or, more dramatically, from Coruisk.

SGURR ALASDAIR   SGURR MHIC CHOINNICH
INACCESSIBLE PINNACLE
Three craggy summits demanding rock-climbing skills for a logical traverse.

SGURR NA BANACHDICH   SGURR A'GHREADAIDH
SGURR A'MHADAIDH
Less assertive peaks further along the ridge demand sustained scrambling.

BRUACH NA FRITHE   AM BASTEIR   SGURR NAN GILLEAN
Sharp teeth, again involving rock-climbing to avoid tiresome diversions.

BLA BHEINN
A well positioned summit giving a grand ascent with interesting views.

Recommended Valley Base Glen Brittle

Maps O.S. 1:50 000 Sheet 32; Bartholomews 1:100 000 Sheet 54; O.S. 1:25 000 *The Cuillin and Torridon Hills*; Scottish Mountaineering Trust. 1:15 000 Sheet *The Black Cuillin, Island of Skye*.

Starting Point/Length and time for main itinerary
Walk 1 Glen Brittle House (411213). 9 miles/3900ft of ascent, 5–8 hours.
Walk 2 Glen Brittle (413208). 9 miles/5600ft of ascent, 6–9 hours.
Walk 3 Glen Brittle (411216). 9 miles/4450ft of ascent, 5–8 hours.
Walk 4 Sligachan (480298). 9 miles/3900ft of ascent, 5–8 hours.
Walk 5 Loch Slapin (561216). 4 miles/3100ft of ascent, 3–5 hours.

The Cuillin of Skye
'Skye weather' is notoriously fickle and frequently the ambitions of climber and walker are thwarted by the heavy mists and incessant rain which many have come to regard as synonymous with the Cuillin. All but one of the 12 mountains in this group lie on a single ridge, which is a series of rocky towers and pinnacles linked by a narrow arête approximately seven miles in length and rarely falling below the 3000ft contour. Navigation presents a serious problem, as the rock is magnetic and the compass is therefore of little value. Such is the attractive force exercised that it is possible to find significant variations within the space of a few yards, and at times the compass needle may go positively berserk. The compass problems are compounded by the inadequacies of the

conventional maps in representing the actual ridge. The old one-inch maps and the newer metric maps are unable to show the various ridges and peaks with sufficient clarity. Only the larger-scale map produced by the Scottish Mountaineering Trust provides a clear picture, and it is highly recommended. Those who visit the Cuillin should familiarize themselves as much as possible with the general layout of the corries, ridges and bealachs (passes) before venturing on to the peaks, for if caught unexpectedly in the mist there is no substitute for a sound knowledge of the potential safe escape routes from the high tops.

CHAPTER 27   WALK 1

Sgurr Dubh Mor 3089ft/944m
Sgurr Dubh na Da Bheinn 3069ft/938m
Sgurr nan Eag 3037ft/924m

A path from the Glen Brittle Memorial Hut crosses the Allt Coire na Banachdich downstream of the Eas Mor (waterfall) joining a similar path from the Glen Brittle campsite, and climbs to the entrance to Coire Lagan. From the campsite a poorer path takes a more direct line across the moors to the foot of Sron na Ciche.

Coir' a' Ghrunnda
Beyond a prominent rock the path turns the base of Sron na Ciche by a steep bank,

where, passing through a natural portal between the hill-slope and a large outcrop, it begins the climb into the hidden bowl of Coir' a' Ghrunnda. Huge plates of rock come into view on the lip of an upper couloir, with the great wall of Sgurr Sgumain appearing to the left. Moving closer to the base of these cliffs the path (well-cairned) treads scree as it continues, scrambling through a large boulderfield, to reach the smooth wall of vertical slabs. Here, look to the left for a narrow cleft. A squeeze up the groove, a short traverse across the rock, and a scramble beside a stream brings to hand a large cairn on the edge of slabs which cross the couloir to Loch Coir' a' Ghrunnda. A backdrop of ragged scree climbs to a ridge-wall where the deep cleft of the infamous Thearlaich-Dubh Gap is seen. The Sgurr Thearlaich side of this is a vertical 80ft pitch of Very Difficult climbing and from below, the lower wall, seen to the right, seems equally precipitous, which it is.

Sgurr nan Eag
The easier exit lies to the right of the corrie on the broken walls of a small point above the Bealach a' Garbh-choire (Pass of the rough corrie), the easiest crossing at the south end of the Cuillin ridge. Moderately-angled scree leads on to the crest at the northern end of Sgurr nan Eag, from where the summit is easily attained. This approach is recommended in preference to the 2000ft of scree on the mountain's southern flank, which is soul-destroying and best avoided.

Sgurr Dubh Mor
An easy scramble up the rock steps on the face left of the prominent boss of Caisteal a'Garbh-choire leads to the ridge and the cairn of Sgurr Dubh na Da Bheinn. On the Coruisk side of the cairn lies a sharp 100ft dip to a short saddle, beyond which a ridge-path can be seen climbing the face of Sgurr Dubh Mor. This twists and turns amongst large blocks to emerge on the crest a little to the west of the cairn. This route should be used on the return to the saddle for a re-ascent of Sgurr Dubh na Da Bheinn, as there are crags to trap the unwary to left and right. To the north, the twin spires of Sgurr Thearlaich and Sgurr Alasdair stand in dramatic silhouette above the notch of the Thearlaich-Dubh gap. Only climbers should attempt to cross the gap (V.Diff) to reach these summits and the return to Glen Brittle by the Great Stone Chute and Coire Lagan (Walk 2). Those of a more modest capability should work their way down the tumble of blocks and scree west of the cairn and return by Coir' a' Ghrunnda.

The Dubh Ridge from Coruisk
The peaks of Sgurr Dubh Mor, Sgurr Dubh na Da Bheinn, and the lesser Sgurr Dubh Beag are collectively referred to as

'The Dubhs', and the classic ascent is from Coruisk. In the summer months, the boat from Elgol to the head of Loch Scavaig gives a grand entrance to the dramatic Coruisk basin, above which the Dubh Ridge rises in a continuous ascent of 3000ft.

The lower part of the route, crossing huge, gently-angled slabs, is graded 'easy', and the firm grip of the gabbro ideal for inspiring confidence in the novice climber. As upward progress continues, the slopes steepen, and on the western face of Sgurr Dubh Beag's summit stack, the first real obstacle is encountered. Here an exposed blade of rock dips to an awkward step of about 60ft, which in its lower section is overhanging. The abseil runs clear of the rock for several feet, and as belaying points are none-too-numerous, it may be found necessary to run out a full rope-length of 120ft from a point above the knife-edge, to ensure that the bottom of the pitch is reached with a sufficient margin of safety. Those disinclined to indulge in such adventures should look on the south side of the peak, where an exposed traverse along a scree and grass ledge will be found at a lower level.

A short arête carries the ridge towards the buttresses guarding Sgurr Dubh Mor. These can be negotiated by a climb of Moderate standard, which quickly attains the jumbled blocks of a short, level crest. Along the ridge to the west of the cairn a path, detected between huge blocks, drops to the short arête leading to the rocks of Sgurr Dubh na Da Bheinn. From here one can either descend easily to Coir' a' Ghrunnda, if continuing to Glen Brittle, or move down and around the knob of Caisteal a' Garbh-choire for a return to Coruisk by the boulder strewn An Garbh-choire. The other Coruisk alternative is to continue south-east on a traverse of the fine ridge linking the three southern peaks of the Cuillin, for a steep scrambly descent of Gars-bheinn's north-east ridge.

CHAPTER 27   WALK 2

Sgurr Alasdair 3309ft/993m
Sgurr Thearlaich 3201ft/984m
Sgurr Sgumain 3104ft/947m
Sgurr Mhic Choinnich 3107ft/948m
Inaccessible Pinnacle 3254ft/986m
Sgurr Dearg 3234ft/978m

A walker can link the summits by a tortuous route involving inconvenient descents and re-ascents but even then the Inaccessible Pinnacle involves a short rock-climb. It is therefore best to be proficient in scrambling and easy rock-climbing (or be accompanied by a rock-climber) when attempting this itinerary and try to avoid poor weather conditions. This sequence of peaks involves scrambling and some rock-climbing, which give some particularly exhilarating moments on the narrow arête between Sgurr Thearlaich and Sgurr Mhic Choinnich.

Sgurr Alasdair

The broad, stony spur of Sron na Ciche (above the Coir' a' Ghrunnda path, Walk 1) climbs easily to the cairn of Sgurr Sgumain, but if continuing along the ridge to Sgurr Alasdair there is a *mauvais pas*, or bad step, with Difficult climbing. This can be by-passed a few yards out on the Coir' a' Ghrunnda side of the ridge, where a less strenuous scramble up a small chimney returns the walker to a narrower arête. Here he is confronted by several rock needles on the edge of the Coire Lagan cliffs. Yet again, the ledges above Coir' a' Ghrunnda give passage to a scramble back on to the ridge below the airy summit of Sgurr Alasdair, the highest point in the Cuillin. Sheer cliffs fall to the floor of Coire Lagan, and though not quite so spectacular, the opposite face of the mountain plunges just as abruptly towards Coir' a' Ghrunnda. The views from Sgurr Alasdair (shared by Sgurr Sgumain) have been described as some of the most enchanting in the world. The wanderer fortunate enough to be standing at the cairn at sunset can linger awhile, knowing that he can make good his escape down the Great Stone Chute.

The Great Stone Chute Approach

In Coire Lagan, the access path circles round the northern side of the tarn to divide at the foot of the massive wall of Sgurr Mhic Choinnich. One route peters out on the An Stac screes at the head of the corrie, and the other crosses towards the foot of a huge fan of boulders, where several cairns below the wall of Sgurr Alasdair point the way ahead, before moving across the throat of the gully to the foot of Sgurr Thearlaich. The Great Stone Chute is a perverse ladder of shifting scree, and there are few who do not reach the stony platform at its head without an intense feeling of relief. Directly overlooked by Sgurr Alasdair and Sgurr Thearlaich, this gap falls rapidly on the opposite side to a cliff-edge, which catapults to the floor of Coir' a' Ghrunnda. From the platform Sgurr Alasdair can be attained by a narrow arête.

Sgurr Thearlaich

From the head of the Stone Chute there is a short, stiff scramble on to Sgurr Thearlaich by way of the upper section of its southern rib, which rises from the Thearlaich-Dubh Gap. From the summit its steep north wall falls abruptly to another gap at the foot of the sharply-profiled Sgurr Mhic Choinnich. Abseiling will probably be required to descend the final section to the gap and there is rock-climbing beyond. (The moderate walker will need to return to Coire Lagan by the Great Stone Chute and regain the ridge by the An Stac screes.) From the gap the easiest continuation moves up a little then traverses round the West Face by Collie's Ledge (Moderate). A more direct route takes King's Chimney (Difficult), the obvious corner on the south side, where conventional rope-work will be required.

Sgurr Mhic Choinnich

The An Stac screes or the rocks on the right lead back up to the ridge from Coire Lagan. Moving right (south-east) scratched rocks between high blocks indicate the start of the climb along slabby pavements above Coruisk. Gigantic walls support the ridge on either hand and, above Coire Lagan, several small ledges give a last delicately-balanced scramble to the cairn. King's Chimney emerges below the cairn and Collie's Ledge gains the ridge a little to the north.

Sgurr Dearg

After returning to the col at the head of the An Stac screes it will be necessary to move down a little to gain a path in the scree (cairns) which moves up the rocky debris under the western edge of An Stac's tower, and keeping to the base of its wall climbs to easier ground. Here a level crest doubles back to the cairn, from which there is a stupendous view of the Inaccessible Pinnacle, which on the Coruisk side has a drop of 2000ft to Coireachan Ruadha.

Sgurr Dearg's Inaccessible Pinnacle has the distinction of being the most difficult 3000ft peak in Britain, its final section involving unavoidable technical climbing, albeit of modest difficulty. The easiest ascent is a Moderate climb along its East Ridge, in places only six inches to a foot wide. Nowhere on the Cuillin Ridge is the sensation of airy height quite so marked and exciting. Fortunately, good 'jug handles' of sound rock give excellent holds on an exhilarating, exposed climb of 150ft. The summit is a tiny sloping table, where a large boulder provides a convenient anchor for the 60ft abseil off the obelisk's shorter side.

The slightly lower summit of Sgurr Dearg is, in mist, probably the most complex in the Cuillin, as a rib of slabs just feet from the summit cairn crosses the main thrust of the ridge towards the giant cliffs above Coruisk, creating very confusing topography. Those continuing along the main ridge to Bealach Coire na Banachdich will need to take great care at this point. Walkers returning to Glen Brittle could retreat back down the screes by the side of the Inaccessible Pinnacle or, in clear weather, continue along Sgurr Dearg's west ridge, with its fine views across to Sgurr Alasdair and Sron na Ciche, for an easy scree-run down to the valley.

CHAPTER 27   WALK 3

Sgurr na Banachdich 3167ft/965m
(centre top) 3104ft/942m
(south top) 3010ft/917m
Sgurr Thormaid 3040ft/927m
Sgurr a' Ghreadaidh 3197ft/973m
(south top) 3180ft/969m
Sgurr a' Mhadaidh 3010ft/918m

Bealach Coire na Banachdich

Above the fall of the Eas Mor, paths climb easily to the rougher ground of an upper basin of Coire na Banachdich. The route does not push ahead to the Bealach Coire na Banachdich, as might be expected, and the rambler should look for cairns to the right, where a gully eats into the cliff-base under the summit of Sgurr Dearg. A cairned route ascends the steepening headwall beneath these crags, turning to the left along a stony gallery to reach the screes climbing to the gap in the ridge. In mist, be sure to keep to the route, more especially on a descent, (usually from Sgurr Dearg, see Walk 2) as there are treacherous bluffs below the upper section of the pass.

If crossing to Coruisk, the loose scree on the opposite (east) side of the pass is decidedly easier, and smooth rocks encountered near the 1800ft contour should be avoided on the right. This is the easiest crossing from Glen Brittle to Coruisk.

Sgurr na Banachdich

To the north of the pass, more steep rock and scree climbs up to the point of Sron Bhuidhe, which, throwing out a short spur, divides Coireachan Ruadha into two smaller corries. On the main ridge, two tops are crossed on the approach to the main peak of Sgurr na Banachdich, the first of which, although not classified as a 'top' by Munro, is generally accepted as being about 3010ft in elevation.

Walkers ascending by the shorter ridge of Sgurr nan Gobhar (2047ft/631m) pay for their audacity on 2000ft of punishing scree. A little further to the north-west of Sgurr na Banachdich's cairn, another shorter ridge pushes out towards Coire a' Ghreadaidh, and between this and the ridge of Sgurr nan Gobhar an easy descent, or ascent, can be made using Coir' an Eich (useful route from the Youth Hostel).

Sgurr Thormaid

A short dip of about 200ft carries the ridge to the foot of the scrambly blocks of Sgurr Thormaid. Here, it is possible to descend to Coire a' Ghreadaidh, but a very rough scramble at the start of this descent needs care to pick a way round a small, short spur (seen on the left), above the easier ground

of the lower corrie. To the north-east of Thormaid's summit, three teeth sitting astride the ridge can be avoided by traversing easy-angled slabs on their left.

Sgurr a' Ghreadaidh

The short arête which follows, though narrow, is quite straightforward, and the fearsome wall of Sgurr a' Ghreadaidh seen earlier is less intimidating than might be imagined, giving a good scrambly route, with lots of fine holds, on the 400ft climb to the southern top of the mountain.

The crest of Sgurr a' Ghreadaidh is the sharpest in the Cuillin, with a spine so narrow in parts that it requires a very fine sense of balance to tread the delicate edge. Again, the adhesion of the gabbro is used to good effect, providing safer stances along first one side and then the other of the blocks lining the ridge, where at times the actual crest is used as a handrail between the tops.

To the north of the highest cairn, a small excrescence overlooking the drop into Coire na Dorus serves as a useful guide always remembering that the route lies on the Coruisk side. Here a fall to a small, narrow gap known as Eag Dubh (black notch) is followed by a further drop to a second gap, An Dorus (the door), at the foot of Sgurr a' Mhadaidh. There is a fairly easy scree-filled gully on the Coire na Dorus side of the gap, but on the Coruisk side a narrow cleft, complicated by several rock pitches, makes ascent or descent more difficult.

Sgurr a' Mhadaidh

There now follows a scramble to the south-west summit of Sgurr a' Mhadaidh, a cairned point 30ft beyond another of similar height. The narrow crest is almost level until it reaches a third point at the northern end of this ridge, wrongly marked 3014ft, and said to be the summit of the mountain on the older one inch maps.

An arête running out to Sgurr Thuilm, which is easily climbed by its south-west slope, provides a more straightforward scramble to Sgurr a' Mhadaidh and this could be used for a descent to Glen Brittle, thereby avoiding the difficulties on the rest of the Sgurr a' Mhadaidh ridge. Another easy route, a scramble known as Foxes' Rake, climbs from the head of Coir' a' Mhadaidh to a chimney, which must be climbed to reach the point where Sgurr Thuilm's ridge meets the flank of Sgurr a' Mhadaidh.

The traverse of the rest of Sgurr a' Mhadaidh, with its three lower tops separated by dips, is complicated by rock-climbing obstacles and conditions causing erratic compass readings. At a small gap below the northern point of this summit crest, the route turns sharply towards the east, rounding a small pinnacle topping the ridge on the Coruisk side, on

the dip to the base of the first of the three smaller summits – Third Peak.

Here the walker is confronted with a wall of gabbro. To the left, crags plunge into Coir' a' Mhadaidh, and the Coruisk face is equally unyielding: the wall must be climbed. Though graded 'difficult', the climb may seem easier because of the grip of the rock, which means that walkers of modest pretentions can second a rope without too much discomfort. On the rise to the next 'top' (Second Peak), a small pillar of gabbro leaning against the side of the hill presents another problem. At the top there is a short step across a narrow gap on to the face of the hill. Another short dip, followed by a modest rise of about 100ft, places the rambler on the north-east summit (First Peak). The slopes falling to the Bealach na Glaic Moire, though fairly steep, are straightforward, and slabs encountered on the final dip to the pass lead to the screes of Coir' a' Mhadaidh (Tairneilar on some older maps), which spills into the moorland basin of Coire na Creiche, next to the road.

CHAPTER 27   WALK 4

Sgurr nan Gillean 3167ft/965m
Am Basteir 3069ft/935m
    Bhasteir Tooth 3005ft/916m
Bruach na Frithe 3143ft/958m
    Sgurr a' Fionn Choire 3068ft/935m

The peaks at the northern end of the Cuillin Ridge can be climbed in one expedition by those with rock-climbing skills. The best route is south to north. The main problems are at the Bhastier Tooth where Naismith's Route (Difficult) provides a direct ascent while the Lota Corrie Route (Moderate) an outflanking line from low on the right. Further difficulties follow on the West Ridge of Sgurr nan Gillean.

The walker, however, will probably opt to climb the peaks individually by their easiest routes, or traverse the ridge from north to south using abseils to pass the difficulties.

Sgurr nan Gillean

Sgurr nan Gillean's pyramid enjoys a commanding position above the expansive moors of Glen Sligachan, and from the hotel the nibbled outline of a ridge can be seen running west to the block of Am Basteir. The mountain also throws down an immensely impressive ridge to the north (the Pinnacle Ridge) though this is not seen to its best advantage from Sligachan. It has four distinct towers, each involving rock-climbing problems, and is therefore best left to cragsmen. Even the West Ridge is guarded by a gendarme known as the Tooth which involves awkard and exposed moves to negotiate. Thus the walker is left with the so-called Tourist Route up the east side of the mountain as the only practical line of ascent.

A path leaving the Carbost road, just beyond the Sligachan Hotel, leads to an old power house. Nearby, a bridge crosses a stream to a moorland path running towards the foot of Sgurr nan Gillean's northern flank. This should be followed to the Allt Dearg Beag, which acts as guide to a cairn, where a turn should be made towards the small tarn below Nead na h-Iolaire. The route, which is indistinct, continues south to another cairn overlooking Coire Riabhach.

Climbing from the hollow, a profusion of cairns appears among boulders and scree below the Pinnacle Ridge, now seen in towering profile above and to the right. Tortuous progress through the boulders and up the scree beyond eventually allows access to the crest of the south-eastern ridge. Here, for the first time, the way to the summit becomes apparent. Cairns mark the way on the pronounced ridge, where there is but one possible route. On the final 100ft of this fine arête, large blocks slanting towards Lota Corrie give an exposed scramble to the top of a vertical wall. Care is needed, and the use of a short rope may provide an insurance on the step up to the airy pedestal of a short, narrow platform which holds the cairn. Those without climbing experience should retrace their steps, as the route towards Am Basteir is not without its difficulties. In mist, care will be needed on the early part of this descent to avoid the tendency to be drawn into Lota Corrie. After the first steep section work back to the north to locate the cairned ridge.

The West Ridge of Sgurr nan Gillean
This ridge is very narrow in parts, and care is needed on the descent to the Tooth (gendarme) of Sgurr nan Gillean, a great boulder which poses a very interesting problem. Even rock-climbers have been known to baulk at this, and the rambler, finding himself thus far, should abseil down Nicholson's Chimney, a narrow cleft to the right (north). This drops to the base of the crag, where a contouring walk can be made across the scree to regain the ridge to the east of Am Basteir. Those who do manage the exposed gyrations around the pinnacle, are then faced with a sudden drop, a few yards to the west, which should be avoided by a climb (or abseil) down a 40ft chimney on the north side of the arête. This leads to the dip of the Bealach a' Bhasteir and the ridge to Am Basteir.

Am Basteir
The walker will usually be content to reach the summit of Am Basteir by way of Coire a' Bhasteir. A path leaving the Carbost road follows the hollow of the Allt Dearg Beag (a small, rocky gorge is best avoided

on the west) to gain the steeper screes of an upper corrie for the climb to the ridge at Bealach a' Bhasteir. Several yards along the ridge to the west, plates of rock tilting towards Lota Corrie create an awkward 10ft step. This is followed by a scramble along a sharp edge above the northern wall of the peak to gain the summit. Walkers are now best advised to retrace their steps from the cairn unless competent to climb down the pitches to the Bhasteir Tooth and thence down to the next pass on the ridge, the Bealach nan Lice. This difficult section can be avoided by a traverse from the Bealach a' Bhasteir along the foot of the northern cliffs to Bealach nan Lice, although such an outflanking manoeuvre will leave out a visit to the Bhasteir Tooth which many regard as de rigeur on any valid exploration of the Cuillin Ridge.

The Bhasteir Tooth
The descent to the Bhasteir Tooth from Am Basteir starts down ledges on the Lota Corrie side for 60ft until the way is barred by a small impending wall. This can be passed by abseil (poor anchorage) or a 20ft 'Difficult' descent pitch down a slightly easier-angled section of the wall to the left (south-east). From the foot of the wall a sloping shelf and ramp leads up to the top of the Bhasteir Tooth which juts out above Bealach na Lice. The Bealach can be reached by another abseil down Naismith's Route. The alternative is a bout of further scrambling down the Lota Corrie flank. From the foot of the impending wall a terrace inclines down towards Lota Corrie. Narrow, sloping galleries and walls (marked by cairns) lead to wider ledges at the foot of the cliffs (cairn) from where 300ft of scree climbing leads back up to Bealach nan Lice. In ascent this Lota Corrie Route is the easiest way to the top of the Bhasteir Tooth. Climbers who choose the south-north traverse may opt for Naismith's Route to make the ascent. This is a challenging Difficult climb up the cracked wall on the south-west face but in poor conditions it is best avoided in favour of the Lota Corrie Route.

Bruach na Frithe
Bruach na Frithe occupies one of the best vantage points on the Cuillin ridge, and is the least difficult of the main peaks to ascend. Above the highest point of the pass between Sligachan and Glen Brittle (Bealach a' Mhaim) a pleasant clamber up 900ft of grassy hillside gives an easy introduction to the hill. Above, a narrow rock ridge, about 150ft long, continues to a wider crest which leads to the summit.

Following the Allt Dearg Mor, an even easier route crosses the grassy bowl of Fionn Choire to gain the ridge at Bealach

nan Lice. Here the walker can move immediately on to rough terraces on Sgurr a' Fionn Choire, which lead to a fine viewpoint overlooking the sterile hollow of Lota Corrie. Scree-slopes continue to the O.S.Pillar on Bruach na Frithe.

From the summit the view to the south is of a long, serpentine ridge rising, curving and falling in a series of spectacular peaks, crags and spurs as far as the eye can see.

Plates of gabbro, tilting slightly towards Lota Corrie, pave the ridge to Sgurr na Bhairnich, which then drops sharply to a gap at the foot of An Caisteal to give an easy descent by Coire na Ciche to the Glen Brittle road. An alternative descent by Fionn Choire leads to the Bealach a' Mhaim path for a direct return to Sligachan.

CHAPTER 27   WALK 5

Bla Bheinn 3044ft/928m
   (south top) 3031ft/924m

Sheriff Nicolson, who made the first ascent of Sgurr Alasdair, considered Bla Bheinn, or Blaven, to be the finest mountain in Skye. The only 3000ft peak not on the main Cuillin ridge, the mountain provides a fine viewpoint of both the Black and the Red Cuillin ranged on either side of Glen Sligachan. The Broadford to Elgol road runs along the mountain's south-eastern flank and provides a start to the climb from the head of Loch Slapin.

Most ascents are made from this side up either of two broad faces divided by a stony gully which is the central feature of this hill's great mass. Both these slopes are steep and grassy, requiring little more than a concerted and continuous push to the respective summit cairns. The top nearest to Clach Glas is the higher of the two, but this goes unnoticed as the arête between has regular slopes which favour neither.

Ascents from the West
Following the Sligachan Burn, the track is sound enough until the main stream turns away into Harta Corrie. A meagre tributary continues to the upper reaches of the glen, where countless peaty pools lie in wait for the unwary. Bla Bheinn's towering north-west wall is split by a deep gully similar to that on the Loch Slapin face. Those tempted to try a scramble will find that, unlike the south-eastern cleft, this may prove troublesome, and a diversion on to the face of the hill must be made to avoid a section of Difficult climbing in one of the upper sections. The southern ridge proves to be a much easier proposition, rising over pleasant grassy terraces above the narrow coastal strip near Camasunary, a quiet haven from which to attempt this popular hill.

SCAFELL, SKIDDAW AND HELVELLYN

England's highest summits are all situated in the Lake District. Considerable ingenuity will be required to find quiet routes, and the paths are all heavily worn. Scafell, and to a lesser degree Helvellyn, offer some scrambling.

SCAFELL PIKE   SCAFELL
Two highly contrasting peaks, the latter involving a dramatic crag climb to reach its summit.

SKIDDAW OR SKIDDAW MAN
Statuesque from a distance but curiously bland on close acquaintance. A round from the north adds interest.

HELVELLYN
Helvellyn has little distant character, but offers interesting valleys and ridges on its eastern flank.

Recommended Valley Base Keswick

Maps O.S. 1:50 000 Sheets 89 and 90; Bartholomews 1:100 000 Sheet 34; O.S. 1:25 000 Sheets *The English Lakes – South West, North West and North East*; O.S. 1:63 360 Sheet *Lake District*.

Starting Point/Length and time for main itinerary
Walk 1 Wasdale Head (186087). 8 miles/3600ft of ascent, 5–8 hours.
Walk 2 Peter House (249323). 8 miles/2800ft of ascent, 4–6 hours.
Walk 3 Patterdale (390161). 7 miles/2700ft of ascent, 4–6 hours.

CHAPTER 28   WALK 1

Scafell 3162ft/964m
Scafell Pike 3206ft/977m
   Ill Crags 3040ft/926m
   Broad Crag 3054ft/931m

England's highest mountains lie some distance from Lakeland's main lines of communication. Of the nearest access points, Borrowdale (to the north) and Langdale (to the east) lie at the start of the longest and least attractive walks. Both walks also involve a complex route from the summit of Scafell if returning to the starting point. Eskdale (to the south) allows an attractive circuit to be made, but on balance the best ascents are from Wasdale (to the west).

Direct ascent from Wasdale
The shortest climb to Scafell Pike is also the most arduous and least attractive. From the head of Wastwater follow the lane to Wasdale Head Hall Farm across the Lingmell Beck and, reaching the bridge at the foot of Lingmell Gill, follow the path behind a belt of trees sheltering the Fell and Rock Climbing Hut. The rise to a footbridge crossing the gill sees the start of a steeper pull to the path's union with a similar trail from Down in the Dale. This second path leaves a corner of the road near the old schoolhouse (finger post) and,

crossing the fields to a footbridge on Lingmell Beck, finds a stile at the start of a diagonal line of ascent across the lower slope of Lingmell. Above a stile in the upper boundary wall the climb continues to a cairn at the foot of Brown Tongue, a grassy ramp between two stream runnels. Here the upward view is increasingly dominated by the headwall of crags above Hollow Stones, a scoop at the head of the stream seen to the right.

At the head of the tongue, a line of cairns to the left points to an easy route below Pikes Crag, whose terminal buttress can be turned to gain Lingmell Col. Here the path from Sty Head (Corridor Route) is joined to follow another line of cairns to the summit of Scafell Pike.

Scafell
The stony path to the south-west of Scafell Pike's massive cairn leads to Mickledore's narrow col. The walker looking for a direct route off the arête may be disappointed. The apparent ease of the stepped blocks abutting the rock face to the left is deceptive. This obstacle is known as Broad Stand, and it is a notorious place for accidents. The tops of the steps slope outwards and can be particularly dangerous when wet, and the narrow exit crack to Broad Stand's slippery slab has a 'bad step' of 20ft of Difficult climbing. Broad Stand is the only feasible route up between the cliffs on the East and North Faces of the mountain, and a long deviation is required to avoid it. This way lies down to the right along an obvious path which skirts the foot of the massive wall of crags seen earlier. Do not take a higher path, which is harder.

Lord's Rake and Deep Ghyll
At the end of the lower traverse, a cross cut into the rock marks the site of the terrible accident of 23 September 1903 when a party of four climbers fell to their deaths

whilst attempting to reach a rocky point on the cliffs above known as Hopkinson's Cairn. The walker may be disquieted at having to pass this memorial just as he is about to enter the confines of Lord's Rake, whose steep scree, so easily dislodged, has also caused many an accident, sometimes with fatal results. Advance with circumspection, and be ever mindful that, as the accepted 'Tourist Route' to Scafell's summit, others unseen may already be climbing ahead. Initially the rake slopes up to a small col-like level, whence the easiest route heads across the mountain face until its rough passage debouches on to easier scree. Here, turning left, there is a short rise to the summit cairn.

Just below the col in the Rake, an easy shelf to the left (The West Wall Traverse) provides an entertaining entrance to Deep Ghyll. Here the walker feels himself really coming to grips with the mountain, for the chasm pierces the very heart of the crags. Walkers should not attempt the lower half of the gully below the traverse, which must be climbed, and is another place where many have unwittingly strayed (usually during descent), with serious consequences. The head of the gully leads to a short grassy table, where, looking to the south-west, the pillar of the summit cairn is seen. To the left, another dark fissure separates the rocky towers of Scafell Pinnacle and Pisgah, and looking through the 'window' between them and Deep Ghyll's western wall an impressive array of Lakeland peaks is revealed.

From the summit of Scafell the selection of the wrong line of descent could be calamitous, and the complex of gills, gully cracks and crags should be investigated carefully, for the cartographers have mapped them in insufficient detail for practical purposes. Below the summit

cairn, in particular, the drop to the head of
Lord's Rake can be a trap for the unwary,
who are often tempted to use Red Gill,
which on the descent, lies a little to the
right (north-east). Although the two routes
converge, the upper section of Red Gill is
decidedly unreliable and walkers unfamiliar with the ground are easily
confused.

Walkers returning to Wasdale Head
should have few problems, as the open
fellside to the west of the crags can be
followed to a rib above a northern line of
crags for the descent to Lingmell Gill.
Easier still is the path to Wasdale Head
Hall Farm, which, if followed, keeps the
walker away from Rakehead Crag, the only
serious obstacle on these broad north-
western slopes.

Ascent from Wasdale by Sty Head

An alternative route from Wasdale, by
easier gradients to Sty Head and Esk
Hause, takes in the tops of Ill Crags and
Broad Crag as short, logical diversions
from the approach path to Scafell Pike.

This itinerary starts at the Wastwater
Hotel and crosses the green to a narrow
lane which cuts through the fields to a
small church, where, turning to the left, a
wider lane is followed to Burnthwaite
farm. A well-trodden path continues along
a green lane between the small enclosures
and reaching Gable Beck bridge, climbs as
an obvious scar across the steep southern
flank of Great Gable on the long drag to Sty
Head. Near an old sheepfold above the
bridge, a second path known as the Valley
Route, branches to the right. This gives a
picturesque clamber, beside the tiny
waterfalls of Lingmell Beck, which,
reaching an attractive confluence at the
foot of Piers Gill, crosses to the south bank,
where zig-zags climb past Spout Head to
emerge on the Sty Head col.

From Sty Head paths lead to the higher
ground of Great Gable, Lingmell col
(Corridor Route), Great End (The Band),
and more importantly, the cross-country
route to Langdale which is used to reach
Esk Hause. This follows a line of cairns to
the east, where, veering to the left at the
foot of the first knot of crags, a natural
portal between the crags of Great Slack
(left) and the rough knots of Great End
(right) will be seen. Fording a stream, the
path cuts across the hollow of Sprinkling
Tarn and thence continues through a gap
to turn south-west near a cross-walled
shelter on the climb to Esk Hause.

This windbreak is often misrepresented
as being at Esk Hause, a name which
properly belongs to the shallow saddle
between Great End and Esk Pike, some
100ft higher (2490ft) and lying 300 yards to
the south-west. This point can be reached
more directly on a path climbing across the
shoulder of Great End.

An obvious path, now profusely cairned,
continues towards a depression separating
a knot to the north of Ill Crags from the
smoother lump of Long Pike. Hereabouts
it is worth taking a short scenic diversion
to the summit of Great End, returning to
the main trail by a path to the south of its
cairns. To the south-west cairns point the
way along a broad undulating crest of
jumbled boulders, with the cairn of Ill
Crags seen on a short rise way out to the
left. Beyond a dip, to the opposite side of
the path a short, diversionary clamber
leads to the cairn of Broad Crag, said to sit
on one of the roughest bouldered summits
in all Lakeland. The main path is regained
near the dip to the head of Rake Gill
where, looking ahead, the stony cap of
Scafell Pike is identified by the size of its
summit cairn. Steps in its south-west
corner allow access to the top for a clearer
view of the many surrounding peaks. To
complete the round follow the path to
Scafell and return to Wasdale.

The Esk Valley circuit

Usually approached from the east, the river
in this quiet valley is first seen near
Whahouse Bridge, at the foot of Hard
Knott Pass. A telephone box identifies the
track to Brotherilkeld, where, passing
through the farmyard, a path below Yew
Crags is followed to a bridge across
Lingcove Beck. Ignore paths climbing to
the right (routes to the Three Tarns and
Bowfell), and continue above the cut of the
river, where, on the climb above the
hidden Esk Falls, Ill Crags appear above a
shoulder of Throstlehow Crag. As the
twisty path emerges into the wider basin of
the Great Moss, Scafell Pike and Scafell
also come into view and increasingly
dominate the near horizon. Turning
towards Dow Crag (Esk Buttress) a
convenient stream crossing sees the path
turning right towards the head of the Esk.

Various ascents are possible from the
wild amphitheatre of the upper valley.
Under the northern edge of Cam Spout
Crag, a stony path crosses a stream
emerging from Cam Spout. Above the
waterfall, by keeping close to the stream
the path threads a rocky defile on the climb
to Mickledore, seen as an obvious dip in
the skyline at the head of a scree rake. A
western tributary of the stream can be
followed to the Foxes Tarn, whose hollow
provides an easier exit to the summit of
Scafell. The walker seeking the summit of
Ill Crags should continue up the valley,
where, turning the northern edge of Dow
Crag's broken face, the dark recess of
Little Narrowcove is discovered. A path
scrambles up its western side on to the
stony ridge to the east of Scafell Pike, with
Ill Crags approached by a branch gully to
the right. Ascents of Scafell Pike and
Scafell are made as previously given, with

problems on the descent again avoided.
The long ridge to Slight Side gives a
high-level promenade above the escarpments of the Esk basin, with small
outcrops encountered at the end of the
ridge easily turned on the right (west), to
reach the streams falling to Cowcove Beck.
The path to Taw House can best be gained
to the east of a short col above the
headwaters of the main stream, and from
it a track runs down to the road.

Ascent from Borrowdale

A stony track from Seathwaite (parking),
to the east of the infant River Derwent
crosses the picturesque Stockley Bridge,
and climbs as a well-defined route to Sty
Head. If seeking a quieter route take the
lane which turns to the right at Seathwaite.
Immediately across the river a path cuts
across the fields on the left (campsite)
towards some old sheepfolds below
Taylorgill Force. This, and the cascades
above it, add to the interest of the path up
this side of the ravine.

From Sty Head follow the route to Esk
Hause and the summits as described in the
ascent from Wasdale Hotel. A shorter and
more interesting alternative is the Corridor
Route, which allows the walker the option
of taking in the tops of Scafell Pike on a
return by Esk Hause.

The Corridor Route

This path, also known as the Guides
Route, leaves the Esk Hause route at the
foot of a small crag, where, cutting through
a tumbledown wall, it descends slightly
before rising again to an open gully known
as Skew Gill. Paths climb the opposite
bank, the higher of the two taking a stream
bed to a red-stoned groove to gain a cairned
terrace, which leads to the head of Piers
Gill. The lower route skirts the head of
Girta Gill and reaches Piers Gill at a
precipitous part, forcing a route up the
hillside on the left (east) to join the terrace
of the higher route. The stream should be
crossed near the head of the gill to reach
the path climbing to the gap of Lingmell
col, where cairns to the left mark out the
route to the summit of Scafell Pike.

Ascent from Langdale

The track from Langdale (parking) is the
longest and most difficult and anyone with
transport would be better advised to cross
to the Esk Valley and make the traverse
from Brotherilkeld. If this is not an option
the walker should be prepared for the
chaos of stones in Rossett Gill at the head
of the Mickleden track, which passes
between the field walls to the west of the
Old Dungeon Ghyll Hotel. At the head of
the gill, Angle Tarn is revealed in a rocky
basin below the crags of Hanging Knots,
with easier gradients ahead providing a
gentle pull to the cross-walled shelter at
2386ft/727m below the rise to Esk Hause.

On returns to starting points in Borrowdale and Langdale the route of ascent is retraced, and therefore the possibility of a problematic descent of Scafell should be anticipated. The only feasible alternative to a descent by Lord's Rake or Deep Ghyll involves a considerable loss of height as the route lies to the south-east of the summit cairn on uneven slopes falling towards Foxes Tarn. From the grassy table at the head of Deep Ghyll a scree rake provides the safest line of descent to the tarn, with the outlet stream acting as the surest guide to the lower ground. This is followed by a tiresome ascent of uneasy scree below the crags of Broad Stand, to regain the ridge at Mickledore. Even this route calls for accurate navigation, especially in mist, factors which further recommend the Wasdale routes.

CHAPTER 28   WALK 2

Skiddaw or Skiddaw Man 3054ft/930m

Visitors approaching Keswick from the south cannot but be aware of Skiddaw, for Derwent Water would seem far less picturesque without the mountain as a backcloth.

From the Spooney Green Lane track and cottages at Thorny Plats just north of Keswick (270243), follow a pleasant path along Latrigg's wooded slope to Gale Road, where, by walking a few yards to the right, the signpost at the start of the Tourist track up the mountain will be found. The motorist can reach this point from Keswick by taking the Crosthwaite Road to the A66 roundabout and then the A591, immediately bearing right at the first junction to the village of Ormathwaite. After the village, take a sharp right turn doubling back along the edge of the hill: this is Gale Road, which leads to the col behind Latrigg where it is possible to park.

The Tourist Track

The obvious track follows a wall to a fence, which continues to a gate where, veering to the left, it climbs towards the crown of Jenkin Hill. At a monument to three men of the Hawell family, shepherds of Lonscale), the steeper slopes of the fell come into view. A small point, Little Man (Low Man), rising above a fold on the left flank of Jenkin Hill is often mistaken for the summit of Skiddaw, as yet unseen beyond it. Ahead the track divides, and here the true line of the original route keeps to the right, whereas a more direct route follows the fence to rejoin the less-direct route at the site of the Skiddaw Hut where, following the opposite side of the wall, on the next 300ft of unrelenting ascent it reaches easier ground. Two peaks appear above the shoulder of Jenkin Hill,

and again are discovered to be the twin humps of Little Man (2837ft), for another fence must be reached before Skiddaw's summit begins to appear.

Little Man or Low Man

If bored by the path, follow the fence towards Little Man, whose convex southern slope makes it a more attractive vantage point than Skiddaw. If taking a more westerly line from the point where the path crosses the fence, the cairn on Lesser Man may be reached (identified by the numerous iron posts sticking out of it). It is worth noting the grassy slopes to the south at this point, which provide an ideal return route off the hill, avoiding the harsh scree below Skiddaw and Little Man.

Skiddaw

To the north of Little Man, the unmistakable scar of the track can be seen on the rounded end of Skiddaw, where the ground is much rougher on the walk up to the cairn on Skiddaw's south top (3034ft). A stone shelter immediately to the north breaks the smooth outline of a broad, bare ridge, where the track takes an unimaginative line to the middle top (3039ft) and the main summit (3054ft) beyond. The views to the north and west, across Bassenthwaite Lake, are best seen from the shelter immediately to the north-west of the summit cairn.

On the return it is best to return to Little Man and take the previously mentioned southern slope. This provides fine views across the impressive southern screes of Skiddaw and Little Man. The descent is terminated by a boundary wall (running across the face of the hill at about the 1200ft contour). It can be followed to the right (west), to reach a path on the bank of Mill Beck, which provides a route back to Millbeck. Alternatively, follow the wall left (east) and descend Howgill Tongue to the road a little to the east of Applethwaite.

Ascent from the north

The way from the north is in many respects more interesting and varied than the well-worn tourist path. The ascent begins at Peter House Farm (250324) south of Orthwaite. Almost opposite the farm is a track to Dash Farm.

The farm track (no cars allowed) should be followed across the fields to Dead Beck on the northern slopes of Cockup, which can be followed to the upper slopes of Broad End. A more interesting walk starts further up the track beyond the rock-face of Dead Crags. Here the cascades of Whitewater Dash add colour to the narrowing valley on the short, sharp pull to a gap carved by the stream. Beyond a gate in the wall at the head of this pass, broad acres of heather to the east of Skiddaw come into view. Little more altitude is gained in continuing along the track towards Skiddaw House, where the

smooth flanks rising to the cairns of Skiddaw offer little challenge. Follow the wall to a broken fence which climbs to the 2700ft contour. Here it turns under the summits to continue to the Tourist Path below Lower Man. In mist a line a little sou'sou'west from this corner of the fence on Broad End helps to find the cairn on the north top of Skiddaw (3024ft), above Gibraltar Crag.

Rather than descending directly to the north by Broad End, to the pastures above Melbecks, there is a more interesting route starting to the south-west. Cross the summit to the cairn of the south top (3024ft). Here, turn south-west and pick your way down the stone detritus to find a tiny pool on a short col at the foot of Broad End (not to be confused with the Broad End to the north of the summit). It is possible to descend from this point to a ruined sheepfold in the upper reaches of Southerndale Beck, and thence by grassy tracks to the fields above Barkbeth. A steep fellside sweeps upwards from this quiet sanctuary to the screes of Skiddaw. To the left it is hemmed in by the sharp ridge of Longside Edge which, from the col, appears as a line of crumbling crags and steep scree-rakes. This ridge is the best route of descent. After crossing the northern flank of Carl Side a path leads to the cairn of Long Side (2405ft), which is separated by a slight dip from the small dome of Ullock Pike. The views of Bassenthwaite Lake from here greatly repay the detour. There is a false northern top which must be crossed to gain the long slant of a ridge aptly named The Edge. The path fades on the lower slopes, and above the intake wall (about 1100ft), a group of rocks known as 'Watches' (rather like a stone circle) should be turned on the Southerndale side, on the drop to the sheepfold on the Southerndale Beck, where the track across the fields above Barkbeth leads to the road. A short walk remains to Peter House.

CHAPTER 28   WALK 3

Helvellyn 3116ft/950m
   Lower Man 3033ft/924m

Helvellyn is perhaps the most popular viewpoint in the Lake District, as it occupies a central position looking out over several of the larger lakes, with distant views to Morecambe Bay.

Approaches from Thirlmere

The shortest routes to the summit are from the west, by paths from the main road along the side of Thirlmere (A591). The Swirls Forest Trail starts from a car-park at 316168. Once through the wicket gate at the corner of the car-park the route ahead is clearly seen above the treeline. A rough path beside Helvellyn Gill promises a stiff 2000ft ascent to the end of Browncove Crags. Once on the ridge of this spur there is an easier rise to the saddle and the cairned path across it which links Lower Man to Helvellyn's summit, here seen to the south-east.

A similar trail from Wythburn Church car park, near the southern end of Thirlmere (look for a signpost, Helvellyn Top 3, Patterdale and Ullswater 7, beside a phone-box just north of the churchyard wall) likewise makes a laboured ascent through the woods to the 1000ft contour. Zig-zags ease the climb to Comb Crags, where the path turns northwards above High Crags on a long diagonal rise, to meet the ridge-path between Dollywaggon Pike and Helvellyn a little to the north of Nethermost Pike.

These two routes might be linked to give variety to a western traverse, but most visitors choose to return to the starting point by the same route.

The Patterdale approaches

Although somewhat longer than the Thirlmere routes, the finest ascents of the mountain are to be made from the east from starts near Patterdale. The classic route from here is the traverse of the ridge of Striding Edge.

The most popular way to Striding Edge leaves the A592 just to the south of Grisedale Bridge in Patterdale, on a narrow road which climbs past the wooded grounds of Patterdale Hall to reach the scattered farmsteads in the Grisedale valley. At a gate at the end of the road (no parking), a track to the right crosses Grisedale Beck and rises gradually to another gate in a wall below a small wood. Turning to the left along the top side of this wall, a well-trodden path, seen earlier, makes a long diagonal climb across the slopes ahead. A branch zig-zagging to the right rises more rapidly to higher ground, and has the advantage that it provides clearer views of Dollywaggon and Nethermost Pikes, at the head of the valley. Near the 1000ft contour and again at the last gateway (on the skyline), paths from Glenridding are joined for the climb to Striding Edge.

Striding Edge

A route along the exact edge has some short easy scrambles, whereas the path, which keeps a little below the crest on its northern side, avoids these and only joins the narrowing arête near its centre. Further along the ridge a rocky knot is encountered which provides more scrambling, though it can be avoided on steep scree to the left. After this a move to the left, then a twist back on ledges, leads

down to a short cleft before the ridge widens again. Another rocky tower almost immediately ahead is best tackled head-on in preference to the loose flanking screes. Broken grassy terraces typify the final part of the climb to the plateau, where the walker finds himself at a commemorative cairn (Gough's Cairn), with the summit of Helvellyn to the right.

Helvellyn and Lower Man

Above a cross-walled shelter a very dilapidated cairn on a knot of bare earth does scant justice to Helvellyn's highest point. A level gravelly ridge to the north-east supports the Ordnance Survey post. Beyond this a rough cairn to the north-west marks the start of the descent of Swirral Edge. To the left (north-west) of this cairn, a profusely-cairned path keeping away from the edge of the escarpments dips 100ft to the broad saddle which precedes the short easy rise to the three broken-down cairns of Lower Man.

Swirral Edge

The descent of Swirral Edge is short but steep, and care is needed, especially when the rocks are wet. The gritty path moves down past rough blocks by a line to their left (north), then it crosses the crest to the right and descends the Red Tarn side by a series of rough steps until easy ledges run down to the col before Catstye Cam (also known as Catstycam or Catchedicam).

From this col, the path swings across the hill-face to the boggy outlet of Red Tarn. Those unable to resist the climb to Catstye Cam for its fine view of Helvellyn's impressive eastern walls can descend rough stony slopes directly to the tarn. Crossing the hollow below it, twin paths run to the gate in the wall at the head of Grisedale Brow for the return to Patterdale. Alternatively a descent down Birkhouse Moor to Keldas gives interesting views of Ullswater, largely unobserved on the Grisedale route.

Helvellyn's southern ridge

From the summit of Helvellyn, walkers have the option of returning to Patterdale by a route that continues at a high level along the ridge to the south. A well-defined, cairned path crosses the top of Nethermost Pike, with grand views down the trough of Grisedale from the craggy headwalls of Nethermost and Ruthwaite Coves. The path skirts the western flank of Dollywaggon Pike, which can be just as easily crossed to regain the path at the top of the zig-zags on the drop to Grisedale Tarn. Here the old packhorse trail crossing from the foot of Dunmail Raise to Patterdale is joined. This turns the foot of Tarn Crag to reveal an easy strolling path along the pleasant vale of Grisedale, to the roadhead above Patterdale Hall.

Ascents from Glenridding

Roads lead up alongside Glenridding Beck to converge at Rattlebeck Bridge. From this point a lane goes up the hill to Miresbeck farm, where a path to the right of the buildings leads to Mires Beck. Above the beck, on the climb to Patterdale path gateway, the path follows a wall, with the continuation of the route seen ahead on the back of a grassy ridge (the end of Striding Edge). The traverse of Helvellyn follows the route described on the Patterdale ascent, with a descent by Swirral Edge to Red Tarn where walkers can return to Glenridding by a path which follows Red Tarn Beck down to Glenridding Beck on a route passing the old mine cottages and Youth Hostel.

The Catstye Cam route

An interesting way of varying an ascent of Helvellyn takes the track to the Glenridding Youth Hostel by the road from opposite the Ullswater Hotel (fork right at the Gillside sign). Above the hostel old mine cottages (outdoor centres) and workings are passed, and looking ahead the crown of Lower Man is seen beyond the long, slanting edge of Catstye Cam. The track continues to an old dam beyond which a stony ridge (left) gives a stiff ascent to Catstye Cam, with Swirral Edge and the walls of Lower Man clearly outlined on the headwall of the cove to the right. At the summit the full splendour of Helvellyn's eastern cwm is suddenly revealed, with Red Tarn nestling in front of the long profile of Striding Edge. The path descends to the foot of Swirral Edge, which provides a stiff final pull to the summit.

There is a choice of return routes. The sporting might opt to fight against the flow of scramblers coming up Striding Edge but a more interesting way heads north.

From the summit of Lower Man a well-trodden route follows the crest of a broad northern ridge, crossing Whiteside Bank (cairn) to a level col at the foot of Raise. Here, take the path to the right around the head of Keppel Cove, which zig-zags down to the ancient track for a return to the Youth Hostel and the Glenridding road. This descent could be further embellished by continuing beyond Raise to Sticks Pass where an easy path heads down to a tarn north of Stang. From here there are two alternatives: a steep hillside path down to the mine cottages, or an interesting diversion over a low col to the east to gain Glencoynedale on a slightly longer return to Glenridding.

SNOWDON, THE GLYDERS AND THE CARNEDDAU

The high peaks of Wales split into two distinct types: the craggy and dramatic; the grassy and rounded. The former offer outstanding scrambling routes.

SNOWDON: YR WYDDFA
Tourist-infested and much abused, Yr Wyddfa is the focal point of a magnificent cirque of peaks.

TRYFAN GLYDER FAWR Y GARN ELIDIR FAWR
Tryfan's dramatic easterly aspect signals the start of a superb expedition.

CARNEDD DAFYDD CARNEDD LLEWELYN FOEL-FRAS
Mountains for the connoisseur – extensive ridge walking into lonely territory.

Recommended Valley Base Capel Curig

Maps O.S. 1:50 000 Sheet 115; Bartholomews 1:100 000 Sheet 20; O.S. 1:25 000 Sheets *Snowdonia National Park – Snowdon, and Conwy Valley*.

Starting Point/Length and time for main itinerary
Walk 1 Pen-y-Pass (647556). 7 miles/3400ft of ascent, 5–8 hours.
Walk 2 Llyn Ogwen (663602). 12 miles/5450ft of ascent, 7–11 hours.
Walk 3 Bethesda (637659). 15 miles/4180ft of ascent, 8–12 hours.

CHAPTER 29   WALK 1

Snowdon:
Yr Wyddfa 3560ft/1085m
Crib-goch 3026ft/922m
Crib-y-ddysgl 3496ft/1065m

Snowdon is a extremely popular mountain with many celebrated routes of ascent. Those wishing to climb the mountain and the two tops are compelled to tackle the famous Horseshoe Route with its airy scrambling on the rocky crest of Crib-goch. In any but perfect conditions the traverse of Crib-goch can be difficult calling for steady and competent scrambling. The ascent of Snowdon alone (Yr Wyddfa) can be a long easy walk by one of a number of routes — the Pig Track being the most varied and interesting. It is well to remember that the mountain's very popularity prompts a lack of respect which is most out of place in winter conditions; at these times virtually all the routes have some sort of difficulty. Moreover the summit is so distanced from the road that a party can rapidly tire on the long easy-angled descents while still at a relatively high altitude.

The most popular routes are those that start from Pen-y-Pass Youth Hostel at the head of the Llanberis Pass, but from here Yr Wyddfa is hidden and it is Crib-goch's rocky point which dominates the scene.

At the south-west corner of the car-park (opposite the hostel), a path winds through boulders under the north edge of the ridge. The path, which has been much improved in recent years, skirts the hillside immediately above the road, gradually gaining height, with short, steep sections alternating with almost-level meanderings. At a ruined sheepfold at the base of crags a faint path branches off to the right along the hillside above Dinas Mot, and thence to a cairn on the northern spur of Crib-goch, which provides an alternative line of ascent. Most will elect to continue to Bwlch y Moch (the gap ahead) on the watershed between the Llanberis Pass and Cwm Dyli.

Crib-goch
At Bwlch y Moch Cwm Dyli's splendour is revealed. There is an enchanting view across Llyn Llydaw to the magnificent crags of Y Lliwedd, with Snowdon to the right. Hereabouts the path divides. The Crib-goch path heads straight up the steep slopes above to the summit, but the Pig Track leads off easily across the southern slopes (left) of Crib-goch providing a more direct route to the summit of Snowdon, by-passing the difficulties of Crib-goch. It eventually links up with the Miners' Track (clearly seen below, crossing the causeway and skirting Llyn Llydaw) above a higher lake — Glaslyn, and thence by zig-zags to Bwlch Glas between Crib-y-ddysgl and Yr Wyddfa.

The climb to Crib-goch takes the narrowing ridge ahead and is much more arduous and intimidating. The ground is stonier and steeper than the Pig Track and scrambling is required to pass a belt of rock-bands halfway up the ridge. Here, a degree of caution will be required. A direct couloir is exposed to stonefall, which is a serious problem when the route is crowded. An alternative route can be worked out up rock steps to the left (south), involving some steep scrambling before ledges allow a move back to the right to regain the ridge. Above, the ridge narrows into a rocky crest which leads directly to the summit cairn (3023ft/921m), where one is suddenly presented with a stunning view. The cairn is placed at the end of the sensationally sharp summit ridge which extends towards craggy pinnacles high above the dark hollow of Glaslyn. The grim walls of Yr Wyddfa dominate beyond. On the right a steep precipice drops into Cwm Glas. It is a position that offers one of the most striking views in the British mountains.

The crest of the ridge is followed to the 'true' summit, which is the pinnacle in the centre of the ridge (3026ft/922m). The ridge is magnificently exposed and precarious for about 400ft and although technically easy it commands respect. If windy or wet conditions prevail, the passage can become a serious undertaking; under ice and snow it is no place for the walker. The pinnacles themselves can be turned on the left by a disjointed path, but near the end the left-hand slopes become more craggy, prompting a direct traverse over the final pinnacle before the descent to Bwlch Coch. In many ways it is best to stick to the airy skyline traverse of the pinnacles, which gives very entertaining scrambling. This may well be the safer way, as the rock is solid and the difficulties minimal, though enhanced by the exposure.

Crib-y-ddysgl
This peak, which is also known as Carnedd Ugain, is reached by a long rocky ridge leading on from Bwlch Coch. The path is broken periodically by easy rock-bands. The general tactic is to tackle these from the left. A good pace can be maintained on this varied ascent and after several steps and bluffs the broad summit plateau begins to take shape. The stony summit carries a triangulation pillar and, though higher than Crib-goch, its views are less outstanding. An easy dip leads to the col of Bwlch Glas (green pass) at 3258ft/993m, where the Pig Track emerges at a point marked by a large, erect stone (The Finger Stone).

Yr Wyddfa
Yr Wyddfa, the burial place, got its name, as an early Welsh tale tells, because Rhita Gawr, killed by King Arthur, was buried in the summit cairn. One of Britain's most

popular mountains it is a place of contrasts. Multitudes flock to its summit, many of them tourists borne aloft on the mountain railway from Llanberis. The 'hotel' at the summit station is a structure of unsurpassed ugliness, but it is unique in providing the highest pint of beer in Britain, a fact that moderates the criticism which might otherwise be heaped on it.

The approach from Bwlch Glas follows the railway. The cairn and triangulation pillar lie a few yards above the summit station. The distant features are too numerous to describe in detail but, on a day of exceptional clarity the Irish coast may be seen beyond the plains of Caernarfon and Anglesey, with the highest of the Lakeland peaks discernible to the north. The summit area of Snowdon is a busy and raucous place where few mountaineers choose to linger. It is still possible to enjoy the mountain in serenity, however, by climbing it in early spring or late autumn.

The Miners' Track from Pen-y-Pass
At the south-east corner of the car-park, the Miners' Track leads round the hillside in a gradual rise into Cwm Dyli, where the full magnificence of Yr Wyddfa is revealed above Llyn Llydaw. A causeway (sometimes flooded) carries the track to the lake's northern shore, where, at a ruined copper-mine building, the route begins its upward scramble into the hidden cwm of Glaslyn. Here, more derelict buildings are passed to reach the steep scree-path climbing to meet the Pig Track at the foot of the zig-zags to Bwlch Glas.

The most rapid descent from Snowdon to Pen-y-Pass is by the Pig or Miners' Tracks, but those who have already completed the first part of the Horseshoe route will doubtless wish to complete it with the traverse of Y Lliwedd. Not only does this give the satisfaction of a full round of Cwm Dyli, but it also provides a fine view of the Crib-goch/Crib-y-ddysgl ridge which is denied on a return by the Pig Track.

The Horseshoe route over Y Lliwedd
From the summit of Snowdon it is necessary to descend the south-west ridge by the Rhyd-Ddu track for a short distance until a finger of rock indicates the top of the Watkin Path, which cuts back across the steep south-eastern flank of the mountain on the left, providing a rapid descent to Bwlch y Saethau. In summer this is a knee-jarring descent on a rubble covered path, but in winter it can become a steep slope of hard-packed snow sometimes calling for good technique with ice-axe and crampons. This is one of the mountain's accident black-spots, and should be treated with caution.

Continuing from the col, various bluffs are crossed on the low section of the ridge

which ends at another col, Bwlch Ciliau, after which the slopes steepen on the climb to Y Lliwedd. This peak is twin summitted — the West Peak is reached first after a steep, stony ascent (entertaining on the left, a slog on the right) followed by a short descent and ascent to East Peak. The cliffs on the Cwm Dyli side are among the biggest and most impressive in Wales. Most of the summer rock-climbs are in the middle grades, but in winter conditions the cliff provides climbs of near alpine proportions and difficulty.

From East Peak the path descends south-east to Lliwedd Bach, beyond which a path leads down the northern slopes to Cwm Dyli, to join the Miners' Track at the Llyn Llydaw causeway. In mist it is important to stay on the ridge and cross Lliwedd Bach before beginning this descent. Before this the northern slopes are steep and treacherous.

Other routes up Snowdon
Yr Wyddfa and Crib-y-ddysgl can be reached easily using one of the other classic routes up Snowdon: the Watkin Path starting from Nantgwynant; the Rhyd-Ddu and Snowdon Ranger tracks starting from points on the A4085 Beddgelert/ Caernarfon road; the Miners' Track from Llanberis. None of these allow easy access to Crib-goch, however. Crib-goch, although technically a top on the criteria used for Scotland, is in all other respects a mountain and it must be climbed by any serious walker aspiring to the Welsh 3000ft peaks.

CHAPTER 29 WALK 2

Tryfan 3010ft/917m
Glyder Fawr 3279ft/999m
  Glyder Fach 3262ft/994m
Y Garn 3104ft/946m
Elidir Fawr 3030ft/924m

The range of peaks between the Pass of Llanberis and the Nant Ffrancon are collectively known as the Glyders. Their southern slopes are broad and grassy broken by scattered outcrops, and only on the steep south-west flank of Esgair Felen are there crags of any note. The north-facing slopes could not be more different, for here the range displays a series of dramatic cwms and cliffs. Proximity to the road gives the peaks an impression of added height, particularly Tryfan, which is splendidly impressive when approached from the Capel Curig direction. Its fine north ridge, which drops directly to the road, is one of the most entertaining and popular scrambles in Britain.

For the Munroist, the peaks of the group are strung out in a convenient chain and can be climbed in one long day, albeit with a degree of inconvenience in getting

back to the starting point. If possible transport should be arranged to allow a start at Llyn Ogwen and a finish at Nant Peris, thereby allowing a straightforward descent from Elidir Fawr at the end of the day.

Tryfan by the North Ridge
Several car-parks along the shore of Llyn Ogwen lie conveniently near the access stile below the Milestone Buttress, the prominent bastion marking the lowest point of Tryfan's West Face. The mountain is covered in crags on both its east and west faces, which meet at the pronounced North Ridge, which provides the logical line of ascent. The path leads to the foot of the buttress and then zig-zags up the scree slopes on the left to a boulder-strewn shoulder on the ridge. This marks a point where several other access paths converge, the most notable being the one that starts at Gwern Gof Uchaf farm to the east of the mountain, which provides a slightly longer but rather more picturesque approach than the Milestone route.

The shoulder also marks the start of the Heather Terrace, a wide shelf that crosses the East Face below the cliffs to give access to the southern end of the mountain.

The steep scree on the ridge leads up to a series of broad rock steps offering a variety of scrambles. These increase in difficulty and unavoidability as height is gained, but there is little exposure. A prominent landmark at half-height is 'The Cannon', a projecting finger of rock on the Ogwen side which can be seen in sharp profile from Ogwen Cottage.

On the rise to the north summit the ridge narrows and steepens dramatically giving honest scrambling aided by the solid incut holds that are typical of Tryfan. Beyond a slight shoulder, gullies coming up on the east and west sides breach the ridge, creating a notch. A steep 20ft descent is required here, which will probably be found to be the most difficult part of the route. Walkers who are unsure of the difficulty, can skirt this on the left by leaving the crest and approach to the notch at a lower level. This still involves scrambling, and though the difficulty is soon passed, it commands respect, for the exposure is quite stimulating.

More energetic scrambling leads to the summit of North Peak. The continuation to the main summit is by a route up runnels and boulders on the west side. The summit boulder-field suddenly arrives, where there is the final challenge of 'Adam and Eve', two rock monoliths projecting from the top of the mountain. Each is about eight feet tall, and the gap between them is just too wide to be a mere step; a definite leap is required to achieve 'The Freedom of Tryfan'. A precipice is near at hand, so a degree of pluck is necessary and the jump is inadvisable if the rock is wet or icy. The narrower block can be scaled from the surrounding rocks, but the fatter, southern obelisk proves slightly more difficult.

Tryfan's South Ridge

For the capable scrambler, the North Ridge provides a direct and rapid route to the top. Walkers who are less sure on rock may find the ascent by the South Ridge a quicker and easier route. The way starts from Ogwen Cottage at the western end of Llyn Ogwen. A well worn path heads towards Tryfan. Soon it becomes grassy and then steepens on the climb to Cwm Bochlwyd. This rather scruffy start is amply compensated by the delightful walk by the side of Llyn Bochlwyd and the easy slopes up to Bwlch Tryfan at the foot of the mountain's South Ridge. After crossing the diminutive Far South Peak easy scrambling leads up the ridge to the summit, various difficult looking clifflets usually being turned on the left (west).

In descent this southern route, though never exposed, requires care and a degree of route-finding skill to locate Bwlch Tryfan. The various obstacles tend to force the route to the west and it is necessary to work back round to the south to gain the col.

Glyder Fach by the Bristly Ridge

Glyder Fach and Glyder Fawr are the twin summits of a broad, stony 3000ft massif that forms the focal point of the Glyder group. Applying a Munro criteria, the two are not separate mountains, but although in some ways complementary they are each different in character (particularly in rock-type) and it is therefore unfortunate that one must suffer the ignominy of being classed only as a 'top'.

The slopes to the south and west are fairly gentle, apart from the precipitous west flank of Esgair Felen, but to the north the peaks are guarded by an abrupt series of faces above Cwm Idwal and Cwm Bochlwyd.

Those tackling Glyder Fach from Bwlch Tryfan have a choice of two routes. Bristly Ridge rises a short distance above the pass, and looks terrifying. This can be avoided on the left by a wide scree-slope which leads directly to the summit plateau. However, if time allows it is best to tackle the ridge, as it is very entertaining. It is comparable in difficulty and quality to the North Ridge of Tryfan, though shorter, steeper and more exposed. A vague path leads up to the left below the base of the lower rocks until it is possible to work up to the right to a break in the ridge. The ridge rises in a series of towers and notches amidst spectacular cliff scenery. The scrambling is straightforward however,

and the holds large and incut. A group of huge teeth appearing to the right signpost the top of the difficulties, where the ridge dips slightly as it reaches the plateau. Cairns lead on to a heap of monolithic blocks of peerless stone the finest of which is the celebrated 'Cantilever' (a huge slab of rock jutting out in perfect balance at the top of one group of blocks). This formation is not quite the summit; which is an even larger pile of rocks a couple of hundred yards to the west. This is a chaotic maze of huge boulders and tilted slabs, and the route through them must be chosen with care. The piles of rock that support the summit and the Cantilever stand on the top of an otherwise level plateau, and in poor visibility they can easily be missed on the way towards Glyder Fawr. A slight descent to rocks surrounding Castell y Gwynt signals the end of the plateau. If crossing the mountain in the opposite direction careful compass work will be needed to locate the top of the Bristly Ridge or its eastern screes.

Glyder Fawr

This western peak of the two Glyders is the highest, though only by the modest margin of 17ft. The route to it from Glyder Fach is indicated by the prominent jagged projections of Castell y Gwynt (Castle of the Winds), one of the weirdest formations to adorn any of the 3000ft peaks in the British Isles. A well-cairned path circumvents it on the left (south), but scrambling addicts will doubtless wish to traverse directly over its splintered crown. The view of Tryfan from this curious stance is disappointing, as it appears small and insignificant against a background of higher Carneddau.

The scrambling and outflanking routes merge at the saddle of Bwlch y Ddwy-Glyder. From here the ridge regains height slowly, the well-trodden path keeping to the south side of the crest. The plateau of Glyder Fawr is so extensive, and the ground everywhere so well-trodden and cairned, that locating the exact summit in mist might be difficult and confusing. Its rock formations are only slightly less arresting than those of Glyder Fach, and of the numerous spikey tors adorning its level crown, the two highest, standing a few yards apart, look decidedly similar. The cautious will tread both to ensure the conquest of the true summit.

In clear conditions the steep descent from Glyder Fawr to the broad col above the Devil's Kitchen is straightforward. The slope is strewn with outcrops and messy screes. It is convex in nature and the exact route only becomes clear after some height has been lost. In misty conditions this descent can become confusing and will call for accurate map work to locate the correct line to Llyn y Cwn. In winter

conditions the steeper sections of the slope can be particularly treacherous, and it may be best to angle down to the west to the head of Cwm Cneifio to avoid this hazard.

Apart from the lake, the main feature of the broad col between Glyder Fawr and Y Garn is the dramatic cleft of the Devil's Kitchen, that breaches the cliffs on the Idwal side. It is possible to break the walk at this point and return to Ogwen, using a ramp that works down cliffs a few hundred yards south-west of the top of the Kitchen to a pile of huge boulders at its foot. It is then an easy walk back to the valley around the end of Llyn Idwal. The more energetic will opt to continue and complete the peaks in one expedition.

Y Garn

When seen from the vicinity of Llyn Ogwen, Y Garn and Foel-goch appear as a long mountain barrier blocking the head of Nant Ffrancon. If the walk has been split at the Devil's Kitchen, Y Garn can be reached directly from Ogwen to start a shorter day. High in its north-east hollow lies tiny Llyn Clyd, enclosed by airy ridges which fall away to Llyn Idwal. These blunt spurs give sporting ascents, the easterly one offering entertaining scrambling.

Heading directly to Y Garn from Glyder Fawr, after passing Llyn y Cwn, the top of the col above the Devil's Kitchen is an extensive area of bogs and rocky outcrops, where in bad weather it is easy to go astray. The grassy slopes of Y Garn are much easier than those of Glyder Fawr, and after about 400ft of re-ascent the path reaches the head of the crags, high above Llyn Idwal and Llyn Clyd. The walk along the crest to the cairn gives a bird's eye view of both, at the same time providing excellent vantage points overlooking the Ogwen Valley, Nant Ffrancon and the wild cwms on the north side of the Glyders.

The way on to Elidir Fawr is complicated by the intervening peaks of Foel-goch (2727ft/831m) and Mynydd Perfedd (2665ft/812m), both of which can be outflanked, respectively, on their western and southern slopes. Unless pressed for time it is worthwhile to include them both in the itinerary, particularly Foel-goch, as it offers excellent views of the Ogwen valley and Pen yr Ole-Wen.

Elidir Fawr

After descending the sharply escarped north-western slope of Y Garn (beware of cornices on the eastern edge in winter conditions), an obvious path contours along the west side of Foel-goch and bears to the left across the shoulder of Mynydd Perfedd to reach the east ridge of Elidir Fawr. Skirting the northern cwm, the path enjoys spacious glimpses of Marchlyn Mawr before deserting the edge of the crags on the last 300ft of the climb to the bouldery summit. This is a series of rocky lumps (greasy when wet), decorated with iron posts standing in line along the ridge.

Elidir Fawr (also known as Carnedd Elidir) is the outlier of the group, and also the mountain most scarred by the activities of man, for the slate quarries above Llanberis rise in massive tiers to over 2000ft on its west side, and its craggy northern hollow, Marchlyn Mawr, has been converted to the upper reservoir of a pumped storage scheme.

The easiest descent is a direct route down the southern slopes to Nant Peris. This involves a height loss of 2700ft. Another way involving 1000ft less descent, crosses Elidir Fach to the north-west and follows the edge of the quarry workings to reach a minor road above Dinorwic. This should not be attempted in gathering darkness or poor weather conditions.

As an alternative, return to Mynydd Perfedd, and move northwards across the ridge to Carnedd y Filiast. Here the steep ridge skirting the north side of Cwm Ceunant provides a way down to Nant Ffrancon, where a pleasant walk along a minor road on the west side of the valley leads back to Ogwen.

Those seeking a more direct way back to Ogwen may encounter problems, as the other slopes above Nant Ffrancon are nearly everywhere steep and precipitous.

CHAPTER 29 WALK 3

Carnedd Dafydd 3427ft/1044m
Pen yr Ole-Wen 3211ft/979m
Carnedd Llewelyn 3485ft/1064m
Yr Elen 3152ft/961m
Foel Grach 3196ft/974m
Garnedd Uchaf 3038ft/926m
Foel-fras 3092ft/942m

The complete crest of the Carneddau, from Pen yr Ole-Wen to Foel-fras, is a fine high-level traverse covering more ground above 3000ft than all the rest of Wales and England put together. There is a problem, however, in that anyone starting at Ogwen and venturing as far as the final summits is left in the middle of a vast, and inhospitable area, from which the easiest escape routes continue further from the starting point. It is therefore worthwhile to arrange for transport to be available at the head of one of the minor roads at the northern end of the group, either that above Aber or the one at Bwlch y Ddeufaen above Ty'n-y-groes in the Conwy valley. Those who are compelled to return to their starting point could either start and finish at Gerlan near Bethesda — from whence a good, if arduous, circular walk can be made — or start at Ogwen, return to Bethesda and then rely on hitch-hiking or road-walking to get back to Ogwen.

Pen yr Ole-Wen

From the bridge at the end of Llyn Ogwen, the steep 2000ft slope of Pen yr Ole-Wen (also know as Penyole-wen or, most correctly, Pen yr Oleu Wen) provides a mortifying start. Across the wall beside the road, broken rocks give a rough ascent to steep grass. This soon deteriorates into a broad, rubble-strewn ridge, studded with small rock outcrops. The ridge is remorselessly steep and notorious as one of the most gruelling ascents in Snowdonia. Indistinct paths pick out an obvious route to the boulders below the summit, but the despairing walker may be fooled by the apparent ease of the ground to the right, which is composed of massive boulders covered in thick bracken and heather.

The connoisseur will seek a route along the Afon Lloer, above Tal-y-llyn Dymen farm to the east (path along the north shore of Llyn Ogwen, or a track from the A5 at the east end of the lake). The Afon Lloer should then be followed to a broad saddle at the foot of the long slant of the mountain's eastern ridge, which also provides fine views of Tryfan and the Glyders.

Carnedd Dafydd

The brutal ascent of Pen yr Ole-Wen is rewarded by easy going along the Carneddau ridge. A brief descent leads to the col to the north from where Carnedd Dafydd, the second highest peak in the group, is easily reached. A mere 400ft of re-ascent leads to the triangulation pillar above the several cairns which line the ridge.

The Gerlan approach

The mountain can be approached from the valley of the Afon Llafar, above Bethesda. A minor road leads from Gerlan to the waterworks near Ty Slatters, at the start of the path leading up to the valley past ruins and through fields. Quit the path where it crosses the upper wall and gain height on the broad ridge ahead, which provides a long but easy ascent to the summit. A south-westerly course on the upper slopes conveniently includes Pen yr Ole-Wen. Alternatively, it may be best to use this route as a descent from a north-east/south-west traverse of the whole massif (see '*A clockwise circuit*').

The ridge to the east of Carnedd Dafydd's cairn runs along the top of the extensive cliffs of Ysgolion Duon, or Black Ladders, where the glimpses into the recesses far below add colour and drama to a mountain which might otherwise appear rather dull. At the eastern end of the cliffs, the point of Craig Llugwy at 3185ft (on one-inch maps) no longer merits a height classification by the Ordnance Survey, though there are some who will still argue and defend the top's claim to be regarded as Wales' sixteenth 3000ft top.

Carnedd Llewelyn

From Carnedd Dafydd it is easy to maintain a steady pace around the head of Cwm Llafar. At the foot of the steeper upper limits of Carnedd Llewelyn a choice has to be made; either contour across the open shoulder to Yr Elen, or head direct for the summit. This is so level and carries so many cairns that the location of the highest point must be a matter of some conjecture. The views from it are extensive, but the top itself is characterless and the mountain's finest features are best appreciated from the four ridges which radiate from it.

The ridge leading from Pen yr Helgi Du provides the best views of Llewelyn's great eastern cliff — the splendid Craig yr ysfa — which dominates the head of Cwm Eigiau.

The Yr Elen ridge is hemmed in to the east by the crag-walled cwm holding the tiny Ffynnon Caseg. In some respects, this peak enjoys a finer situation than the parent peak, for it looks directly in at the shattered cliffs of the Black Ladders. As previously indicated, the main ridge of Carnedd Llewelyn can be left by a traverse along its south-western flank to reach Yr Elen's ridge at the col above Ffynnon Caseg. Once the start of the route has been located, the way to the col appears as a well-trodden path. In poor weather however, walkers may prefer to get an accurate compass bearing on Yr Elen's ridge from the summit of Carnedd Llewelyn.

To the north of Carnedd Llewelyn, the fourth ridge heads out to the most remote of the Welsh 3000ft peaks, Foel Grach and Foel-fras. Both are humps on a huge, grassy whaleback, which throughout its length barely falls below the 2950ft/900m contour. Foel-fras is worthy of recognition as a separate mountain, distanced as it is from Carnedd Llewelyn. Foel Grach is really just a 'top', but as it must be crossed to reach the northern peak, such a distinction is purely academic.

The re-ascent to Foel Grach from the col to the north of Carnedd Llewelyn is barely 100ft. There is a cairn and a crude refuge on the summit, and beyond, is the long walk to the grassy hump of Foel-fras. The large, triangular rise of Garnedd Uchaf (highest cairn) must be be crossed to reach Foel-fras. This has numerous cairns and tracks, and in mist compass work will be required to identify a turn in the ridge.

Possibly due to the remiss use of contours on the one-inch maps this hill was never considered to be in excess of 3000ft. However the 1:50,000 maps have changed all this as a summit is shown within a 920m contour, and a 'top' said to be 926m, or 3038ft, making it Wales' fifteenth 3000ft top.

Foel-fras

The final rise to Foel-fras is gentle and a triangulation pillar to the west of the wall marks the summit.

The way off the hill will depend on the ultimate destination of the walker. To the north-west, Llwytmor's broad ridge falls easily to Afon Goch or Afon Anafon above Aber on the main Bangor-Conwy road. The walker bound for Bethesda must return to the slopes of Garnedd Uchaf and then to the shoulder of Yr Aryg and the ridge of Gyrn Wigau which leads down to Gerlan and Bethesda. The main Carnedd ridge continues north-east over Drum and Drosgl to the roadhead at Bwlch y Ddeufaen.

The clockwise circuit

Perhaps the most sensible and convenient route to link the Carneddau tops is the clockwise circuit from Gerlan. A left fork is taken by the bus shelter at the end of the village, and the road, which peters out into a track, taken to some sheep-pens at the entrance to Cwm Caseg. A stiff pull up the prow of the grassy ridge above these leads to Gyrn Wigau, and the pleasant, curving whaleback is then followed in a semi-circle past the rocky tors of Drosgl, Bera Bach and Yr Aryg until a contour path traverses the northern slope of Garnedd Uchaf before heading off in a north-easterly direction to the triangulation pillar on Foel-fras. From here, steps must be re-traced for half-a-mile before heading south over Garnedd Uchaf to Foel Grach. The route as previously described is then taken in reverse as far as Pen yr Ole-Wen, from which a descent can be made due north across grassy slopes to reach the gradual ridge above Cwm Llafar, which is taken down to Gerlan.

CHAPTER 30

IRELAND'S HIGHEST PEAKS

Scattered across the breadth of southern Ireland, these mountains provide walks to suit every taste. The relevant transport and accommodation details listed here are set out as they relate to the individual mountains.

LUGNAQUILLIA
A fine hill for an afternoon stroll, with picturesque valley approaches.

GALTYMORE
Grassy tops set in the heart of pastoral Ireland.

CUMMEENNAPEASTA
Continually interesting and varied, with a craggy start and a steep descent.

CARRAUNTOOHIL   CAHER   BEENKERAGH
A fine expedition enhanced by spectacular aretes and crag-rimmed corries.

BRANDON MOUNTAIN
A romantic coastal peak commanding captivating views.

CHAPTER 30	WALK 1

Lugnaquillia 3039ft/927m

Lugnaquillia (Log na Coille) is a rounded grassy hill with two broken escarpments guarding the north and south sides of its flattened summit. To the west, at the head of the Glen of Imail, there is an artillery range around Camarahill and military signs posted in the area should be checked to see if red warning flags are flying before proceeding on to the hill.

Ascent from Glen of Imail

The best motorable road follows the Little Slaney River to the foot of Ballineddan Mountain. One of the military signs stands at a junction with a track a little south of a ford on the Little Slaney River (convenient parking space). Nearby, an iron gate opens on to a grassy track leading to ruins hidden amongst the gorse. Beyond, the soft ground along the side of Ballineddan Mountain and Slievemaan can be contoured to the upper reaches of the river, here little more than a stream, which should be crossed to gain the higher ground to the east of Camarahill.

This spur also provides a useful route of ascent as the short heather and grass along its broad ridge make for a swift ascent to the 2000ft contour. Signs of a path appear once two outcrops are passed and cairns appear below the steeper, rock-strewn face on the climb to the level crown leading to Percy's Table. The route across Slievemaan is not so pleasant, as the ground here is very wet and soft. Turning on to the col between the headwaters of the Little Slaney and Ow rivers, thick oozy peat-banks must be avoided to reach the stone-speckled slopes on the western fringe of Lugnaquillia. Here the route from Camarahill is joined, with cairns to show the way across the summit table, where a red military warning sign appears ahead, closely followed by a triangulation pillar on a low plinth of rock.

Endless waves of bare brown hills to the north excite little interest, the better views being eastwards to the sea, or west to the central plains of Ireland.

Ascent from Glenmalur

The Avonbeg River has carved out a convenient route to the eastern base of the mountain, which is served by a road and track running to the Gleann Moolura Youth Hostel. The shortest route from this side starts below the waterfalls of the Carrawaystick Brook, where a farm track will be found leading to a footbridge across the river. The brook is then crossed on stepping-stones to reach a farm, behind which a series of zig-zags lifts the path up the side of the valley. As upward progress is maintained the broad ridge of Clohernagh gradually takes shape and the path disappears, to be replaced on the higher, heathery ground by another path found slightly to the north of the ridgeline. This later skirts the bluffs above the Carrawaystick Brook, which should be seen in a deep fold to the left. The route hereabouts lies almost due west, the easy grass

Recommended Valley Bases Baltinglass and Killarney

Maps *Walk 1* O.S. 1:63 360 Sheet *Wicklow*, and O.S. 1:126 720 Sheet 16: *Walk 2* O.S. 1:126 720 Sheets 18 and 22: *Walks 3 and 4* O.S. 1:63 360 Sheet *Killarney*, and O.S. 1:126 720 Sheets 20 and 21: *Walk 5* O.S. 1:126 720 Sheet 20.

Starting Point/Length and time for main itinerary
Walk 1 Glen of Imail (984917). 6 miles/2200ft of ascent, 3–5 hours.
Walk 2 Glen of Aherlow (874280). 6 miles/2700ft of ascent, 3–5 hours.
Walk 3 Corran Tuathail Youth Hostel (832882). 9 miles/3500ft of ascent, 5–8 hours.
Walk 4 Breanlee Bridge (768868). 6 miles/3750ft of ascent, 4–6 hours.
Walk 5 Cloghane (512118). 7 miles/3100ft of ascent, 4–6 hours.

punctuated here and there by sizeable peat-hags, which are the only impediment to speedy progress. The bald top of Lugnaquillia lies straight ahead, and as it draws nearer, the broken edge of the South Prison should be turned to gain the summit. If continuing due west, the walker will find himself overlooking the rough hollow of North Prison, whose escarpment gives a second pronounced edge to the summit table. This walk from Glenmalur is one for the real moorland enthusiast as, on balance, the western approach is to be preferred.

CHAPTER 30   WALK 2

Galtymore 3018ft/920m

The Galty Mountains, or Galtees, derive their name from the Irish Gaelic, Sliabh Coillte, mountain of the woods, Galtymore being the highest of this rolling range of seven tops.

The route from the south

Anyone travelling by public transport will probably find their footsteps directed to the southern approaches as the N8(T6) Caher to Mitchelstown road is used by buses serving these towns, which are the nearest sizeable centres of population. Being so alike the numerous side-roads leading off this artery may confuse. If travelling from Mitchelstown, the most convenient of these bohreens, as they are called, is best located by first identifying the crossroads at Skeheenaranky with its attendant 'Shell' garage and inn. Continue eastwards for a further half-mile to find the lane. Anyone travelling from Caher should ask to be set down at the third turning on the right (northern arm of a crossroads) beyond the Cuilleannach (Mountain Lodge) Youth Hostel access, a route well-signposted and the nearest useful guide. Looking west from the crossroads, the Shell garage sign at Skeheenaranky should be just visible, as the N8 hereabouts runs arrow-straight for several miles.

Climbing steadily in a line almost due north the narrow lane, shielded by hedges, veers imperceptibly towards a small tributary of the Shanbally River, hidden in a dip to the right. Several tracks and lanes leading off to the left and right should be ignored, bearing in mind that the ascent is continuous until the great moorland spread of Galtymore appears above a clump of trees beside the road's upper limits. A short level stretch precedes a gate at the start of an unfenced cart-track, known locally as 'The Black Road' (cars may be parked hereabouts). Passing through a second gate the rutted trail runs beside the tributary of the Shanbally, bears right at a rough fork, and crosses the open moors of Knockeenatoung to peter out on

a broad, peaty spur to the south of Galtybeg. Here a large cairn, almost at the end of the track, signals a convenient turn to the north-west, where the hump of Galtymore is seen across a wide heathery basin. This route may well be wet and spongy, though preferable in dry conditions to the peat-hags on the col to the west of Galtybeg. These are unusual in that they break up on the very edge of the cliffs overlooking Lough Diheen. These great mossed terraces also shore up the north-eastern corner of the summit and the route along their peaty parapet reveals the homely farmsteads in the Glen of Aherlow, with the wider vale of Tipperary to the north.

The route from the north

The shortest route to the summit starts from a road along the southern margins of this pleasant glen, where a farm lane (easily missed), seen twenty yards to the east of Clydagh Bridge, provides a most convenient access to the hill. Forestry plantations hemming in the first section of the walk stand aside as the narrow bohreen climbs above the farms and fields of Glencoshabinnia, to the broad flank of the Galtees, above a tiny farmstead at the head of the lane (very limited car parking — ask at the farm). Trees again shield rough tracks leading to high pastures, that to the right passing through a gate to reveal a steepening hillside climbing towards the vegetated crags above a hidden Lough Diheen. On either hand of the moraine which holds back the tarn steep ground rears to the crowns of Galtybeg and Galtymore, to give routes which prove to be equally demanding.

A white Celtic cross, commemorating the 1,500th anniversary of the landing of St. Patrick, stands near the edge of weathered blocks looking down on the Clydagh River and the Glen of Aherlow, but it is left to an untidy mound of stones to mark the highest point of the mountain (Dawson's Table). Lyracappul and Slievecushnabinnia are best seen from the western end of the summit's broad crest, and a longer ridge walk could easily take in these summits. For those returning to Mountain Lodge Youth Hostel, a look at the tor of O'Loughnan's Castle, to the east, might add interest to the day.

CHAPTER 30   WALK 3

Macgillycuddy's Reeks (East):
Cummeennapeasta 3191ft/972m
  Cruach Mhor 3062ft/933m
  Lackagarrin 3100ft/944m
  Bearna Rua 3159ft/962m
  Cnoc an Chuilinn 3141ft/957m

Macgillycuddy's Reeks comprise four mountains and six tops. Poor maps and

misleading or non-existent mountain names make this range a nomenclature-nightmare. There are five main sources of information. The Ordnance Survey; The Irish Mountaineering Club; Claud W. Wall, the original guidebook author; E.W.Hodge of The Scottish Mountaineering Club; and R.Hayward's book *In the Kingdom of Kerry*. Each of the latter four authorities give the mountains different names in an effort to fill the vacuum brought about by the failure of the Ordnance Survey to identify peak names. In this book the Ordnance Survey names are used together with the most likely names for the other peaks. The following conversion table will enable some of the confusion to be resolved.

3062ft/933m: Cruach Mhor (Ordnance Survey); Knocknapeasta (Wall — the Irish M.C.Journal March 1951 states this name was invented by Wall); Foil na Breachain or Faill na bPreachan (Hayward):Cruach (Hodge).
3100ft/944m: Unnamed (O.S.); Lackagarrin (Hayward); Fiaclan (Owner Beaufort Hotel); Cruach (Irish MC Journal).
3191ft/972m: Un-named (O.S.); Cummeennapeasta (Hodge); Knocknapeasta (other published sources).
3159ft/962m: Un-named (O.S.); Bearna Rua/Barna Ruadh/ Barraruadh (Hodge); Ballaghnageeha/Bealach na nGaotha (Hayward); Barrabwee (Wall).
3141ft/957m: Cnoc an Chuilinn (O.S.); Knockacullion (Hodge); Foil na Gower/ Faill na nGabhar (Hayward).

Although the Reeks can be climbed in one long expedition from Kate Kearney's cottage to Lough Acoose, the peaks to the north and west of Carrauntoohil are awkwardly placed and will involve re-tracking. It is therefore better to split the mountains into two groups, the western and eastern tops, to allow a start and return to the same point and to give time for a more leisurely appreciation of these interesting mountains.

The eastern peaks of Macgillycuddy's Reeks are linked by a continuous ridge, which, for the greater part of its length, rarely strays below the 2750ft contour. An east-west traverse is best as this avoids having to attempt a crossing of the awkward ridges of Cummeennapeasta and Lackagarrin late in the day, or when mist obscures the tops. As the most spectacular corries lie to the north of the range the choice of route to the first summit naturally tends to direct the walkers' footsteps along the corridor of the Gaddagh River, the lane above the Corran Tuathail Youth Hostel being the best.

Cruach Mhor

Cars may be parked at the head of the lane for a small consideration (enquire at the farm cottage). To the right of the building go through a gate and across the soft pasture to a rough bohreen found between a tumbledown wall and fence (look to the left boundary of the fields). This stony pathway should be followed to the Black Stream where, reaching the peaty moors, a steep conical hill appears to the left, apparently topped by a large tor. Grassy slopes beside a tributary of the Black Stream lead to the edge of a moraine holding back the tarn of Lough Cummeennapeasta, where the climb becomes increasingly more rocky, so that the walker has to pick his way through a confusion of slabs and outcrops to reach the massive summit cairn (the tor seen earlier, which proves to be a grotto).

Those making the ascent from the Gap of Dunloe road should follow the Derrycarna River and then climb to the broad ridge at the eastern end of the range. From Cnoc an Bhraca the ridge strides westwards to a col, where a curious narrow chasm falls down the northern slope to twin tarns just below the 1250ft contour. Continuing beyond this gap the walker finds a broken crest on the steeper rib leading to the summit of Cruach Mhor.

Lackagarrin

Looking south from the grotto, several rock stacks are seen to block the passage along a knife-edge ridge. Those disinclined to try their scrambling should seek out a route along the steep face above Lough Cummeennapeasta. Using various blocks and ledges beneath the stacks it is possible to continue across the face to an open gully, where, climbing diagonally back to the ridge ahead, the walker should find himself on a slabby step at the foot of the highest craggy tower. Here large blocks provide a short, exposed scramble (approx 20ft) to a low cairn perched on the one square of grass atop Lackagarrin's summit. The feeling of space is quite marked and again caution must be exercised on the delicate step across a small slab (the rough flagstone which gave the peak the 'name Lackagarrin) just beyond the cairn. The head of a steep gully (left) is now crossed to more rocks on a crest falling away to the deep hollow of Lough Googh, which, with the loughs in the deeper Cummeenduff Glen further emphasizes the magnificence of this airy viewpoint. Here keep to the left (south) of an obvious rib formed by the tilt of the rock, where a series of ledges provide a stairway down to two large slabs, crossed on their upper edge, to reach a short col.

Cummeennapeasta

Outcrops on the ridge ahead are best outflanked on the left (south) as the arête here is a razor's edge on the cliff-top above Lough Cummeennapeasta. Passing beneath a block of crag on the third outcrop the walker should look for a wide, grassy rake which regains the ridge approximately 40ft below the cairn on the summit of Cummeennapeasta. From it a convex spur with an edge of crag drops away to Cummeenduff Glen. This, if used on an ascent, is a less taxing clamber than that of the rougher arête of the northern ridge.

Bearna Rua

The grassy crest ahead turns, dips gently in a shallow curve to the right and rises gently once more to the small windbreak which acts as a cairn on the crown of Bearna Rua. About nine yards to the north-east a solitary iron post peers down the green cliffs above the well of Lough Cummeenmore. This is a useful guide-post at the head of 'The Bone', whose narrow spur is the one useful escape route from the centre of the ridge on this side.

Cnoc an Chuilinn

The broken edge of the northern corrie sharpens the ridge and again there is a wonderful sensation of space on the easy ground high above the Hag's Glen and the great convex slopes which fall away to Cummeenduff Glen. This lazy promenade is cut short by Cnoc an Chuilinn, which demands a purposeful push before summit stones pave the way to its large cairn.

Here the ridge turns slightly to the north-west, as a nose above the northern corrie, but a line a little to the west, especially in mist, avoids the possibility of getting too close to the grassy ledges at the cliff edge. A 500ft descent finds a col, where a broken-down cairn stands at the head of a pronounced gully falling directly to Lough Callee. A wall and fence cross the route a few yards to the west and, from their joint termination on the cliff-top, the giant buttresses of the peaks above Lough Cummeenmore are seen.

The long level crown of Cnoc na Toinne is supported on a broad acreage of steep grass. At the end of the ridge ahead, the 1000ft slant of Carrauntoohil's pyramid appears massive, and on its southern flank the near-vertical slope of Caher is equally imposing. To the west of the cairn there are some patches of thick peat on the narrow ridge dropping to the head of the Devil's Ladder. If descending to the Hag's Glen keep to the gully's western side, as this gives the most stable passage down its treacherous screes to the stream in the lower couloir. On reaching the flatter ground at the head of the valley cairns appear and these should be followed to the track beside the Gaddagh River. Walkers returning to Corran Tuathail Youth Hostel are advised to cross the river near the. outfall of Lough Callee, as the lower ford is often impassable and dangerous. Before leaving this wild amphitheatre pause to look at the magnificent cliffs on Carrauntoohil and Beenkeragh, for their savage beauty and grandeur is rarely surpassed in these islands.

On the south side of the ridge, immediately opposite the cut of the Devil's Ladder, a break in the escarpments allows a steep, grassy descent to be made to the hollow of Curraghmore Lake. A tributary of the Cummeenduff River can then be followed to the rough track, which leads in to the road in the lower valley. The walker making an ascent from the south is also able to take advantage of a shorter traverse, should he so wish, by returning directly from the summit of Cnoc an Chuilinn across the grassy hump of Brassel Mountain. The eastern nose of this hill provides the easiest descent to the road, which should be reached a good mile to the west of the hostel. For those whose only interest is a short ascent of Carrauntoohil (see Walk 4), either of these routes provide the best route of ascent from the south.

CHAPTER 30	WALK 4

Macgillycuddy's Reeks (West):
Carrauntoohil 3414ft/1040m
  Tooth 3000ft/914m
Caher 3250ft/990m
  (north-west top) 3200ft/975m
Beenkeragh 3314ft/1010m

The three western peaks of Macgillycuddy's Reeks are the highest mountains in Ireland. Carrauntoohil also known as Corran Tuathail, the premier peak, provides the link between a magnificent horseshoe above Coomloughra Glen and the long serpentine ridge of the eastern tops (see Walk 3). There are two obvious approaches: one from the Glencar road near Lough Acoose, the other from the direction of the Gaddagh River.

Lough Acoose approach

At the northern end of Lough Acoose a minor road passing through a gate gives access to the eastern side of the lake. Here a group of outcrops immediately above the road should be turned on the left (north) where grassy moorland folds are easily crossed to reach the flank of Caher beyond. The going is straightforward enough, the gentler initial rise being replaced by more persistent slopes on the stonier approach to the twin cairns of Caher's north-western summit.

Should Beenkeragh be your first objective it is advisable to try to avoid the worst of the boggy tracts below Coomloughra Lough by striking out towards Skregmore. Alternatively, leave the Glencar/Killorglin road a little to the north of the stream draining Lough Eighter, to cross moorland stretching to the steeper grass directly below this hill's western flank (path from the cottages south of Breanlee Bridge). A broad ridge runs south-east from Skregmore to Beenkeragh. Here, the slopes above Coomloughra Glen fall away more sharply than the contours on the map seem to suggest and those unfamiliar with the ground may well speculate upon the narrowness of the crest atop Caher's great cliff, whose massive wall increasingly dominates the scene on the opposite side of the glen.

Gaddagh River approach

The positions of Caher and Beenkeragh relative to Carrauntoohil do not readily lend themselves to an easy completion of the entire traverse of all the summits of the Reeks (see Walk 3). But, as none of the more interesting and sensational sections of the traverse are lost by using the northern approaches, this does not detract from the attraction of these ascents, especially when, as frequently happens, days must be cut short because of the vagaries of the weather and tops missed have to be climbed later.

From Gearha a minor road follows the river's western bank to a point immediately beyond a bridge crossing the Glasheencorgood Stream. Here two rough tracks divide, that to the left climbing steadily towards several small farmhouses above the Gaddagh River. This is the easiest route into the Hag's Glen, and thence to the foot of the Devil's Ladder, and the cairns of the path climbing Carrauntoohil's eastern slope.

Beenkeragh

Alternatively, above the last farmstead take to the heathery slopes of Knockbrinnea, an outrider of Beenkeragh. Follow a route overlooking the Gaddagh River to reach the cairn (2782ft) above the broken pinnacles of the Hags Teeth. To the right a broken edge of Beenkeragh falls away to expose an enormous buttress and the serrated crest of the ridge to Carrauntoohil. The broad, stone-spattered spur sweeps round to another cairned mound a little to the north-west, where decaying escarpments can be seen pushing a northern flank out to the grey screes of Skregmore.

Turning to the south-west, a short grassy col crosses to rough blocks which provide a stairway up the summit slope of Beenkeragh.

Beenkeragh — Carrauntoohil arête

Immediately to the west of Beenkeragh's cairn the rough lip of the Eagle's Nest crater dips and turns on to the narrow blade of a jagged arête. Here large blocks should be turned on the right, where a path may be detected amongst the boulders at the head of precipitous scree-slopes falling away to the twin tarns of Lough Eagher and Coomloughra Lough, seen far below. A sharp dip carries the rocky rib to a short grassy level, leading to the first squat pinnacle on the crest of the arête. A path

showing the way ahead divides briefly on a second knob and ruffs of vegetated crag on either hand support the narrow ridge as it continues to rockier tors, the highest of which is the Tooth, or Knockoughter. Stepping across these rocky knots, tilted slabs are seen on the opposite wall of a scree-filled gully cutting back into the crest. This is the narrowest section of the arête for the delicately-balanced steps rising to the next rocky lump tread the very edge of the cliff, to give an exposed scramble overlooking the Eagle's Nest. This can be avoided by following the gully to the foot of the slabs (right), which are then turned on steep screes above Coomloughra Glen.

The screes climb back to a wider crown of rubble and grass at the foot of Carrauntoohil's bulging flank, where the earthy path finds itself at the head of a deep gully and then above the edge of a gigantic cliff on the final pull to a small, flattened crown, where a turn to the north reveals a cairn, a pole, and a huge metal cross.

Carrauntoohil

There can be few symbols of the Christian faith which stand on so grand a pedestal, for the cross commands superb views on every hand. To the south of the congested summit a stone-littered slope spreads a steep flank above broken escarpments lipping the hollow of Curraghmore Lake. Above this edge, at about the 2750ft contour, an almost-level traverse can be made between the head of the Devil's Ladder and the col at the eastern end of Caher, a route which can be used to advantage when attempting the longer traverse of the Reeks ridges from the north side on an east-west traverse.

If returning to the Hag's Glen down the 1000ft slope to the east, cairns following the line of the northern precipices provide a useful guide to the col at the top of the Ladder.

The descent to the col at the foot of Caher's narrow spine is less clear and in mist careful navigation will be needed to locate the start of the route, which lies along the top of a craggy headwall of Coomloughra Glen. On the regular incline of the broad slope to it, take a line almost due south, in an attempt to catch the craggy lip of this western corrie, at the same time avoiding a line too far south as this leads to difficulties on the rocky ground beneath the southern edge of the col.

Caher

Claud Wall came to the conclusion that Caher was an abbreviation of Cahernaveen, or Cathair na bhfian, Fort of the Fianna, for on a visit to the mountain he met a shepherd who referred to the peak by that name. The logic of this seems confirmed by the fact that near the northern base of

the mountain there is a Derrynaveen which is invariably translated as 'the wood of the Fianna'.

The configuration of the mountain is so positive that the only route to its summit from the east is that along the blade of an obvious ridge. A path leaves the col to reach the foot of Caher's blunt eastern snout at the head of a massive gully, then zig-zags above the broken wall of the chasm on the climb to grassy ledges on the upper limits of a precipitous southern flank. The tiny summit cairn sits on a small knot of the narrow crest, gazing across the void of Coomloughra Glen to the stacks of Beenkeragh and Carrauntoohil.

A short nose jutting out above the massive cliffs (a little west of a second cairn 30ft below the summit) can be avoided on a grassy slope which leads more directly to the neck of a short saddle at the foot of another prominent peak. Here a wall and fence crossing the route come to an abrupt halt at the edge of a cliff split by two rotten gullies. A sturdier bastion buttresses the north-western summit, whose twin cairns enjoy wonderfully clear views to the south and west. The descent takes easy slopes to Lough Eighter to complete the Coomloughra Horseshoe on the path beside the stream to Breanlee. Those who have made an ascent from the north should retrack across the main summit to the southern flanks of Carrauntoohil which should then be contoured to the top of the Devil's Ladder for a descent to the Hag's Glen (see Walk 3) and the Gaddagh River track. If returning to Cummeenduff Glen try the broad ridge of Curraghmore West (Curraghmore on the maps), as its lower slopes are less steep than those on the route from the head of the Devil's Ladder to Curraghmore Lake (see Walk 3).

CHAPTER 30   WALK 5

Brandon Mountain 3127ft/953m

St Brendan chose a fine mountain on which to establish his retreat, and the route he took to the summit from the west is still known as 'The Saint's Road'. A better ascent by far is 'The Pilgrim's Route', climbing the opposite side of the mountain above Brandon Bay.

'The Pilgrim's Route'

Half-a-mile to the north of Cloghane a signpost (Cnoc Bhreadain : Mount Brandon) indicates the start of a narrow lane climbing to the tiny farmstead at Faha (permission to park a car can be obtained at the farmhouse). Here another signpost points to a track passing through a gate to the rear of the cottage and continuing along the side of a wall crossing the face of the hill. Leave the track and, moving uphill, cross a stream in the direction of a walled enclosure housing a small religious shrine dedicated to Our Lady of the Mountains, where, looking along the slope, a rough moorland path may be detected as an oblique line crossing the gaps in two broken walls. At the second wall, a rusting iron post carrying a triangular sign, 'Aire Cnoc Gear' (Take care dangerous hill), is encountered, the first of several such waymarks which pick out the next section of the route.

The path passes through another tumbledown wall to reach the entrance to a rocky cwm. To the left, slopes plummet into a deep, narrow corridor where numerous tarns are seen to cascade one to the other on the fall to Lough Nalacken 1000ft below. Towering above the opposite side Brandon Mountain asserts its mastery of the skyline, where a large cairn and cross stand atop a crumbling cliff.

The path turns northwards to creep along the side of the cwm beneath crags buttressing the eastern spur of the hill. Rounding large slabs paving the floor of the upper corrie, the path wriggles past several waterholes, beside a streamlet and across plates of rock, as it follows the arrows pointing to the foot of the cliffs below the summit cairn. Other symbols painted on the rocks continue to mark out a route which struggles to establish a foothold on rocks at the foot of the steep terraces of a grassy rake. Looking across the head of the cwm, a short horn flanked

by slabs is seen to guard the eastern side of a gap, and it is obvious that an eastern ridge narrows to an arête of no mean difficulty.

The path finds its way up the base of the crags to a large rock decorated with a sizeable cross, which marks the foot of the grassy steps exiting to the ridge. This should be noted as a useful guide should the walker later find himself having to retrace his steps in mist.

Only 100ft now separate the walker from the summit cairn, which is quickly attained by following the obvious crest of the ridge along the cliff-top. To the south-west, narrow sea-girt peninsulas come into view, poking out into the Atlantic; the very view which inspired St. Brendan to go in search of new worlds. The remains of his oratory stand a few yards to the north of a large summit cairn and a cross made from iron rods. Those wishing to return to Faha may choose to return down the lake-studded valley leading down to Lough Cruttia, which is rough and trackless but enlivened by spectacular scenery. Alternatively, the crags of the eastern slopes can be viewed from above by continuing along the ridge towards Brandon Peak, another mountain shaped by the glacier which ripped out the basin of Lough Cruttia, seen far below. To the south-west, a few rudimentary cairns signpost the way down to Ballybrack by 'The Saint's Road'.

'The Saint's Road'

The approach from the west starts at the cottages at Ballybrack, which are reached by a small road leading off the Dingle to Brandon Creek road immediately to the north of a narrow bridge across the Feohanagh River. A bohreen squeezes between grass-covered walls thick with brambles, turning eastwards in the hamlet to seek a track climbing towards the open moors. Brandon Mountain is the large lump dominating the skyline ahead, and which stays in view throughout the ascent.

The track ends at a gateway in a broken wall and a moorland path continues up by a streambed to follow the line of a tumbledown wall. Some distance above the head of the wall a rocky stump in the centre of a large mound of stones confirms the upward passage. Higher up Lough Eightragh comes into full view, tucked under the western base of the hill. Several cairns plot the route up the broad flank below the summit, but continued upward progress is just as effective as following the cairns, and will eventually bring the walker to the brown earth immediately below the cairn, where the infinitely more dramatic eastern flank of the mountain appears.

An alternative return can be made along the ridge to Brandon Peak with a descent by the steep grassy western flank towards the Feohanagh River for a walk down to Ballybrack.

INDEX

Log Book

CHAPTER 1 / WALK 1   **Ben Lomond**

date   weather   time taken

companions

CHAPTER 1 / WALK 2   **Beinn Ime etc.**

date   weather   time taken

companions

CHAPTER 1 / WALK 3   **Ben Vorlich (Loch Lomond)**

date   weather   time taken

companions

CHAPTER 1 / WALK 4   **Beinn an Lochain**

date   weather   time taken

companions

CHAPTER 1 / WALK 5   **Beinn Bhuidhe**

date   weather   time taken

companions

CHAPTER 2 / WALK 1   **Ben More (Crianlarich) etc.**

date   weather   time taken

companions

CHAPTER 2 / WALK 2   **Cruach Ardrain etc.**

date   weather   time taken

companions

CHAPTER 2 / WALK 3　　　　　　　　　　　　　　　　　　　　　　　**Beinn Laoigh etc.**

date　　　　　　　　weather　　　　　　　　time taken

companions

CHAPTER 3 / WALK 1　　　　　　　　　　　　　　　　　　**Ben Vorlich (Loch Earn) etc.**

date　　　　　　　　weather　　　　　　　　time taken

companions

CHAPTER 3 / WALK 2　　　　　　　　　　　　　　　　　　　　　　　　**Ben Chonzie**

date　　　　　　　　weather　　　　　　　　time taken

companions

CHAPTER 4 / WALK 1　　　　　　　　　　　　　　　　　　　　　　　**Ben Cruachan etc.**

date　　　　　　　　weather　　　　　　　　time taken

companions

CHAPTER 4 / WALK 2　　　　　　　　　　　　　　　　　　　　　　　**Beinn Eunaich etc.**

date　　　　　　　　weather　　　　　　　　time taken

companions

CHAPTER 4 / WALK 3　　　　　　　　　　　　　　　　　　　　　　　**Beinn Sgulaird**

date　　　　　　　　weather　　　　　　　　time taken

companions

CHAPTER 4 / WALK 4　　　　　　　　　　　　　　　　　　　　　　　**Beinn Fhionnlaidh**

date　　　　　　　　weather　　　　　　　　time taken

companions

CHAPTER 4 / WALK 5　　　　　　　　　　　　　　　　　　　　　　　**Ben More (Mull)**

date　　　　　　　　weather　　　　　　　　time taken

companions

CHAPTER 5 / WALK 1　　　　　　　　　　　　　　　　　　　　　　　**Ben Starav etc.**

date　　　　　　　　weather　　　　　　　　time taken

companions

CHAPTER 5 / WALK 2   **Buachaille Etive Mor**

date   weather   time taken

companions

CHAPTER 5 / WALK 3   **Buachaille Etive Beag**

date   weather   time taken

companions

CHAPTER 5 / WALK 4   **Bidean nam Bian**

date   weather   time taken

companions

CHAPTER 5 / WALK 5   **Sgor na h-Ulaidh**

date   weather   time taken

companions

CHAPTER 5 / WALK 6   **The Aonach Eagach**

date   weather   time taken

companions

CHAPTER 5 / WALK 7   **Beinn a'Bheithir**

date   weather   time taken

companions

CHAPTER 6 / WALK 1   **Beinn Dorain etc.**

date   weather   time taken

companions

CHAPTER 6 / WALK 2   **Beinn Mhanach**

date   weather   time taken

companions

CHAPTER 6 / WALK 3   **Stob Ghabhar etc.**

date   weather   time taken

companions

CHAPTER 6 / WALK 4   **Creise etc.**

date   weather   time taken

companions

CHAPTER 7 / WALK 1   **Beinn Heasgarnich etc.**

date   weather   time taken

companions

CHAPTER 7 / WALK 2   **Meall Glas etc.**

date   weather   time taken

companions

CHAPTER 7 / WALK 3   **Meall Ghaordie**

date   weather   time taken

companions

CHAPTER 7 / WALK 4   **Meall nan Tarmachan**

date   weather   time taken

companions

CHAPTER 7 / WALK 5   **Ben Lawers etc.**

date   weather   time taken

companions

CHAPTER 8 / WALK 1   **Carn Mairg etc.**

date   weather   time taken

companions

CHAPTER 8 / WALK 2   **Schiehallion**

date   weather   time taken

companions

CHAPTER 8 / WALK 3   **Stuchd an Lochain**

date   weather   time taken

companions

CHAPTER 8 / WALK 4 — Meall Buidhe

date   weather   time taken

companions

CHAPTER 9 / WALK 1 — Ben Alder etc.

date   weather   time taken

companions

CHAPTER 9 / WALK 2 — Beinn Eibhinn etc.

date   weather   time taken

companions

CHAPTER 9 / WALK 3 — Sgor Gaibhre etc.

date   weather   time taken

companions

CHAPTER 9 / WALK 4 — Chno Dearg etc.

date   weather   time taken

companions

CHAPTER 10 / WALK 1 — The Mamores

date   weather   time taken

companions

CHAPTER 10 / WALK 2 — Ben Nevis etc.

date   weather   time taken

companions

CHAPTER 10 / WALK 3 — The Aonachs

date   weather   time taken

companions

CHAPTER 10 / WALK 4 — The Grey Corries

date   weather   time taken

companions

CHAPTER 10 / WALK 5   **Stob Coire Easain etc.**

date   weather   time taken

companions

CHAPTER 11 / WALK 1   **Beinn a'Chlachair etc.**

date   weather   time taken

companions

CHAPTER 11 / WALK 2   **Beinn a'Chaoruinn etc.**

date   weather   time taken

companions

CHAPTER 11 / WALK 3   **Creag Meagaidh etc.**

date   weather   time taken

companions

CHAPTER 11 / WALK 4   **The Monadhlaith**

date   weather   time taken

companions

CHAPTER 12 / WALK 1   **Beinn Udlamain (Drumochter) etc.**

date   weather   time taken

companions

CHAPTER 12 / WALK 2   **Meall Chuaich**

date   weather   time taken

companions

CHAPTER 12 / WALK 3   **Carn na Caim etc.**

date   weather   time taken

companions

CHAPTER 12 / WALK 4   **Beinn Dearg (Atholl)**

date   weather   time taken

companions

CHAPTER 12 / WALK 5   **Carn a'Chlamain**

date   weather   time taken

companions

CHAPTER 12 / WALK 6   **Beinn a'Ghio etc.**

date   weather   time taken

companions

CHAPTER 13 / WALK 1   **Cairn Gorm**

date   weather   time taken

companions

CHAPTER 13 / WALK 2   **Bynack Mor etc.**

date   weather   time taken

companions

CHAPTER 13 / WALK 3   **The Feshie Five**

date   weather   time taken

companions

CHAPTER 13 / WALK 4   **Braeriach**

date   weather   time taken

companions

CHAPTER 14 / WALK 1   **Cairn Toul etc.**

date   weather   time taken

companions

CHAPTER 14 / WALK 2   **Beinn Bhrotain etc.**

date   weather   time taken

companions

CHAPTER 14 / WALK 3   **Ben Macdui etc.**

date   weather   time taken

companions

CHAPTER 14 / WALK 4   Derry Cairngorm etc.

date   weather   time taken

companions

CHAPTER 14 / WALK 5   Ben Avon etc.

date   weather   time taken

companions

CHAPTER 14 / WALK 6   Beinn a'Chaorruinn etc.

date   weather   time taken

companions

CHAPTER 15 / WALK 1   Glas Tulaichean etc.

date   weather   time taken

companions

CHAPTER 15 / WALK 2   Carn a'Gheoidh etc.

date   weather   time taken

companions

CHAPTER 15 / WALK 3   An Sgarsoch etc.

date   weather   time taken

companions

CHAPTER 16 / WALK 1   Glas Maol etc.

date   weather   time taken

companions

CHAPTER 16 / WALK 2   Broad Cairn etc.

date   weather   time taken

companions

CHAPTER 16 / WALK 3   Lochnagar etc.

date   weather   time taken

companions

CHAPTER 16 / WALK 4   Driesh etc.

date   weather   time taken

companions

CHAPTER 16 / WALK 5   Mount Keen

date   weather   time taken

companions

CHAPTER 17 / WALK 1   Meall na Teanga etc.

date   weather   time taken

companions

CHAPTER 17 / WALK 2   Gulvain

date   weather   time taken

companions

CHAPTER 17 / WALK 3   Sgurr Thuilm etc.

date   weather   time taken

companions

CHAPTER 18 / WALK 1   Ladhar Bheinn

date   weather   time taken

companions

CHAPTER 18 / WALK 2   Luinne Bheinn etc.

date   weather   time taken

companions

CHAPTER 18 / WALK 3   Sgurr na Ciche etc.

date   weather   time taken

companions

CHAPTER 18 / WALK 4   Sgurr nan Coireachan etc.

date   weather   time taken

companions

CHAPTER 18 / WALK 5   **Gairich**

date   weather   time taken

companions

CHAPTER 18 / WALK 6   **Sgurr a'Mhaoraich**

date   weather   time taken

companions

CHAPTER 18 / WALK 7   **Gleouraich etc.**

date   weather   time taken

companions

CHAPTER 19 / WALK 1   **Beinn Sgritheall**

date   weather   time taken

companions

CHAPTER 19 / WALK 2   **The Saddle etc.**

date   weather   time taken

companions

CHAPTER 19 / WALK 3   **The South Cluanie Ridge**

date   weather   time taken

companions

CHAPTER 20 / WALK 1   **The Five Sisters Ridge**

date   weather   time taken

companions

CHAPTER 20 / WALK 2   **Ciste Dhubh etc.**

date   weather   time taken

companions

CHAPTER 20 / WALK 3   **Beinn Fhada**

date   weather   time taken

companions

CHAPTER 20 / WALK 4   **A'Ghlas-bheinn**

date   weather   time taken

companions

CHAPTER 20 / WALK 5   **The Cluanie Horseshoe**

date   weather   time taken

companions

CHAPTER 21 / WALK 1   **Sgurr nan Ceathreamhnan etc.**

date   weather   time taken

companions

CHAPTER 21 / WALK 2   **Mam Sodhail etc.**

date   weather   time taken

companions

CHAPTER 21 / WALK 3   **The Mullardoch Peaks**

date   weather   time taken

companions

CHAPTER 21 / WALK 4   **Sgurr a'Choire Ghlais etc.**

date   weather   time taken

companions

CHAPTER 22 / WALK 1   **Maoile Lunndaidh etc.**

date   weather   time taken

companions

CHAPTER 22 / WALK 2   **Bidein a'Choire Sheasgaich etc.**

date   weather   time taken

companions

CHAPTER 22 / WALK 3   **Moruisg etc.**

date   weather   time taken

companions

CHAPTER 22 / WALK 4   Sgurr Ruadh etc.

date   weather   time taken

companions

CHAPTER 22 / WALK 5   Maol Chean-dearg

date   weather   time taken

companions

CHAPTER 22 / WALK 6   Fionn Bheinn

date   weather   time taken

companions

CHAPTER 23 / WALK 1   Beinn Alligin

date   weather   time taken

companions

CHAPTER 23 / WALK 2   Liathach

date   weather   time taken

companions

CHAPTER 23 / WALK 3   Beinn Dearg (Torridon)

date   weather   time taken

companions

CHAPTER 23 / WALK 4   Beinn Eighe

date   weather   time taken

companions

CHAPTER 23 / WALK 5   Slioch

date   weather   time taken

companions

CHAPTER 24 / WALK 1   A'Mhaigdean etc.

date   weather   time taken

companions

CHAPTER 24 / WALK 2   **Mullach Coire Mhic Fhearchair etc.**

date _____ weather _____ time taken _____

companions _____

CHAPTER 24 / WALK 3   **An Teallach**

date _____ weather _____ time taken _____

companions _____

CHAPTER 25 / WALK 1   **The Fannichs**

date _____ weather _____ time taken _____

companions _____

CHAPTER 25 / WALK 2   **Sgurr Breac etc.**

date _____ weather _____ time taken _____

companions _____

CHAPTER 25 / WALK 3   **Ben Wyvis**

date _____ weather _____ time taken _____

companions _____

CHAPTER 25 / WALK 4   **Am Faochagach**

date _____ weather _____ time taken _____

companions _____

CHAPTER 25 / WALK 5   **Beinn Dearg (Ullapool) etc.**

date _____ weather _____ time taken _____

companions _____

CHAPTER 25 / WALK 6   **Seana Bhraigh**

date _____ weather _____ time taken _____

companions _____

CHAPTER 26 / WALK 1   **Ben Hope**

date _____ weather _____ time taken _____

companions _____

CHAPTER 26 / WALK 2   **Ben Klibreck**

date   weather   time taken

companions

CHAPTER 26 / WALK 3   **Ben More Assynt etc.**

date   weather   time taken

companions

CHAPTER 27 / WALK 1   **Sgurr Dubh Mor etc.**

date   weather   time taken

companions

CHAPTER 27 / WALK 2   **Sgurr Alasdair etc.**

date   weather   time taken

companions

CHAPTER 27 / WALK 3   **Sgurr a'Ghreadaidh etc.**

date   weather   time taken

companions

CHAPTER 27 / WALK 4   **Sgurr nan Gillean etc.**

date   weather   time taken

companions

CHAPTER 27 / WALK 5   **Bla Bheinn**

date   weather   time taken

companions

CHAPTER 28 / WALK 1   **Scafell Pike etc.**

date   weather   time taken

companions

CHAPTER 28 / WALK 2   **Skiddaw**

date   weather   time taken

companions

CHAPTER 28 / WALK 3   **Helvellyn**

date   weather   time taken
companions

CHAPTER 29 / WALK 1   **Snowdon**

date   weather   time taken
companions

CHAPTER 29 / WALK 2   **The Glyders**

date   weather   time taken
companions

CHAPTER 29 / WALK 3   **The Carneddau**

date   weather   time taken
companions

CHAPTER 30 / WALK 1   **Lugnaquillia**

date   weather   time taken
companions

CHAPTER 30 / WALK 2   **Galtymore**

date   weather   time taken
companions

CHAPTER 30 / WALK 3   **Macgillycuddy's Reeks (East)**

date   weather   time taken
companions

CHAPTER 30 / WALK 4   **Macgillycuddy's Reeks (West)**

date   weather   time taken
companions

CHAPTER 30 / WALK 5   **Brandon Mountain**

date   weather   time taken
companions